The Art
of Charlie Chaplin

The Art of Charlie Chaplin

A Film-by-Film Analysis

KYP HARNESS

McFarland & Company, Inc., Publishers
Jefferson, North Carolina, and London

Library of Congress Cataloguing-in-Publication Data

Harness, Kyp, 1964–
    The art of Charlie Chaplin : a film-by-film analysis /
Kyp Harness.
        p.   cm.
    Includes bibliographical references and index.

    ISBN-13: 978-0-7864-3193-9
    softcover : 50# alkaline paper ∞

    1. Chaplin, Charlie, 1889–1977 — Criticism and interpretation.
I. Title.
    PN2287.C5H33   2008
    791.4302'8092 — dc22   2007036790

British Library cataloguing data are available

Cover photograph ©2008 Shutterstock

Manufactured in the United States of America

McFarland & Company, Inc., Publishers
    Box 611, Jefferson, North Carolina 28640
    www.mcfarlandpub.com

Table of Contents

For Allison,
Ava and Clay

Preface

S ometimes the iconic status of an artist obscures the real achievements and accomplishments of that artist — and the human being behind the artist.

This seems especially true in the case of Charles Chaplin, whose image has come to be accepted as a symbol of the premiere art form of the twentieth century, which he played a large role in creating and developing.

When images become so familiar, it is difficult to see them anew — to appreciate the reality for which the symbol is a metaphor.

This has been my task in creating the present volume. I sought and viewed every one of Chaplin's films in chronological order, the better to become acquainted with the reality behind the symbol, the artist behind the icon.

In my previous book, I used the same technique with the films of the comedy team Laurel and Hardy formed by Chaplin's old music hall touring roommate Stan Laurel. In the case of Stan and Ollie, I had made the point that they achieved profundity and greatness through their sheer lack of pretension, through their pure devotion to simple comedy.

Chaplin was quite different in that from his earliest films he was hugely ambitious, and throughout his career sought to enlarge his art to include drama, tragedy, political and social commentary, and philosophy.

His story is the story of the better part of the twentieth century, of which he was, in the popular sense, the defining artist. His films take us from the rustic suburbs of Edendale, California, in 1914 to Pinewood Studios of London, England, in 1967. We are able to observe a clown from the British Music Hall introduce an evolving art form as he progresses from the flickering cartoonlike antics of his earliest silent films to the dramatic, sophisticated, complex, and often sharply satiric comedy for which he has become known.

As in my previous book, I have relied here on two basic volumes to provide historical background.

David Robinson's *Chaplin: His Life and Art* is likely to remain the definitive work on Chaplin — exhaustive and extensive, it was written with full access to the Chaplin archives, and is the best overall view of Chaplin personally and professionally.

As well, there is Chaplin's own volume, *My Autobiography*, an impressive, engrossing, idiosyncratic work which is, of course, invaluable to anyone with an interest in Chaplin.

To trace the growth of Chaplin's art has been a privilege, and to have experienced the totality of his insights into the human experience is to be awed by this dynamic, brilliant, still controversial figure, who looms—despite his small size—in our collective subconscious.

1

The Tramp

Who was Charlie Chaplin? A half-century ago, or even a quarter-century ago, it would have seemed preposterous to even ask the question. He was the first of the global superstars, a defining figure of the twentieth century. The image of the alter ego he created, the Tramp, was a symbol to all the human population of cinema, of laughter, of Everyman — of humanity itself, coping in a life and a world spinning out of balance, always triumphing, just barely, over a grim and ruthless reality.

The symbol survives, surfacing in the most unlikely places, recognizable to those oblivious of its creator, nearly a century after the Tramp first tumbled into the world's consciousness. But what lives behind the symbol, what hidden world gave birth to the tiny splay-footed creature who haunts this place, even peripherally, as generation after generation passes through? Who was Charlie Chaplin?

First and foremost, Chaplin was a clown. Presumably, the human animal has had at the heart of its existence, since the time of its achievement of consciousness, the need to laugh, at itself and others. Presumably there have been those since the dawn of time who have preformed the function of fulfilling that need, of giving their fellow humans something to laugh at. At the most basic level, the clowns who induce the purest laughter are those who have made of their bodies instruments entirely attuned to the activity of arousing amusement, in a sphere beyond words, beyond rational thought.

Certainly innumerable such clowns came and went on waves of laughter in the vast stretches of time before the invention of the motion picture camera. But it is hard to believe that any of them were more accomplished, more supernaturally gifted and ethereally graceful, more sublimely comical and connected to the root and heart of all laughter than Charlie Chaplin.

He was a master of pantomime — silence was the domain over which he was most assuredly the king. He had absolute body control, and his gestures — the mere flick of his fingers, the tiniest glint of his eye — conveyed more thought and emotion than pages of dialogue from the most profound of writers. His artistry was in the very subtlety of his movements, his gestures — uniquely human truths were sensitively observed and sensitively, exquisitely expressed through the small body made into a vessel through which passed all the beauty, pain, struggle, joy, terror and poetry of being human and being truly alive. Far from the rarefied demonstrations of technique which constitute the performances of most mimes of today, Chaplin's artistry always stayed connected to human truth, to the sheer ridiculousness and absurdity of existence itself — and to gallantry and faith in the face of that absurdity.

His gifts in this arena extended to his abilities as an athlete and an acrobat. Chaplin performs stunts in his films which seem to defy the laws of gravity — which, at the very least, arouse awe and wonderment as well as laughter. His teetering on the ladder in *The Pawnshop* (1916) comes to mind, as do his hijinks on roller skates in *The Rink* (1916) and *Modern Times* (1936). Even as an older man of fifty-six in *Monsieur Verdoux* (1947), he takes a tumble off a couch onto the floor, all the while holding a cup of tea out of which never spills a drop. He was extraordinarily agile, almost impossibly malleable and flexible — even his lesser works offer the pleasures of seeing him leaping through windows and over fences in his inimitable manner — and, especially in the films by which he earned the world's love, his performances are always dazzlingly energetic and enthusiastic. However subtle and poetic his pantomime was, it was always accompanied by this athletic vitality, the physical élan of both the ballet dancer and the gymnast. There lived in him the desire to slash away at the grey brutality of life with the extravagant beauty of his gestures.

Primary among his gifts was the natural gift of the body he was born in. He was a small man, 5'6", slender, and small-boned. People meeting him were known to express surprise especially at the smallness of his hands and arms. His smallness aided and accentuated his agility, as well as providing him with instant sympathy. It was instrumental in his portrayal of his Tramp clown character — a character of such "small" societal status that his world barely allows him to exist at all.

Chaplin's head, however, was large in comparison with the rest of his body — giving him the look, proportion-wise, of an eternal child. His appearance always signals a primordial identification with our own childhood in our collective memory. His larger head size was of benefit to him as an actor whether on the stage or on screen, as it would ensure that the incomparable precision of his expressions of emotion and thought would always reach the back row. As well, he was blessed with large, dark, incredibly expressive eyes, which, as his one-time roommate Stan Laurel remarked, "Absolutely forced you to look at them."[1] Chaplin's eyes, searing, dark, emotional, glow like coals at the heart of every piece of celluloid he appears on. There seems something in the depths of them, even in the midst of gaiety, which is deathly serious, and sad.

All of these attributes contributed to his superiority as a clown. As important as these, he was simply funny — he moved funny, and he had a talent for sheer ridiculousness of gesture. One of his wives remarked on the intellectualizing that was done about the meaning behind her husband's clowning, saying, "Charlie usually didn't mean anything. He just has his funny little ways."[2] One only has to summon up the memory of his Tramp character's waddling walk — or his twitching of his mustache — to know the truth of that statement. They are funny for their own sake. They need no explanation, and none is possible.

One can't talk about such mannerisms at all, though, without appreciating Chaplin's genius in creating his clown character, the Tramp. Tramp comedians had been popular in the British music halls of Chaplin's youth, and throughout human history the figure at the bottom of the societal ladder, the one who counted least of all in the world, has always been the figure of laughter and fun to his fellow humans. Chaplin's genius was to develop his own take on that archetype and bring it to a level previously unknown. His Tramp is not one whose seediness and poverty are jokes in themselves, but one who conducts himself as though these facts are the most ephemeral of illusions — much in the way that the comic drunk who effects a bogus air of sobriety is much funnier than the one who merely acts flamboyantly drunk. The Tramp is on the bottom, on the periphery, he is last, but as if in some strange fulfillment of the Gospels, he is actually first — however minimized or victimized by the looming world around him, by its violence and its callous indifference, he always stands, miraculously, ridiculously, with nobility and dignity intact.

The Tramp was Chaplin's alter ego. He played him for twenty-five years, from the age of 25 to 50, and during that time Chaplin never stopped developing the Tramp. The Tramp changed as Chaplin changed — though so intertwined and interchangeable were they that one is tempted to say the reverse is also true. The Tramp could be earnest, mischievous, vengeful, moral, romantic, cruel, gallant, joyful, clumsy, graceful, sad, heroic, pitiful. His character seems somehow to encompass the whole range of human experience, and we are fixed upon with a growing conviction as we watch him that he represents us all, that he struggles in the midst of the cogs and angry policemen on behalf of us, all of us.

In creating such a finely-detailed self-portrait over 25 years, Chaplin created not just a mirror for himself but for all the vanity and tragedy of the human condition — all the glory and folly our existence is shot through with. And his instrument of this depiction was his inhabiting the character of one who is a nullity, who is one of the least among us.

So effective was this depiction that the Tramp captured the attention of the world; he was a global phenomenon. As impressive as this accomplishment is, it is less important than the reason behind it — that the Tramp was and remains one of the most compelling and complex characters ever created in any medium.

Undoubtedly, Chaplin's skill as an actor contributed to the arresting quality of the Tramp — Laurence Olivier called him "the greatest actor who ever lived"[3] — as well as the authenticity of the character being an essential expression of Chaplin's own true self. Beyond these are the scenarios and gags Chaplin devised for the Tramp through his genius as a writer and director. Though many other clowns had created their own personas, none were able to create the volume of brilliantly effective gags and stories as Chaplin did over his career. He was one of the great gag writers of all time and, importantly, his gags always revealed, or made comment on, something in human nature, and were relevant to the theme of his films as a whole.

A gag which immediately leaps to mind is his reaction, as a drunken husband, to the news his wife has left him in *The Idle Class* (1921). He puts down her letter, turns his back to the camera, bows his head with his arms before him, and begins shaking. We believe we see him in the depths of anguished remorse. But when he turns, we see he has merely been taking the opportunity to shake himself a martini — which he then neatly pours, and sips at contentedly.

The gag is funny for the cleverness of its construction, the dependable mastery of its execution. But beyond this it is a defining snapshot of the character — he really is so cold and unfeeling that his honest reaction to his wife's departure is merely to nonchalantly fix himself a drink — a display of the very type of behavior which drove his wife away. In our momentary delusion that the character is capable of remorse, we share the ever frustrated hopes of the alcoholic's wife, who has been, like us, fooled into believing that he is capable of generating any type of emotion in himself which doesn't involve his beverage of choice — we have been fooled into thinking he is alive, when he is dead. The gag contains something sad and disturbing, too.

Another gag which comes to mind is in *Modern Times* (1936). The Tramp, recently released from jail, ambles down the street. A lumber truck passes him, and the (presumably red) flag falls off the end of the truck. Charlie picks up the flag, dashing after the truck, calling to the driver. At that moment a protest march rounds the corner and falls into step behind him as he strides, waving the flag and yelling to the driver. The police descend, and Charlie is arrested for leading the march.

The construction again is impeccable — and the gag defines the theme of the film overall, which is a portrait of the precariousness and insecurity of the poor as they make their way between the feet of the behemoths of Business and Law. Charlie's journey in the film is to make a round robin between work, jail, and vagabondage — he is completely at the mercy, the film repeatedly tells us, of societal forces which are beyond his control. How better to display the irrational vicissitudes of fate which swirl about Charlie than this sequence, where society seems only to exist as a force determined to throw him into jail, where he leads a protest march against that society in utter oblivion, turning to see his comrades only in the final moments?

As well, in the image of the looming throng suddenly marching passionately behind the Tramp we see the writhing crowds which have always appeared in times of political upheaval, and to see them steadfastly continuing in their mission behind an unknowing clown brings to mind the random and arbitrary nature of all our political constructs.

Another gag, too good not to mention, is in *City Lights* (1931). The Tramp has made the friendship of a drunken millionaire, who allows Charlie to use his limousine after a night they've spent out partying. Charlie pulls off in the car, but soon feels a craving for a smoke. He doesn't have any cigars, so he scans the street. He sees a man walking, smoking a cigar — Charlie edges along in the car, watching him furtively, waiting for him to drop the butt. When he does, another bum approaches to grab it. Charlie stops the car, leaps out, violently kicks the bum out of the way, grabs the cigar, and puffs at it as he gets back into the car, glaring angrily at the bum — who sits on the pavement staring dumbfoundedly at Charlie as he drives off.

Simply to have the Tramp creeping along in the car, waiting for the butt to fall, is gag enough in itself. But in the kicking of the other tramp, we are inspired to imagine the bum's shocked amazement at the figure who's just leapt from his stately limousine to scuffle over a cigar. As well, we're connected to the theme of the movie as a whole, which, with its relationship of the Tramp and his millionaire friend — who embraces or rejects Charlie according to his level of intoxication — and the interwoven relationship of the Tramp and a blind flower girl — who believes the Tramp to be wealthy, never seeing his rags — is a meditation on the roles we all play, and those we give to others, based upon material wherewithal real, imagined, or presumed.

Beyond the multitude of brilliant gags which adorn his work are the narrative structures of his films through which these gags are woven like a necklace of gems. His growth as a writer can be traced from the early madcap slapstick shorts, into which he ambitiously began adding more sophisticated narrative twists and turns, from the subtleties of *Police* (1916), *The Immigrant* (1917) and *Easy Street* (1917), to the full-on sweeping story-telling arcs of *The Kid* (1921), *The Gold Rush* (1925), *City Lights*, and *Modern Times*. His greatest stories have the grand inevitably of archetypal legends, and each produces visions or tableaus which define them and the statement they make on our common plight — whether that be Charlie on the cogs in *Modern Times*, his dance of the rolls in *The Gold Rush* (or is it his eating of his shoe?), his beatific, hopeful gaze at the end of *City Lights*, or his dance, as Hynkel, with the globe in *The Great Dictator* (1941). He repeatedly created iconic images within his narratives which comment comically, beautifully, on humanity's destiny.

Chaplin was a true humorist, a satirist, and a sharp observer of human nature. He expressed a view of life through his films — and from the moment he gained control over them, he began making each of them very personal statements about himself and the world around him, first unconsciously, then, increasingly consciously — some would say, at times, to the detriment of his art. Nonetheless, his great ambition as an artist, as he increasingly called himself as the years went by, marks him off from other clowns.

There was an intensity in his need to create. Friends and family spoke of his all-consuming drive and absorption when making a film, to the harm of personal relationships and his own health, immersed entirely as he was in his great need to express what was so important for him to express.

This is all to say that Chaplin, as a master of his craft of clowning, revolutionized it and transformed it into a uniquely personal and intimate form by which to express his own very singular — yet universal — sensibility, thereby raising his craft to high art in his field, as astonishingly as Shakespeare, Beethoven, and Picasso did in theirs. Chaplin, like these others, transcends his form and may be regarded, beyond a clown, actor or filmmaker, as an archetype of a revolutionary genius artist.

As an artist, he was inspired to comment on virtually all the phenomena of reality. He was a product of his times and was created by them as much as he came to define and embody them for others— and since he lived and felt them so deeply, so completely, his art transcends its time as it does all time. If on occasion, in addressing the issues he felt called upon to comment on, he faltered and did so unwisely or unsuccessfully, his passion could never be doubted, nor his sincerity in daring to tackle all the questions existence put to him. Even in his lesser — mostly later — work, we never see him lukewarm, bland, complacent. Always his sensibility is pushing forward, hungrily encountering new truths and falsehoods to expose, encountering more reality and life to transmute into art.

Clown, acrobat, writer, director, humorist, composer (when sound came in, he began writing the music for his films)— visual poet of the pratfall and philosopher of the ass-kick — all of these unite and constitute a totality which is beyond calculation, but which finds residence beneath the encompassing term of "artist." And, like all truly great artists, he only had one real subject: himself. To begin to ask who Charlie Chaplin was— or rather, who Charlie Chaplin is— we go again to encounter his living sensibility preserved on celluloid, the Tramp whom laughter makes immortal, we go to see that heart and soul again, shining on the screen, preserved in the light, sharing in our struggle, our mystery and folly.

2

Keystone

When the 24 year old Charles Chaplin stepped onto the lot of the Keystone Studios in California in December 1913, he initiated the rude, crude, primitive beginnings of his cinematic career at a studio in the throes of its own rude, crude beginnings, in a medium still weathering through its own beginnings—beginnings which were rude, crude, and primitive, as seen from our contemporary viewpoint.

Thomas Edison had patented the kinetoscopic camera—which allowed one to photograph a series of pictures in succession—only 22 years before, in 1891. Edison had been inspired by a meeting he'd had in 1888 with Eadweard Muybridge, a man who'd achieved some fame with his zoopraxiscope projector. The zoopraxiscope device projected Muybridge's own photographic images from rotating glass discs. From 1880 on, Muybridge had toured with his device in America and Europe, displaying the short sequences of illusory movement, including the legendary sequence which had begun his obsession with approximating life—the images of a horse trotting he'd taken to settle a longstanding debate among racing men about whether all four of a horse's hooves left the earth at any time during its trotting.[1]

Edison assigned his assistant, William Kennedy Laurie Dickson—a photographer with much interest in the simulation of movement—to study Muybridge's work and to work on a similar device. Assisted by the invention of a new, thin, flexible film by George Eastman, the passionately dedicated Dickson designed the kinetoscope, the first cinema camera, in 1889. This was patented by Edison along with the kinetograph, the device through which the film taken by the kinetoscope could be viewed. It was a lighted box, the handle of which was turned by the viewer to pass a film strip of pictures over a light bulb.

These were first called arcade peep shows, then nickelodeons, and by 1894 their popularity had spread throughout North America and Europe.

By 1896—and with a studio set up to make films for the kinetographs—Dickson was aware that inventors in other countries were steadily improving upon and surpassing his original device. He was aware as well that the Lumiere

Brothers in France were making inroads on a device to project images, and argued with Edison that they should do the same. Edison saw no future in a machine which projected images for crowds of people to watch, but Dickson persisted on his own.[2]

Dickson became aware of a man named Thomas Armat who had developed a projection device, and who had demonstrated it at the Chicago Exhibition Fair. Armat, having sunk his life savings into his machine, was broke, so Dickson convinced him to sell the rights to his machine to Edison. Edison patented it under his own name and named it the Vitascope.

At this juncture, Edison and Dickson suffered a falling-out. Dickson left Edison and formed the American Mutograph Company. When Dickson soon developed his own version of the projection machine, called the Biograph, the company became the American Mutograph and Biograph Company in 1899, and then, simply, the Biograph Company.[3]

Biograph was one of the first film studios, producing hundreds of films, and by 1908 it had a stock company of actors which included Dorothy and Lillian Gish, Mary Pickford, and Lionel Barrymore. An out-of-work actor and failed playwright named D.W. Griffith came to Biograph as well and in assuming directorial duties he developed much of the language of cinema — of editing, of camera shots — that we know today. Later, Chaplin would call him "the teacher of us all."

Mack Sennett, an aspiring comic and singer, came to Biograph in 1908. Originally from Richmond, Quebec, Sennett studied Griffith's methods and began writing scenarios. He displayed a flair for comedy, so Griffith appointed him the principal director of comic productions — an area Griffith wasn't interested in. Sennett directed over eighty one-reel (ten minute long) comedies between 1911 and 1912.

It was at this point that Sennett was contacted by the New York Motion Picture Company to run a new comedy arm it was establishing in California. Sennett accepted the job, moved to California and created the Keystone Company, bringing Biograph actors with him such as Mabel Normand, Ford Sterling, and Fred Mace. The studio flourished, turning out eight reels a week by 1913.

The secret of Sennett's success, as Chaplin himself later noted, was his enthusiasm.[4] The Sennett vision as manifested at Keystone was a knockabout free-for-all which owed much to the anarchic energy of the comedies coming from Pathé in France. Yet it also was crossbred with the dusty roads and small-town mores of early twentieth century America. The films were exuberant, calamitous, quick-cutting circuses of mugging, flirtation, mayhem and pratfalls. They were demonic mirror reflections of the country in its adolescent strainings at the beginning of the century. There was no restraint, no pause for second thought — just a barrage of action culminating in a chase. The Keystone Kops became known the world over as a catchphrase for an aberrant force of destructive incompetence.

As brilliant as Sennett was in surrounding himself with talent — most of the greatest clowns of the time passed through his studio — he was as equally unlucky at holding onto talent. His male lead, Ford Sterling, was beginning to ask for more money and to speak of moving on to another studio. Sennett looked around to replace Sterling, and, according to legend, recalled Charles Chaplin, whom he'd seen performing in a British vaudeville troupe a year before. The performance had so impressed Sennett at the time that he claimed he'd vowed to sign Chaplin if he ever got the chance. Now the opportunity presented itself.

Chaplin had been born in 1889, in Walworth, London, England. His father, also named Charles Chaplin, and his mother, Hannah, were both music hall singer-entertainers. Their union lasted only two years after Charles Jr.'s birth, however, so that as Chaplin later noted, he was "hardly conscious of having a father at all."[5] In 1891, with Chaplin Sr. achieving some notoriety as a singer, he left Hannah and Charles behind — along with Charles' half-brother Sydney, Hannah's son from a previous union.

Chaplin's brother Sydney was instrumental to his survival of these years, and throughout Chaplin's life he fulfilled the same purpose as did Theo Van Gogh and Roy Disney for their brothers — he exercised a watchful, almost paternal care over his brother, giving him the grounding necessary to ascend his artistic heights while tending to the mundane, necessary material realities on his behalf. In Hollywood, Sydney would later negotiate for Chaplin the greatest salary ever paid to an entertainer up to that time. In addition, Sydney would attain some success as a film comedian in his own right, and would co-star in a few films of Chaplin's.

Chaplin's mother had a difficult time making ends meet after the departure of her husband. Chaplin would later remember her with great fondness — he would state, "If I have amounted to anything, it will be due to her,"[6] and as a child he was greatly entertained by her talent for mimicry — and was moved by her emotional reading of the Gospels.[7]

She did the odd singing engagement, and it was during one in 1894 that Chaplin, at the age of five, made his first stage appearance. Hannah's voice had begun to weaken, and when it failed her onstage, precipitating the catcalls and boos of the audience, the stagehands shoved her son on, having seen him sing and dance backstage.

The young Chaplin immediately won the crowd over with his natural talent, moving them to throw coins at his feet. At one point, he felt the need to stop his song and inform them that he would resume singing after he'd gathered all the money from the floor.

Ever after, Chaplin would link his first stage appearance, and what turned out to be his mother's last — and the gathering of the money — with the failing of his mother's voice, and with her subsequent deterioration and decline.[8]

In the next year, Hannah fell ill, and was admitted to an infirmary. Sydney was placed in an institution, the seven year old Charles was sent to live with relatives. When Hannah did not recover, both boys were sent to a workhouse in 1896. While there, Chaplin contracted ringworm, necessitating the humiliation of having his head shaved and being set apart from the other children.

After eighteen months the boys returned to live with their mother, now at least partially recovered. They lived in a succession of dingy back rooms over a six-month period before being forced to readmit themselves to the workhouse.

Shortly after, Hannah announced her intention to remove her sons from the workhouse — the authorities released them, along with her. She only desired to spend a day of fun with them in the park, however, and once the day had passed she presented herself along with them to be readmitted, much to the consternation of the authorities, much to the delight of her two boys.

Shortly after this she fell ill again. She was taken from the workhouse to the infirmary, and her worsening, delusional mental condition caused her to be committed to an asylum. Her own mother had gone mad and had been committed only five years before.

By this time the courts had tracked Chaplin Sr. down in order to enforce his paternal obligations. The boys were taken out of the workhouse and discharged into his care. He was an alcoholic engaged in a stormy relationship with an alcoholic woman, who harbored a vicious hatred for Sydney.

Hannah became well enough to be released from the asylum. She was reunited with her sons. At this point, Charles, at age 9, entered show business. He began clog dancing with a group of boys, the Lancashire Lads, touring England throughout 1899–1900. After this, he returned to live with Hannah — Sydney had gone off to sea as a steward.

In 1901, Chaplin's father died at age thirty-seven from alcoholism, his career having fallen off several years before. Young Chaplin tried his hand at a variety of odd jobs on the London streets in order to contribute to the meager household he shared with his mother. On a spring day in 1903 he returned home to be told by some neighborhood children that his mother had gone mad. He found her beyond communication, and took her to the infirmary. She was quickly committed to an asylum.

The fourteen year old survived as best he could on the streets of London until his brother came home from sea. Upon Sydney's return, they visited their mother in the asylum. Chaplin would long be haunted by her words: "If you had only given me a cup of tea, I would have been all right."

Sydney had come back with a burning ambition to become an actor — an ambition his brother shared. Charles procured himself an agent and quickly landed a supporting role in a touring production of *Sherlock Holmes*. The play toured Britain throughout 1903–4, with one reviewer singling out Chaplin as "a bright and vigorous child actor," remarking that he "hop[ed] to hear great things of him in the near future."[9]

Sydney toured with the play as well, and for a period their mother was released from the asylum and traveled with her sons. In 1905, she relapsed and was committed for the final time. Chaplin joined a company of boy comedians called Casey's Court Circus and toured with them until 1907, sharpening his comedic skills and becoming the star of the show.

By this time Sydney was employed as a pantomimist by the legendary Fred Karno, leader of a comic pantomime troupe which had ten companies touring the music halls across Britain, performing a repertoire of original sketches. British pantomime was not entirely silent; the 18th-century edict which forbade dialogue on any stage save the Royal ones had pretty much faded by this time. But Karno's sketches depended mostly upon physical action, with dialogue merely facilitating and punctuating the slapstick, which was always played with an undercurrent of "wistfulness." Karno's name at the time in England was synonymous with the madcap, yet gentle, knockabout comedy he specialized in. Sydney implored Karno to hire his brother, and in 1908 Chaplin was signed on.

Chaplin's talent asserted itself and he was quickly given many of the best roles in the repertoire of sketches. Over the five years he was with Karno, Chaplin would play many roles, but it seems beyond dispute that his most effective one was as the "Drunk" in the sketch "Mumming Birds," known later as "A Night in an English Music Hall." The premise of the sketch — later to be recreated in one of Chaplin's films — was that of a show within a show, facilitated by another proscenium and stage constructed within the stage the troupe appeared on. The faux proscenium was complete with a box into which was escorted the Drunk as played by Chaplin, and the sketch consisted mainly of his outraged reactions to the godawful parade of horrendous singers and execrable joke-tellers the "show" was composed of. Chaplin took many drunken falls in and out of the box, and his Drunk, alternating between sodden disdain and animated disgust, finally ended in a fight to the finish with the show's "Wrestler" as the sketch came to its clamorous end. The Drunk was a rogue and a rake, a type Chaplin would resuscitate periodically in his films such as *The Cure* (1917), *One A.M.* (1917), and *The Idle Class* (1921) — and whose outraged sense of propriety would find a permanent home in the Tramp.

Stan Jefferson — later Laurel, of Laurel and Hardy — and Albert Austin, who would perform in many Chaplin films, were also in the troupe. From 1908 to 1913 they toured throughout England and in France, and most momentously, made two trips to America. The first, beginning in September 1910 and lasting until June 1912, began unpromisingly as the troupe had been ordered to perform a sketch which was inferior and which they were uncomfortable performing for that reason. Greater success came later in the tour when they switched to "Mumming Birds," which became a big hit. Chaplin's performance was repeatedly singled out for praise, becoming something of a sensation in and of itself — and certainly the key element in the troupe's success as a whole. As the tour progressed, his name was advertised above the name of the troupe.

"One of the best pantomimists we have seen here," read a Montana review. "Charles Chaplin as the inebriated swell is a revelation," read another.[10] One read: "Charles Chaplin has been described, by some critics, as a genius. To say the least he carries the hallmarks of genius..."[11] Chaplin was called "the world's greatest impersonator of inebriates and the biggest laughmaker on the vaudeville stage."[12] Groucho Marx, never one to hand out compliments easily, saw "Mumming Birds" while appearing in vaudeville with his brothers and reported back to the other Marxes: "I just saw greatest comedian in the world."[13] Over sixty years later he would remember it as "the greatest thing I'd ever seen."[14]

It was during the first tour of America that Mack Sennett claimed to have seen Chaplin's performance and to have been bowled over by it. It was during the second tour, begun only four months later in October 1913, that Sennett, searching for a replacement for Ford Sterling, contacted Chaplin and offered him employment at Keystone.

Chaplin was ready to move on — he was enticed by the money Sennett offered as well as by the notion that after a year in the motion picture business he could return to vaudeville an international star. He wrote to Sydney that after working five years in the movies he figured he'd be "independent for life."[15] After completing his obligations to Karno, he traveled to Edendale, a half-industrial, half-residential suburb of Los Angeles, and came to the Keystone Studio, a rustic, ramshackle operation built on the grounds of what once had been a farm, with a barn serving as the dressing room for many of its actors.

Chaplin reported for work, and Sennett, for reasons best known to himself, kept him waiting around the lot for some time. All the while, Chaplin worried, fearful that his more subtle comedy would not jibe with the Keystone style of altercations and chases. "I knew that nothing transcended personality," Chaplin would remember.[16]

This edict was proven in January 1914 when he was given the role of a reporter in *Making a Living*, a "documentary" about the printing press — which at Keystone meant a slapstick comedy based around some footage shot at a real printing press. The story was improvised as they went along — in fact no Chaplin film used a complete script until *The Great Dictator* in 1940.

He enters the screen in a frock coat, wearing a top hat. He is sporting a handlebar mustache, necessary since Sennett had expressed concern at Chaplin's youthful appearance (the comedian had been made up to look like a man in his fifties as the "Drunk"). The mustache, not entirely successful in disguising the youth of the 24 year old Chaplin, also serves notice that his character is a rake, a rogue, in the parlance of the day, a "dude" — and probably somewhat similar to the Drunk of "Mumming Birds." He makes his sprightly way along the avenue and encounters the other main character of the film, a reporter played by the film's director, Henry Lehrman. Hailing him, he strikes up an amiable conversation, exchanging a few pleasantries which are good-naturedly bantered with by Lehrman, who then bids a cordial good-bye and turns to go.

Chaplin, in a quick, desperate movement, grabs his elbow, and then in a straightforward manner tells him through his gestures that he's somewhat up against it, and by the by, would it be possible for his new friend to loan him a few...? Lehrman turns brusquely away. Chaplin seizes his elbow again and once more appeals to him, this time more plaintively, with a more pitiful, sorrowful tale of need. Lehrman, either because he's affected by the tale or just wants to get Chaplin off his back, reaches into his pocket for some funds— Chaplin breaks from his distraught mode to gaze at the money cunningly, with icy assessment in a quick darting look. Lehrman offers the bills to Chaplin, who moves to refuse them, as if in some sudden resurgence of pride. Shrugging, Lehrman starts to put the money back into his pocket, but Chaplin quickly forestalls him from doing so.

Remarkably, this is all done in one shot, the first shot of Chaplin's career. He conveys, silently, all that we need to know of this character. We see his false bonhomie, his calculating charm, his attempt to bluff his way into a position far beyond his station. We see the desperation his effusive banter vainly attempts to mask, and we see the furtive lack of scruples at the heart of him, the cheerful amorality of a man who's quite prepared to do anything for money — he's really no better than a beggar or a thief. We see the joyful hypocrisy, the enthusiastic skullduggery.

This is built upon in the next scene when Chaplin comes upon a young woman and her mother. He flirts with both, giving a ring to the young woman and charming the mother. As it turns out, he has stolen the girlfriend of his benefactor in the previous scene, who enters and engages in a knockabout fight with Chaplin. For some reason, after this, Chaplin comes upon the printing press where Lehrman works, and applies for a job as a reporter. Lehrman intervenes with the editor and Chaplin is refused. Chaplin, however, witnesses a car crash, and while others gather around to help, he steals a photographer's plates and runs back to the press.

What is notable about the film is the quantity of comic business which Chaplin brings to his character. In kissing the hand of the woman, he twists his mouth and smacks his lips appraisingly, judging the taste — after giving her the ring he is more bold, kissing all the way up her arm to her shoulder. When pleading with the editor for a job, he pounds his fist on the man's knee repeatedly, demanding to be heard — when the knee is moved away, he moves it back so it can be pounded on again. He grabs the man by his bald pate and twists his head around to get his attention — and later on, after receiving a job from the man, he kisses the same bald pate.

The film accelerates into the final fight and chases as was expected of all Keystones. But before this, Chaplin has succeeded in injecting a fair amount of himself into the film — the psychological subtlety that was so much a part of his art, the "personality" which transcended all else. He was bitterly disappointed by the finished product, feeling that many of his best improvisations had been cut. Even so, what remains is the enthusiasm of a young comedian playing a scoundrel and a good-for-nothing with all the energy and genius at his disposal, working every minute he's on the screen in the pursuit of funniness and fame.

After this he was shoved into another film by Sennett as an afterthought. Told to grab a costume and add some gags to a Mabel Normand comedy in progress, he dashed to the wardrobe department and returned dressed in the clothes and makeup that, with very little alteration, he would wear for the next thirty-five years.

Chaplin would later describe the dual birth of the Tramp costume and character—for, as he said, one gave rise, magically, to the other—as a sort of mystic, miraculous birth. Miraculous as his sudden inspiration arguably was, many elements of the costume in which he arrived at the hotel lobby set had their precedents in the past. The derby he wore had been the signature headwear of British music hall comedians since before Chaplin's birth. The mustache he donned was, again, for the appearance of age, but now it was clipped back from the handlebar style of his previous film to allow for more freedom of expression—its more minute proportions are similar to the mustache he is seen wearing in a backstage photograph of the Karno troupe from three years before. Though Chaplin would later remember that the baggy pants and oversized shoes were also born instantaneously on the way to *Mabel's Strange Predicament*—the title of the film—we see today that his pants here are only moderately loose, his shoes normal-sized. The waddling gait, which Stan Laurel remembered him using in the Karno days,[17] isn't quite so pronounced here—it would assert itself in time.

Told to enter the hotel lobby set and provide some "business," Chaplin shambled before the cameras and improvised a series of gags which to all accounts entranced the Keystone crew, winning over the dubious Sennett and securing Chaplin's place at the company.

The Tramp lingers around the lobby, flirting with women who are manifestly scornful and uninterested. He ambles about, leisurely smoking a cigarette. His actions are of themselves not funny, but it is his attitude which is funny—and preposterous. Chaplin had decided that the character was one who did not belong in the lobby—who was pretending to belong, but was really only a tramp looking for shelter and warmth. In the film we see a creature feigning insouciance who does not belong in the space he's in—who has no business being there, and, as far as we can tell, no has no idea what it is he thinks he's doing there. He keeps failing in his attempts to sit in a chair for no apparent reason—though the ineptitude increases as he begins taking hits from his pocket flask.

He isn't a real tramp—at one point he hands a porter some bills for helping him back into his chair. Yet he is not entirely a comic drunk either. His outrageous come-hithers to the young ladies are absurd rather than crude. He simply does silly things — like grabbing a passing dog's tail in order to right himself from the chair, and slapping a man across the buttocks with his cane without provocation. He moves in strange, jerky, yet graceful rhythms and movements.

He is like a person superimposed upon the world, an image projected on it, yet not part of it. All the other characters go about their missions with defined objectives, a sober focus. But he merely floats among them like a ghost, his mission, his raison d'etre, forever a mystery, if it exists at all.

The strange predicament of the title is one typical of the Keystones and of the effervescent, luminous Mabel Normand: Mabel is occupying a room in a hotel with her dog, planning to meet up with her lover later; across the hall an old crone and her husband are lodging. All the unsubtle confoundments which can be wrung from that set-up are wrung — people hiding under beds, etc. — and Charlie wanders through it, not exactly part of it, just another dash of chaos to add to the proceedings. He carries on with his flirtation when his lasciviousness is aroused by the sight of Mabel in her pajamas in the hotel hall.

Some traits of the Tramp are already present. We see him do the back-kick gesture — where he kicks behind him to send a discarded object or piece of waste spiraling disdainfully into the ether — two times, in one case using it as a bizarre gesture of flirtation. As well, his bamboo cane is present and accounted for, enlivened into its own unique existence by the overflow of energy and life from Charlie, in whose hands it assumes shapes and purposes heretofore undreamed of — he performs the familiar gag of swinging it around and hitting himself on the head with it several times. As he had in his prior film, he performs a series of remarkable falls throughout, each time leaping high into the air and going into a half-backflip, landing on the small of his back, his buttocks protruding and his legs spread-eagled. At one point he goes to kick someone, misses, and flies backwards, seemingly landing on his neck.

Chaplin dominates the film — he is what we take away from it. He would later remember that they let the camera run on as he improvised in his opening scene, letting the take last longer than customary for a Keystone film. And so we see him here already adapting the medium to his talent, mastering it to serve the demands of his comedy of personality, of attitude.

It was these attributes of his comedy which would account for his rapid rise to stardom from this moment on. Ford Sterling, Mabel Normand, Chester Conklin, Roscoe Arbuckle, and Ben Turpin were all great, hilarious performers. But it was the psychological depth of Chaplin's performances, the attitude behind the ridiculous actions, difficult though it was to define, which gave him the edge on virtually all other comedians, and made his work revolutionary. His ability to portray this depth in a subtle way as a performer would translate itself into the sensitivity and sophistication he would develop as a filmmaker when he began to take over writing and directing as well.

What also made Chaplin different from other screen comics up to that time was the comic business he performed. The gags he improvised were of a different tone than what the American comedians did—Chaplin's actions were unpredictable, often nonsensical, and audacious. They came from the broad behavioral surrealism of the British music hall, and the foolish absurd actions flowed easily in all their cheerful illogic through the character of the Tramp in a way that they couldn't have through the character Chaplin had adopted in his previous film, the comic villain. The Tramp is less restricted, undefined, a man from nowhere, a blank canvas, an empty vessel, an open door into the graceful madness behind the pillars of Victorian England.

After such a breakthrough, there was little doubt as to what costume Chaplin would wear in his next film. Sennett needed to get some footage to fill out half of a reel (each reel lasting ten minutes) and so a crew was dispatched to photograph some children's go-kart races in nearby Venice, California. In typical Keystone fashion, the event was used as the found backdrop for the creation of comedy, and so the film, *Kid Auto Races at Venice*, consists simply of Chaplin as the Tramp improvising around and in the midst of the races of the title.

Kid Auto Races was released before *Mabel's Strange Predicament*, though made after it—and so it is cosmically suitable that the first film to introduce the Tramp to the world is essentially a five-minute character portrait of what would become cinema's greatest and most recognizable figure. It simply consists of the Tramp—there are no other characters—loitering, lollygagging, and getting in the way of the "newsreel" crew trying to photograph the kid auto races. The figure who would actually come to symbolize film the world over is here seen darting in and out of frame, insinuating himself into the cinematic proceedings—he shows an active interest in the camera, peering quizzically into it, positioning himself in front of it with faux nonchalance.

It is a film with no plot, no chase—it's merely a wide-open, free spectacle of Chaplin as the Tramp ad-libbing comedy before our eyes and before the eyes of the crowd of real-life race enthusiasts, who are far more interested in the said race than in the diminutive, twitching Englishman who is creating one of the most enduring characters of the twentieth century in their midst.

The Tramp, again, does not belong here. Perhaps he does not belong anywhere. He ambles about, smoking a cigarette, ever so casually finding himself in front of the camera once again, and when he is repeatedly pushed out of camera view he is affronted, but undaunted in his determination to drift back into frame, to be photographed. As with the rejection of his flirtations in the previous film, he seems to take no offense at the angry punches and kicks which the cameramen dole out to him, sending him catapulting onto his backside—he only begins positioning himself once again with outrageous insouciance, strolling between the cameras and the go-karts. At one point, for no apparent reason, he takes off and runs maniacally down the length of the track. The film ends with him shoving his face directly into the lens of the camera, twisting his features into a childish grimace.

By now it must have been seen that the Tramp costume and character were too good to give up. He was inserted into *Between Showers*, a more elaborate and typical Keystone comedy, and one which displays the elemental simplicity of the Keystone method. *Between Showers* is a film concerning itself with the peregrinations of an umbrella. Ford Sterling trades in his tattered wreck of an umbrella for the more desirable, functional one of Charlie Conklin, unbeknownst to Conklin. Later, Sterling helps a desirable female across a puddle — he leaves to get a board for the purpose, handing her the umbrella, but when he has returned, a handsome policeman has already performed the service for the damsel, and she refuses to give Sterling the umbrella back. He begins to remonstrate with her, and the Tramp intervenes, defending the woman. In the end another policeman is summoned, who turns out to be Conklin, the original owner of the umbrella — he hauls Sterling off to jail.

All of the action, as was the custom, is merely an excuse for the characters to pummel and kick each other, to wring each other's necks and take preposterous pratfalls. Again, Charlie is the outsider, who wanders into the conflict — at times he "comments" on it directly to the camera, laughing joyfully with his hand over his mouth in what will soon become a familiar gesture. This puckish, mischievous quality will be another aspect which will propel Chaplin to stardom — his great charm as a performer, his "cuteness," is coming to the fore.

As well, and as attractive to audiences, there is his obvious disdain for any sort of authority. Here, as in *Mabel's Strange Predicament* and *Kid Auto Races*, he is fond of sticking his tongue out at anyone who would reprimand him — mostly behind their back — and he thumbs his nose at a policeman.

His next two films are rather less interesting, seemingly more hastily contrived, makeshift affairs. *A Film Johnnie* has at its heart a gambit that Chaplin himself would use in two films of his own in the future — when lacking an idea, simply use filmmaking itself as an idea for a film, pressing the studio and cameras into service as a backdrop for comedy. The Tramp here comes to seek employment at a film studio, his penniless desperation at the outset marking him definitively, for perhaps the first time, as a genuine tramp. Slapstick, even less motivated than in other films of the period, ensues, along with a suspiciously authentic-looking fire, but beyond providing more screen time for the Tramp, there is little that dignifies the film.

Tango Tangles is the result of Sennett sending several of his stars down to a real-life dance hall to improvise some footage. So off-the-cuff was this production that the actors did not even bother to get into costume and makeup. They simply wore their daily attire, so we see Chaplin, playing drunk again, but in a natty suit, with a clean-shaven face. He dances, and as usual, flips and falls down repeatedly, but we see, in its absence, the necessity of his make-up, of his mustache. As graceful and as athletically inventive as ever, Chaplin is here a handsome, debonair young man —compelling, but hardly the figure of fun and eerie surrealism he is when wearing the clown mask of the Tramp. A film of defiant silliness, *Tango Tangles* also boasts the appearance of Roscoe "Fatty" Arbuckle, who contributes several outrageously gymnastic pratfalls of his own.

The Tramp is back with a vengeance in *His Favorite Pastime*, which opens in a bar and has Chaplin mining drunkenness for laughs once again. What is most striking about the Tramp in this film is his hostility and cruelty. When a barfly (Arbuckle) begs for a sip of his beer, the Tramp taunts him with it, allowing him to blow the head off it, and repeatedly making as if to offer him some — before downing the whole thing himself. Later, a restroom attendant puts his hand out for a tip and the Tramp burns it with a lit match. He fights a losing battle with the swinging restroom door, which springs back to belt him again and again as he attempts to exit — he finally gives in and crawls under the door. But mostly the Tramp's battles are with other men, and he lays thoroughly unprovoked beatings on several of them, sending them caroming from one room into another throughout the film.

In the next film, *Cruel, Cruel Love*, he abandons the Tramp costume and character; here his mustache is more dainty and stylish, and he seems to be wearing the frock coat from *Making a Living*. He is a lover, whose budding romance with Minta Durfee is derailed when she mistakenly believes him to be involved with her maid. She sends him off, and he is so distraught that he attempts to commit suicide by drinking poison — as he believes life to be ebbing from him, he has a bizarre vision of himself in the fiery regions of hell, devils tormenting him at each side. Water had been substituted for the poison by his roommate, so Chaplin does not die, and his chastened lover, learning the truth, comes to embrace him once again. Before that, there is plenty of roughhousing, with Chaplin unveiling a new move — leaping high into the air to kick someone in the chest — along with plenty of the standard "people being thrown from one room into another" shots. The film is mainly a curiosity. Chaplin's performance is energetic, but his character seems a regression after what he's been developing as the Tramp — and the "suicidal" plotline isn't conducive to big laughs. Presumably, as Chaplin was still a mere actor-for-hire, he had little choice about scenarios or the characters he was assigned to play within them.

Somewhat better is *The Star Boarder*. Back in Tramp costume again, Chaplin is the boarder of the film's title, who is having a casual, not-so-clandestine affair with his landlady — which understandably annoys her husband. Chaplin has an opportunity to belt himself in the nose with a tennis ball on one of his dates with the landlady, and to send himself spiraling to the ground during a serve — Chaplin's physical dexterity in itself provides the most compelling reason to view these early comedies. Later, the Tramp consumes an icebox full of alcohol, once more descending into comic drunkenness. The Tramp's assignation with the landlady is captured by a young boy photographer, who also catches the landlady's husband in some compromising poses. He is able to project them on the wall with a "magic lantern" in the final scenes, precipitating the expected knock-down drag-out festival of pummeling and kicking.

Chaplin was next thrown into *Mabel at the Wheel*, a production starring Mabel Normand, by whom it was also directed. Intended as a satire on the Pearl White serial thrillers of the time, the film features Mabel being courted by a car racer, who is temporarily usurped by a villain. He makes off with Mabel on his motorcycle, but is defeated when Mabel returns to her boyfriend. The villain takes his revenge by attempting to sabotage Mabel's car in the race which concludes the film. The villain is played by Chaplin, who enters into the part with demonic gusto, aggressively mugging his way through a series of dastardly actions. His tiny mustache is here augmented by a slight goatee, adding a devilish flair to his appearance — he seems also to be wearing his frock coat again from *Making a Living*.

As always, he gives his all to the performance, and his nasty little sociopath — who walks about sticking hapless bystanders with a pin — provides most of what life there is in the film. But *Mabel at the Wheel*'s prime significance derives from events which took place off-screen. Chaplin adored Mabel Normand as a co-worker and as an actress, but he considered her unqualified to direct him — when he tried to suggest a gag to improve a scene and was rebuffed, he strode away and seated himself on a curb, refusing to work, informing her of his lack of confidence in her as a director. It was near the end of the day, so not much work was lost, but Normand was distraught, and the crew members had to be talked out of slugging "the Limey," as they called Chaplin. Since Normand and Mack Sennett were lovers, it was widely assumed that Chaplin had completed his final day of work at Keystone.[18]

For Chaplin, Normand in and of herself was not the main problem — though he was correct in his assessment of her as an ineffective director and of the film as uninspired and substandard. He had in fact been frustrated and infuriated by all of his directors to date, save Sennett himself, who had allowed him freer range and expression in *Mabel's Strange Predicament*. Henry Lehrman and "Pop" Nichols, the other directors, rejected Chaplin's suggestions, edited out his improvisations. His attempts to inject gags into the films were met with dismissive cries of "There's no time!"[19]— meaning that the tempo always had to be quick, the film always has to be racing along to its conclusive chase. He had attained a reputation as being difficult, and he had pleaded Sennett to allow him to write and direct his own films.

Chaplin was called into Sennett's office the next day, fully expecting to be fired. Sennett was more than conciliatory — because, as Chaplin would learn months later, word had recently come from New York on the immense popularity of the films which had featured Chaplin to date, and orders were pouring in for more Chaplin films. Chaplin boldly put himself forth as director again, promising to put up the money for the film in the event it flopped. Sennett assented, and it was now Chaplin's task to apply himself to the Keystone method, to infuse it with his comedy of personality and attitude.[20]

The Keystone method, as restrictive as Chaplin apparently found it, was successful because it was a fun-house mirror of American society in 1914. All of the men in the films are skirt-chasing scoundrels and/or drunks. All of the women are either flirtatious young beauties or old withered crones. The characters are all driven by lust, greed, vengeance, or by some ludicrous combination of all three — and within the final five minutes of any given ten-minute film worth its salt, these various ingredients have combined to send the characters tumbling about the screen, throttling, pummeling, gouging, kicking, biting like barnyard animals — leaping into the air like porpoises and falling on their keisters like befuddled toddlers. The films are hyper, electrified, spasmic eruptions bursting through the last fraying bonds of Victorian morals and values — contemporary reviewers found their frank, frenzied sexuality and energetic, remorseless violence quite vulgar.

The films, with their highly stylized acting and symbolic gestures, have their own language, and their unvarying structure gives them a sense of ritual. Much like the Model Ts which Henry Ford had recently begun to mass produce and which figure prominently in these films, the Keystones are uniform in their sturdy, dependable, mechanical assembly-line way. For Chaplin, their rapid production had allowed him to become familiar with the new medium and to put before the public a consistent, recognizable character who had found favor in only two months. Now, his task was to enlarge upon the nuanced touches — so important to his art — which he had been able to inject into the rapid Keystone style up to that date.

There is some question as to which film is Chaplin's first as scenarist and director. Chaplin remembered it to be *Caught in the Rain*, but *Twenty Minutes of Love* was released first, and certainly bears all the earmarks of being the work of a first-time director — similar in its elementality to *Between Showers*, it chooses a simple storyline, so as not to go too far wrong. The film utilizes several of the Keystone mainstays — it is set in a park, and as in the Shakespearean comedies, love is everywhere, couples canoodling on every bench and behind every bush.

The Tramp enters, first disgustedly mocking the spooning couple on a nearby bench, then actively interfering with their lovemaking. Meanwhile, another couple is experiencing problems — she demands that he go off and provide some money for her. The man stalks off, and steals a pocket watch from a man sleeping on a bench. Before he can present it to her, it is in turn pickpocketed from him by Charlie, who presents it to the guy's girlfriend in his absence. When the man comes upon this he angrily demands the watch back, and Charlie snatches it away and runs off.

Here Chaplin works in a gag whose cleverness looks ahead to the intricate gags which will become typical of his work. In running off with the watch, the Tramp comes upon the sleeping man from whom the watch was stolen in the first place, unbeknownst to the Tramp. Charlie wakes the guy up, and hurriedly tells him — all in mime — to hold onto the watch for him, pretend it's his, as his pursuers get nearer. The man, waking up, looks at the watch and says that it is, in fact, his watch. Yes, yes, Charlie tells him through his gestures, that's fine, just what I want—of course, it's "yours." But the man, laying his hands proprietarily on the watch, says, This—is—my watch. And the Tramp then begins fighting with him.

The film ends with the original pickpocket, his girlfriend, and the sleeping man all beating up on Charlie. But before this, we have seen a perfectly serviceable direction of a solid comedy, with perhaps a few longer takes than are commonly seen in a Keystone comedy of the time—with perhaps a storyline a bit more focused and uncluttered, some shots which are composed more carefully. It is in fact a rather ingenious little film, and its lightness bears witness to Chaplin's remembrance that it was shot entirely in one afternoon.

Chaplin was again put under the directorship of Mabel Normand—presumably a new understanding had been reached between them—for *Caught in a Cabaret*. Here the Tramp is a waiter in the cabaret of the title who masquerades as the Greek ambassador on his off-time, courting Mabel. There is the contrast between the aristocratic bearing Chaplin assumes as the ambassador and his lowly status as a worker in the very cheap-looking honky-tonk—and Chaplin will return to the idea of a lower-class person impersonating a dignitary in future films. In the end, Mabel stops in at the café when Charlie is working there, leading him to frenziedly attempt to conceal his real status. In the resulting fracas, Charlie's Herculean boss at the café—played by the stalwart Edgar Kennedy—flies off the handle and pulls out a handgun, shooting indiscriminately in every direction. A rather stark and disturbing conclusion.

Caught in a Cabaret is the first of only a handful of two-reeler (twenty-minute length) films Chaplin made at Keystone. It doesn't sustain its added length particularly well.

Chaplin is back in the director's chair for *Caught in the Rain*, sometimes designated as his first directorial effort. He is out walking in the park when he comes upon the matronly wife of Mack Swain. Swain, here in his first role with Chaplin, is the first in a progression of large, mountain-like men, who will perform the role of "Goliath" to Charlie's "David" throughout the Chaplin canon. Charlie is quite taken with Swain's wife, infuriating the larger man. The problem is compounded when Mack and his wife turn in at their hotel for the night, only to find that Charlie, now well-intoxicated, is boarding in the room across the hall. Later, Swain's wife sleepwalks, and finds herself in the Tramp's room. Their frenzied attempts to conceal this situation from Swain as he returns comprise the last third of the film—Charlie ends up hiding out on the balcony in the rain. The Keystone Kops spy him, shooting at him to make him come down. In the end, as always, chaos reigns, and Chaplin has created another solid comedy—though perhaps a shade less amusing and inventive than *Twenty Minutes of Love*.

As if to verify the erratic and idiosyncratic strain of the releases to date, the next film is one of the split-reel (five-minute) releases created when Sen-nett ordered his camera crew and actors out to a special event that was hap-pening in the area, to utilize it as a premise around which to improvise some comedy. Here, the event is a marching band and parade. Oddly, Chaplin decided not to perform as the Tramp, but spends the entire duration of the film as a new character — a woman.

In *A Busy Day*, his character is a sour-faced little urchin, a mean-spirited ridiculous busybody who is ever jealous of the actions of her philandering hus-band. She is a spitfire who spends the film leaping at and attacking her hus-band and virtually all the men with whom she comes in contact. In one of Chaplin's most violent performances, she is thrown, and throws others, in and out of frame throughout — though at one point she pauses to do an ungainly, appalling dance to the music of the marching band. At the end of this strange five minutes of spasmodic convulsions, the obstreperous little fishwife is thrown from a dock and left to gurgle beneath the waves — mourned by no one.

The Fatal Mallet is another crude and simple film, this time directed by, and co-starring, Mack Sennett himself. Here, as in real life, Mack and Mabel Normand are lovers, until they are disrupted by the jealous Charlie, who expresses his ire by throwing bricks at them. They throw bricks back at him, and Sennett and the Tramp become involved in a fight of their own, as Mabel swiftly becomes involved with a third suitor, the immense Mack Swain. The Tramp and Sennett now unite to take Swain out of the picture, approaching him with armloads of bricks which are flung at his head to no apparent effect. At this point, Charlie and Sennett discover the large mallet of the film's title and utilize it to dispatch Swain, carrying his supine body into a barn. After they've laid him out — Charlie characteristically bestowing a goodnight kiss on his brow — we are given a display of just how much of a disreputable double-crosser the early Tramp could be: he knocks Sennett out with the mallet as well and skips off to meet Mabel on his own. The film ends with Sennett and Swain coming to; the former pitches Charlie and Swain into a nearby pond, as Mabel and Mack Sennett are united once again.

After *The Fatal Mallet* — a silly and brutal comic strip trifle — a film named *Her Friend the Bandit* usually follows in most filmographies. The film is now lost, the only one of the Chaplin Keystones to bear that sad designation — what with the flammable nature of nitrate film, and the offhanded manner with which these films have been treated over the past ninety years, we are fortu-nate to have the majority of them even in the patchy, washed-out state so many of them are in. From the scant information we have on *Her Friend the Bandit*, we know that Chaplin was the thief of the title and that his co-star was Mabel Normand, so presumably it was another collaboration between the two.

Chaplin was then recruited for a cameo in *The Knockout*, a Roscoe "Fatty" Arbuckle two-reeler. Arbuckle agrees to enter a boxing match with Cyclone Flynn. He makes an agreement with someone whom he believes to be Flynn but is actually an imposter, to throw the fight and to split the money. Before the fight, Mack Swain informs Arbuckle that he has bet big money on him, so he'd better win — or he'll shoot him. In addition, the real Flynn comes to town, and climbs into the ring. Chaplin appears late in the film in his bit part as the referee for the fight, and adds a few gags to this very ordinary comedy. He moves with balletic grace and manages to get himself mixed up in the fight, but unfortunately the entire sequence is ineptly photographed in long shot.

Again, what's noticeable here is Chaplin's ability in these very broad films to invest his performance with so much nuance and character. The other actors in these films simply aren't able to communicate emotion as clearly and appealingly as does Chaplin. His attention-grabbing makeup as the Tramp — the smudge of a mustache over his upper lip, the thick exclamation point — like marks above his eyebrows— make his facial expressions easier to read, and they define his face in a way the faces of those around him are not defined. At times, Chaplin's performances are so refined compared to those around him that they scarcely seem to be practicing the same art.

He was teamed again with Mabel Normand in yet another Keystone use of a local event to serve as background for a comedy, this event being a car race. The film, *Mabel's Busy Day*, features Mabel trying to sell hot dogs at the event, with Charlie interfering. The action seems largely improvised and, on Chaplin's part, again consists mostly of a series of kicks, clouts, and slaps.

It is clear from all of these films, but especially with *Mabel's Busy Day*, how deeply important violence was to Chaplin's early comedy. Slapstick was common to Keystone before his arrival, but no one lifts a leg into the air, aims it at an opponent, and straightens it out into a kick that sends the malefactor sprawling out of frame with as much dash and panache as Chaplin. There is a savage and vicious pleasure he takes in the boffs on the head he dishes out to his enemies which send them tumbling to the earth in dazed confusion. There is a curt yet deep satisfaction he takes in grabbing someone by the face and dismissing him from his proximity with a disdainful sweep of the arm. Often, such actions are taken for no discernible reason at all. Chaplin's athletic, graceful and enthusiastic displays of violence are statements in and of themselves. Chaplin's delight in leaping into the air and kicking someone in the chest is undeniable — and infectious.

If it is true, as Chaplin remembered, that no one was ever injured in any of the slapstick stunts in his films,[21] it is a tribute to his skills, and the skills of all the other actors particularly in films like these, that they were able to present such impeccable simulations of violence. It was all choreographed, he remembered, like a dance.

After these digressions, Chaplin was again able to direct — *Mabel's Married Life*, for which he collaborated on the scenario with Normand. Charlie and Mabel are married, but Charlie is made jealous by the large Mack Swain. In an extended gag which he'll use in future films (*Easy Street*), Chaplin attacks Mack's backside with his foot and his cane as the larger man woos Mabel — but all of Charlie's feverish exertions count for nothing, as his opponent remains completely unaffected by Chaplin's exertions.

The most notable scene in the film occurs later, when Charlie arrives home after a night of drinking. During the day, Mabel bought a boxing mannequin and has left it standing in the living room — with its sweater and cap, it very much resembles Chaplin's rival of that afternoon — and so the drunken Charlie is quite taken aback to see him there, standing before him in such an insolent manner. Chaplin looks back at the door, thinking that maybe he's entered the wrong apartment. Then he approaches the mannequin, and calmly tries to reason with it. His anger grows as the mannequin refuses to answer him. He opens the door, demanding that the mannequin leave. He pushes against the mannequin's chest, and is quite outraged that the mannequin pivots back at him on its rounded bottom. Chaplin takes off his coat, determined to have it out with the defiant intruder once and for all.

What's incredible about this fairly long shot (for Keystone) is Charlie's unshakeable conviction that the faceless mannequin is his rival of earlier that day, and the reality of Chaplin's growing vexation as the mannequin refuses to speak to him, to explain itself. It is the first extended incidence of Chaplin's power to give life to inanimate objects, simply through the depth and strength of his conviction, through his physical reaction to, and interaction with them. He is somehow able to recreate reality so that it corresponds to his temperament, his feelings about it, his psychological needs. When he does something as simple and as silly as mistaking a dummy for a real person, he is not merely foolish, for there is something deadly serious and utterly sincere in his belief that the mannequin is mocking him. What he does here, as he will increasingly do in the future, is to call into question the very concept of objective reality — for this character, the universe is simply there to be reordered according to his mood. This non-acceptance of the defined limits of reality which the Tramp will display again and again is, ultimately, madness — or would be looked upon as such outside of the cinematic world the Tramp inhabits. Here, in film, Chaplin's inability to come to terms with reality, his insistence in reordering it, recreating it, giving new, strange, unexpected life to it, allows him to triumph over and transcend it, even from his lowly status.

Chaplin's next directorial effort is *Laughing Gas*, a comedy set in a dentist's office where Charlie works as a dental assistant. The setting of this undistinguished film isn't important — it's just another in the series of ultra-violent dust-ups, with Charlie kicking and punching everyone from his small co-worker in the office to the patients in the waiting room, mostly without any provocation whatever. The Chaplin of these early films is just a mischievous, vicious imp, who evidently feels inspired to slap someone across the side of the head at every opportunity.

Following in this mode is *The Property Man*, which features Chaplin in the eponymous occupation at a vaudeville theatre. Likely based on Chaplin's own observations as a traveling performer, the film is a two-reeler, perhaps reflective of the more elaborate setting, which is composed of the stage and backstage of a theatre. The tone of *The Property Man* is set in its first moments, as Charlie sits backstage with his co-worker, a frail old man with a long white beard — the Tramp is drinking from a pitcher of beer and the old man asks him for some. The Tramp twists his ear and spits a mouthful of the liquid into the old fellow's face. This is merely a prelude to the twenty minutes of abuse the geriatric sidekick is subjected to: Chaplin repeatedly hits him, kicks him in the face, throws a giant trunk on the old man's back, and when it pins him to the ground, leaps onto the trunk and kicks the old man in the face again — there is a meanness to the "comedy" which kills any humor intended. The film seems interminably long and the Tramp here is nothing more than a crude, violent menace with no redeeming qualities whatever. Mack Sennett plays as a boisterous audience member, his performance signaling once again that his real talents lay on the other side of the camera. In the end, Charlie turns a hose on the audience, drenching them as the film fades out.

Chaplin's next film, *The Face on the Bar Room Floor*, was something of an experiment for him — he based the film on the well-known folk poem of the same name by H.A. d'Arcy. The poem is a hoary tale of a an artist who tells his barroom companions about his betrayal at the hands of a friend who stole his lover away; at the conclusion of his tale he falls dead across the portrait of his beloved he's etched on the barroom floor. The poem was well known to the public of the day, and Chaplin satirizes it (he does several drunken pratfalls across the portrait before dying), as well as using it for the plot and structure of his film. The result is only moderately successful.

Likewise is *Recreation*, a split-reel comedy (five minutes) which was needed to fill out a reel for another film, and seems to have been improvised in great haste for that purpose. It is another park-bench comedy, in which two men get into a fight over a girl in a park, leading to an eruption of brick-throwing. It's the least inspired of the genre so far, and contains nothing particularly memorable.

Perhaps inspiration continued to lag, for the next film, *The Masquerader*, utilizes the old trick of using the studio itself as a backdrop. We see Chaplin himself, clean-shaven, arriving at Keystone for a day's work. Roscoe Arbuckle shares his dressing room, and if this film is correct, the two were just as boisterous and argumentative in real life as on the screen. Chaplin dons the costume of the Tramp, but skirmishes continue until he is ousted from the studio and told not to come back. Cunningly, he returns and gets himself re-employed — as a woman.

Notably, this female impersonation is quite different from the last, in *A Busy Day*, the split-reel in which he played a furious, scolding little battleaxe. Here, he is glamorous, beautiful, flirtatious — he smiles winningly at the boss who had only hours before thrown him out, and who is now smitten with him. It is, again, puzzling and eerie, the degree to which Chaplin is able to bend reality to his will — the comedy lies not in the awkward clown trying to pass in drag, but in his utter effortlessness in doing so, the seamless, fluid, completely convincing adoption of feminine movement and spirit, of a face which projects delicacy and feminine whimsy. He even turns his nose up with catty disdain at other women observing him and the strange hold he has on the men around him. We are in uneasy awe at his ability to erase totally the comforting line of gender division. For he is now so unmistakably "woman" that he mocks us along with all the other dupes in the film — he good-naturedly mocks our presumptions and definitions of gender from the other side of the line, laughing at us like the shape-shifting ephemeral sprite he is.

With *His New Profession*, Chaplin is back in the park, mischievously interfering with a young couple's romance once again. He is given the job of wheeling around the bandaged-footed uncle of the young man of the couple (played by the young Charley Chase). Charlie performs his new job reasonably well, barring a series of bangs and jabs tendered to the bandaged foot — but later, when the old man falls asleep, the Tramp parks him on the street, stealing another handicapped man's "Crippled — Please Help" sign and tin cup, placing them on the slumbering uncle's lap. As donations come in, the Tramp uses them to procure alcohol in the nearest bar — another darkly cunning maneuver from the Chaplin mind.

Chaplin uses Roscoe Arbuckle again in his next film, this time teaming with him in a very conscious way. In *The Rounders* they are both prodigious drunks who have alienated their wives. Chaplin is back in his "Mumming Birds" rake mode, and Arbuckle is his counterpart — they set off staggering into the night together in order to get away from their wives. They are paired as equals, both men's energy as star comedians feeding off each other, but never finding a place to combine and interact — there is the sense that they're actively trying to upstage one another. They stumble into a nightclub and make themselves at home in a fairly lengthy scene, Charlie urbanely striking a match on a man's bald head, and later leaning casually on that head, while Arbuckle stretches out on the floor, using a tablecloth as a blanket. Later, after creating the requisite mayhem, they are chased by their wives and an angry crowd down to the river shore, where they hide, leaping into a rowboat and pretending to sleep. As the film fades out, they slowly sink beneath the river's surface, still snoring away as they are submerged — a memorable image.

This type of calamity, especially with a sidekick as talented as Arbuckle, is amusing, but of all the films of this period, the one which presages most closely the Chaplin that is to come is *The New Janitor*. Charlie is a janitor in an office building, and naturally it isn't long before his antics cause him to be fired. He trudges off, dejected, and there is the slightest hint of pathos. Later, a worker in the office needs to pay off a gambling debt, and so tries to take the money from the safe. A woman in the office discovers him and he gets into a scuffle with her. Charlie enters and saves the woman, catches the would-be thief, and is rewarded.

What Chaplin has devised here is essentially a serious plot, rather than a simple situation which can be accelerated into a chase and/or a conflagration. There is a moment in the middle of the film where Chaplin as director becomes quite interested in fleshing out the straight plot, and we don't see the Tramp for several moments. When Charlie enters and foils the thief, he performs his graceful and magical violence in a heroic manner, not merely as a reflex of his perversely anarchic spirit. He knocks the pistol from the thief's hand with his cane, and as the Tramp bends to pick it up, the guy moves to attack him from behind. In a remarkable feat, the Tramp, unperturbed, bent over, trains the gun on the thief from between his legs.

In showing Charlie capable of performing gallant, heroic actions, Chaplin invests him with more humanity, with deeper meaning—making him, for this moment, less a gyrating one-dimensional cartoon character, more a creature who can reach for something higher than himself even as he struggles for basic survival. While the Tramp's abusive savagery is funny, Chaplin is beginning to see here that he is able to entertain higher ideals and to strive towards them in his splay-footed manner—in doing so, the audience becomes more emotionally invested in him. As the ultimate underdog he has our sympathy, our vote—we're rooting for him all the way. At the same time, he is able to perform acts and gestures which are magical, sublime, beyond all of us. He is from the bottom, beneath us, yet somehow he communes with powers at the very top, in the magic of his actions, in the purity of his ideals. He is absurd because of the incongruity of his aspirations and his lowly status. This is the nature of his strange heroism.

As well, the context in which the Tramp's display of gallantry occurs is important—within the plot Chaplin has constructed, it performs the function of redeeming him, of vindicating him after his earlier, ignominious dismissal. The idea of the Tramp as a character being capable of redemption, of aspiring to noble ideals, is one that will be returned to in the future.

For his next film, Chaplin teamed himself with Chester Conklin, a player in many of the films so far, and a man Chaplin once referred to as "the funniest man in the world."[22] Conklin invariably performed in glasses and a walrus-like mustache, mining, as did Ford Sterling, the then-current comic stereotype of the phlegmatic Dutchman. *Those Love Pangs* features Charlie and Chester as rival suitors, first for a woman in their boarding house, then for a variety of women in the world as large. It's another Keystone film about the eternal erotic pursuit, but there is much charm in the execution here, largely emanating from Chaplin's reactions and performance. When Conklin jabs Charlie with a fork through a curtain as Charlie's trying to make time with a woman, the Tramp's reaction is convincing and ridiculous at the same time—ridiculous as his later strange and impenetrable gestures as he skirmishes with Conklin. Later, he departs from the house with Conklin, his cane hooked around Conklin's neck and dragging him down the steps. Then there are Charlie's vigorous stares of stunned and appalled disbelief as he sees that the walrus-mustached, beady-eyed Conklin has somehow connected with a beautiful damsel in the park (it's quite easy to lip-read her calling to him —"Hey, Chester!"). At the sight of the gnome-like man being caressed by the girl, Charlie is so overcome with disgust that he has to lie down on a park bench — then he contemplates drowning himself in a pond.

Charlie begins taking a shine to another woman in the park — he starts to flirt with her, but her boyfriend appears, foiling his attempts. At one point he fights with the man, and they animatedly argue on the bank of the pond. In their furious gesticulations, Charlie keeps tipping back, stumbling and almost falling into the pond behind him. His opponent reaches forward each time, grabbing him and steadying him. This happens four times. Then Chaplin neatly hooks his cane around his opponent's neck, deftly catapults him into the pond, kicks him in the head, and runs away.

He soon dispatches Chester Conklin in a similarly vicious manner, helping himself to his money. He observes Conklin's and the man's girlfriends heading into a cinema, so he follows. We see him then gaily seated between the two women in the theatre, his arms around their shoulders, regaling them with exquisite small talk as his legs and feet, inexplicably held aloft, are presumably communicating in some obscure form of sign language. But Chester and the man have recovered and arrive at the theater to exact their revenge. Havoc ensues, and Charlie is pitched through the movie screen.

This ending is one similar to those before — the Tramp so infuriating the other people with whom he comes in contact that they unite to pay him back for the chaos he's created (*Twenty Minutes of Love*, *The Masquerader*, *A Busy Day*, *The Rounders*). It's like an admission that Charlie can only keep kicking people around and acting in his violently antisocial manner for so long before he has to pay the price for it.

He is unpredictably and energetically brutal for such a small man, and his double-crossing, deceptive and spiteful actions— except for his foiling of the robbery in *The New Janitor*— attest to the fact that he has no scruples, and no loyalty to anyone but himself. In his assiduous pursuit of flesh and money he is without sentiment, and he is one for whom the end justifies any means, no matter how savage. He has no remorse or repentance, nothing but a steely eye for the main chance. It's no wonder that the crowd races to condemn him by the film's end.

His kicks and punches are shocking — that's why we laugh at their athletic outlandishness. But also we appreciate the honesty and courage of his sad grasp on life's grim and bitter truth, his connection to the essential violence of existence which so much of our behavior is designed to avoid or conceal. There is a strong strain of the sadist in Chaplin — and with it, the knowledge that life, too, is sadistic. Chaplin is connected viscerally to this essential violence of life, this unvarnished, primal battle to escape extinction that he, unlike the rest of us, refuses to deny. This is why the crowds chase him as well.

Feeling his oats as a director/scenarist, Chaplin next fashioned *Dough and Dynamite*, reportedly with some help on the writing from Mack Sennett. It is more ambitious in terms of plot: Charlie is a waiter at a café/bakery in which the unhappy bakers react to their boss's refusal to increase their wages by going on strike. Charlie is pressed into service as a worker in the bakery, while the angry bakers try to sabotage the establishment by inserting a stick of dynamite into a loaf of bread.

The plot is more elaborate as well as using for its basis something real and gritty — as he would do in the future, Chaplin utilizes events which could be torn from the headlines of a newspaper, which are prosaic, serious and not comic at all, and builds comedy around them. This will later be seen in his depiction of poverty, squalor, alcoholism, drug addiction, war, starvation and child abandonment in his comedies, and it is seen here in his depiction of a labor dispute. So absorbed was he in this more substantive plot that Chaplin exceeded his budget, nearly doubling it. Sennett insisted that the film be a two-reeler in order to recoup its expense, and it was a great success.

In his role as the waiter-turned-baker, Charlie performs several neat tricks — balancing a tray on his head which remains in position as he swiftly turns his body beneath it, fashioning bracelets of dough around his wrists which then become doughnuts — but mostly he is engaged in his usual occupations: flirting cutely with any female who happens to be present, and kicking and slapping any male in the vicinity. His target for the latter activity is mostly Chester Conklin, featured prominently once more. At one point, in response to one of Charlie's more egregious attacks, Chester administers a rapid-fire flurry of ass-kicks to the Chaplin posterior. The film ends as the strikers get a young girl to bring the dynamite-laden loaf of bread into the bakery, ostensibly "returning" it. Charlie notes that it needs to be baked some more, and the resulting explosion destroys the bakery, burying him under a massive blob of dough.

Less ambitious is Chaplin's next film, *Gentlemen of Nerve* — it returns to the old tack of ambushing a real-life event and improvising comedy on the fly. Here, it is a car race, and we can see the amused reactions of the onlookers to the escapades of Charlie and his friends — the popularity of the films ensured that the crowds could not be indifferent as they were in *Kid Auto Races in Venice*, eight months earlier. Mabel and Chester Conklin attend the races, though Chester must first contend with the flirtatious advances of Mack Swain towards his girlfriend before they enter the arena. Once in, Chester begins doing a little flirting of his own towards another woman. Outside the gates, the Tramp happens upon the scene and tries to finagle his way in — with Mack, he discovers a hole in the fence which they try to put to use. Swain's massive frame becomes stuck in the fence and several hundred feet of film are spent with Charlie trying to push him through the fence. Inside, the Tramp wastes no time in making time with Mabel, and when Chester comes upon them he attacks the Tramp, who sends both Conklin and Swain sprawling against a policeman. The officer duly escorts them out, leaving Charlie in bliss with Mabel. The film is simply another exercise in rowdiness, with the Tramp dishing out some especially vicious beatings on all and sundry, at one point purposely burning Swain's face with his cigarette.

By contrast, *His Musical Career* is a neatly constructed comedy in which Chaplin again makes use of Mack Swain. They are movers who are given the job of delivering a piano to one address, and repossessing a piano from another. Struggling and straining with the piano out to their rickety mule-driven cart, they naturally deliver the piano to the house they are supposed to collect from ("Mr. Poor's" residence), and go and seize a piano from the home they are supposed to deliver to ("Mr. Rich"). There is some good byplay between Chaplin and Swain, and an interesting, "impossible" gag — at the first residence, Charlie lifts the piano onto his shoulders, carrying it around as Mack and the proprietor debate about where it should be placed. At the end, after they have made off with the piano from the second house, they encounter its well-heeled owner. He attacks them, demanding his piano back. The piano goes rolling down a hill, along with Mack and Charlie — and into a river, Charlie merrily tinkling the ivories as they sink beneath the waves.

In *His Trysting Place*, Charlie is married to Mabel Normand, and they have a son. The Tramp would seem to be a well-intentioned, if unconventional, father — at one point he lifts his son by the scruff of the neck to give him a kiss. Charlie is sent out by Mabel to get a baby bottle — at the same time as Mack Swain departs his wife. Swain is given an envelope by a woman to mail for her: it contains a love note advising her beloved to meet her at their favorite "trysting place." Swain and Chaplin go to the same restaurant and exchange coats by mistake — resulting in Charlie's wife finding the note apparently beckoning him to an assignation, and Mack's wife finding the baby bottle, leading her to suspect him of rather more intensive dalliances.

Before this, Charlie has entered the restaurant, and for no apparent reason, picks a bun off a bearded man's plate and starts eating it. The man turns to glare angrily at him. Quite unconcerned about the man's ire, Charlie calmly wipes his fingers on his beard. Then Chaplin and Swain share a great scene as the two of them eat at the diner counter. The large and perspiring Mack hungrily slurps his soup down as Charlie observes him with withering disgust — at one point he mimes playing a fiddle to give some idea of the ungodly sounds Mack makes as he sucks the liquid from his spoon. The scene is the first of many in Chaplin's films which will concern themselves with food — its mastication, digestion, and excretion as well, if one takes into account the concern he shows for the posterior in his films, not only in terms of the punishment it takes from the constant kicking, but in the solicitude and care with which the Tramp tends to his own rear after a fall or mishap.

Repellent scenes of individuals eating with appalling table manners is a constant throughout Chaplin's work, and here Swain follows up his ghastly soup guzzling with several sneezes in the direction of Charlie's plate. The Tramp, as always, is abhorred by this grotesque and unseemly conduct, despite his being no great follower of social etiquette himself. He gnaws a large meat bone, trying to shield it from further precipitation from Swain—when Mack reaches in front of him for the salt, Charlie bites into his arm instead of the bone. This is all played out in one take—as with Charlie's earlier struggle with the boxing mannequin in *Mabel's Married Life*, Chaplin has slowed the frenzied Keystone pace to concentrate on character; in this case, the subtle interactions between two characters. In the end, after the expected misunderstandings and confrontations, Mabel and Charlie are united once again, and with their child; they embrace, in an oddly moving ending. Mabel Normand, as always, is sympathetic and charismatic throughout.

By this time, Chaplin had made great inroads as a director and scenarist, as well as in evolving the Tramp character which was becoming steadily more popular with the public. Perhaps it was irksome to him that Sennett then recruited him to star in an ambitious production under Sennett's direction. It was Sennett's ambition to produce the first full-length comedy feature—to gain backing, he engaged the world-famous stage performer, Cobourg, Ontario-born Marie Dressler, and set about converting her great stage success, *Tillie's Nightmare*, into a screenplay. Renamed *Tillie's Punctured Romance* for the film, it's a melodrama parody, with the innocent young Tillie—the large, boisterous Marie Dressler—being taken from her country home by an unscrupulous city slicker whose only objective is to separate Tillie from the currency he's gotten her to steal from her homestead. In the city, having secured her money, he abandons her, returning to his girlfriend of before. Shortly thereafter the cad gets wind that Tillie's the sole heir to her millionaire uncle's fortune, after the unfortunate uncle has perished in a mountain climbing accident. The city slicker than seeks Tillie out at the diner where she's waitressing and hurriedly marries her. They move into the mansion they believe they've inherited. But then word comes that uncle didn't die after all—that he's miraculously revived at the bottom of that mountain....

Chaplin was assigned the role of the deceitful city slicker, one which allowed him to play an entirely unsympathetic, thoroughly reprehensible character with no holds barred. If a savage, antisocial hostility can be seen in some of his performances as the Tramp, it is right in the foreground of his performance here. Chaplin would later give short shrift to this film in his autobiography, stating that he felt it didn't have much merit, and that he was glad to get back to directing when it was over.[23] But by all accounts the film was a hit at the time, and was a big factor in further establishing Chaplin with the public. Tellingly, in a letter to his brother Sydney just after completing the film, he referred to it as the "best thing I ever did."[24]

Chaplin's performance in the film is full of energy, dynamic and inventive — he goes right to the limit in his depiction of the amoral, tawdry villainy of his character. The film is a revelation of his ability to successfully create comedy with a character mostly unlike the Tramp. Each scene he is in contains sharply observed nuances as well as a broad commitment to the utterly contemptible viciousness he portrays. He also manages to punctuate each scene with several outlandish pratfalls.

Even his entrance is provocative. After seeing carefree Tillie gamboling about on her lawn with her dog, we see Chaplin, shot from the back, smoking a cigarette. Even from the back, we can see that he is a disreputable character — one of the first instances of Chaplin "acting with his back," conveying emotion and personality with his face turned away from the camera as he will do several times in the future (most notably in *The Gold Rush*). He turns to face us and we see him not as the Tramp, nor as the shyster from *Making a Living*, the character closest in temperament to his persona here; we see he now has a tinier, daintier mustache — two Gallic dots hovering over his lips. He is a dandy, a smooth operator looking for his next mark — and he soon finds it in the gullible Tillie.

Knocked unconscious by the brick Tillie had thrown in playing with her dog, he is brought into her farmhouse, and meets her father. We see the nature of Chaplin's snobbish character when he refuses to shake the hand which the lowly farmhand proffers to him. When he gets a gander at her father's stash of currency, however, he is overtaken with a lust for its immediate acquisition. He charmingly courts Tillie and convinces her to run off with him, emphasizing the necessity that she procure her father's money from its hiding place. She goes to carry this out as he waits for her nervously outside.

A farmhand accosts him and asks him some questions. Chaplin spits his lit cigarette into the man's face, flips him down onto the ground, than whacks him on the buttocks smartly with his cane as the man scurries out of frame.

There are certain sequences in which Chaplin's violence is so savage that it enters the realm of the demonic. His efficient dispatching of the man here is shocking not in the hostility it expresses, but in the complete dispassion in which it is undertaken — Chaplin is angry, but mostly annoyed that he has to dismiss the interfering fool. It is simply something which needs to be done, which stands between him and the successful execution of his crime. The fact is that there is nothing that he will not do for money.

This is seen as well when Tillie emerges, all dressed up in a gaudy, ludicrous dress of which she is quite proud. Chaplin is unsparing in conveying to us how horrendous he considers her apparel to be — but is quite appreciative and complimentary of her wardrobe to her face.

This is at the heart of the film — his venal, contemptuous exploitation of the Marie Dressler character. Later, when he is reunited with his former girlfriend (played by Mabel Normand), they watch the massive Tillie dancing grotesquely at a cabaret, falling on her backside — and they laugh at her quite delightedly. At one point, when another man touches Tillie he even feigns jealousy, solely for the amusement of Mabel (preceded with a "Watch this!" gesture to her). Throughout the film, his character makes it clear that he has no use for Dressler aside from her as a conduit for monetary gain — he thumbs his nose at her as he makes off with her money early in the film, he kicks her away when he realizes she has no money at the end. Along the way he slaps a newsboy across the head, blows cigarette smoke into a servant's face, mocks an effeminate partygoer, and, for no apparent reason, engages in perhaps the most intense, savage knock-down fight yet with Chester Conklin, his guest at a high society party in the film.

He seems motivated entirely by hostility. Again, this is an aspect of the Tramp's character as well, which was instrumental in his great popularity with the public. But here, Chaplin delights in taking it to its apotheosis. But we must ask ourselves — why is his violence so intoxicating, exhilarating, hilarious? Is it Chaplin's firm grasp on the dread reality of life again, a reality he has known all too well through the humiliation and deprivation of poverty, the mad scrabble for mere survival which causes him to rain down such remorselessly savage blows on Chester Conklin, and which causes us to react with delight and joy and awe at the sight of the spectacle? His balletic, merciless infliction of pain is terrifying as well as being terrible — and at times there is horror mixed in with the shock before laughter comes. There is nothing cute or empathy-arousing about this incarnation of Chaplin.

The gusto of Chaplin's performance is also seen in his reactions, in a film whose rambunctious broadness means that no double take can be too huge. In Chaplin's own self-directed films, such as *Those Love Pangs*, he has been experimenting with delayed reaction — where a character has been overcome by his nemesis but doesn't know it yet (like Charlie in the movie theater when Conklin and another man hover over him as he regales their girlfriends). The suspense is built as the main character's obliviousness is drawn out, as the audience anticipates the reaction to come — only heightening the laughter when the final explosion arrives. Chaplin has two occasions to use this device here, and his milking of our expectations is more than repaid in full each time.

The first instance is when he is with Tillie in the city and is about to meet up with his former girlfriend, Mabel, for the first time. He walks along with Dressler and comes to a corner, around which Normand stands watching him. We watch for awhile as Chaplin stands arguing with Dressler before they turn the corner — then he glances around and sees Normand. He yelps, stiffens out straight as a board, and slides down against the wall to the pavement.

The second instance is when he is in a café with Normand, and is just about to turn and discover that the woman he abandoned — Dressler — is now his waitress. He chats for awhile before he turns and sees her — he shrieks with horror as he pitches straight backwards in his chair, the plates from Tillie's now upended tray smashing over his head as he falls.

The film ends with a chase replete with the Keystone Kops — Sennett was determined to put everything he had into the production — and it remains one of the most lively comedies ever filmed. Marie Dressler is a wonder to watch, and her teaming with Chaplin is inspired — the absurd incongruity of their frames is particularly striking in the dance sequence in the last quarter of the movie. But Chaplin by this time was not interested in co-starring with anyone, nor was he interested in being directed by anyone but himself.

His next short is *Getting Acquainted*, and notably, it uses the same basic cast as did his last short, *His Trysting Place*. Again, he uses Mack Swain as his nemesis, but here Chaplin is married to the matronly Phyllis Allen, who played Swain's wife in the former film, while Swain is married to Mabel Normand. Mack and Mabel are out for a walk when Mack hastens to help a man fix his new automobile. Left alone, Mabel is fair game for Charlie as he ambles by, having left his wife back sleeping on a park bench. She repels his advances. At the same time, Mack Swain happens upon Charlie's wife, and is quite taken by her — but she is offended by his lascivious intent. There is more of the leaping and running around the park that we've become accustomed to, and an instant each where the wives get together and introduce their husbands to each other — the panicked husbands trying to stifle the revelation of their adulterous desires. It's all fast farce, skillfully done by Chaplin the director/scenarist. The most memorable parts are the small touches, such as Charlie inadvertently (?) lifting Mabel's dress with the crook of his cane as he flirts with her — then angrily chastising his cane for its impudence, administering a firm spanking to it for good measure. The multi-functional cane, suitable for keeping enemies at bay, whacking them across the buttocks or the head, or dragging them by the neck, and even useful for cleaning one's fingernails or picking one's teeth, has acquired its own separate, autonomous personality at last.

Chaplin's next film was a takeoff on the then contemporary fascination with all things prehistoric. *His Prehistoric Past* features the Tramp clothed in animal skin in B.C. times, but with derby miraculously intact. He comes as an outsider to the community presided over by King Mack Swain and his many wives. Charlie dispatches Swain over the side of a cliff, but the King returns just as Charlie is getting together with his favorite wife. Swain starts pummeling Chaplin — as the dream evaporates, and we see a policeman pummeling the Tramp on a park bench, waking him up from his sleep.

His Prehistoric Past is a slight piece, and more of a novelty than anything else — likely because, as Chaplin later admitted, he was distracted by other matters during its making.[25] His contract with Sennett was coming to an end, and, because of the popularity of the films he'd made at Keystone over the past year, other companies were making offers for his services. Chaplin, with the canny sense of the worth of his talents which would remain constant throughout his career, was making financial demands which Sennett was unwilling or unable to fulfill. Thus, Sennett, remaining true to his reputation as one who was skill-ful at finding talent but not so skillful at keeping it, let Chaplin go—to sign with the Essanay company, which was receptive to Chaplin's demand of $1250 per week plus a $10,000 bonus. Chaplin had started at Keystone at a salary of $150 per week.

Chaplin was genuinely fond of Sennett, but, as he wrote to his brother Sydney, "business is business."[26] For the rest of his life Chaplin would retain warm memories of Mack Sennett, Mabel Normand and Roscoe Arbuckle. As well, he would use Chester Conklin in his films twenty-five years into the future, in *Modern Times* (1936) and *The Great Dictator* (1940); he would bring back Mack Swain as a comic villain in several shorts in the twenties as well as in, most notably, his masterpiece, *The Gold Rush* (1925); and Hank Mann would find employment in such future works as *City Lights, Modern Times,* and *The Great Dictator.*

The thirty-five films Chaplin made at Keystone established him with the public and put him in the position to write his own ticket. Astoundingly, the Keystone films were all made and released entirely in one year—1914—and flooded into the cinemas at an average rate of three per month. The public was mesmerized by this mischievous, acrobatic, at times savage little man—who, to be exact, wasn't really known as a "tramp" yet—who wandered into situa-tions, stirred up trouble, flirted with the attractive women—often sneaking a peek at their buttocks in calm appraisal—kicked people in the chest and ass, then waddled merrily on, thumbing his nose or sticking his tongue out at his beaten adversaries as a final gesture. In a medium of motion and movement, he was motion and movement—and, as portrayed comically in *Kid Auto Races at Venice*, he strode straight to the center of the frame and commanded the attention of the world—for, as a British critic observed at the time, "he does things we have never seen done on the screen before."[27]

Ninety years later, from the contemporary perspective, it is still possible to experience the excitement and freshness Chaplin brought to the screen— though these films, having been in the public domain for so long, now circu-late in sadly tattered, mutilated, often washed-out prints. They are the closest we can get to seeing the young man who created such a sensation in vaudeville houses as part of the Karno troupe, and they are a fascinating window into Chaplin's hurried, vigorous birth as a film performer, and his growth as a filmmaker.

Beyond their academic interest, many of the films are very funny—the silent film viewer in the early twentieth century had a more developed sensi-tivity towards gesture and body language than does the contemporary viewer, with the result that we might have to watch one of these films several times to comprehend the meaning of what was readily apparent to them at once. Much is expressed in movements which escape our attention, and intertitles are at a minimum. Superficially, the films are all chaos and exaggeration, frenetic, meaningless movement. But looking closer, there is satire, humanity, a view of existence both wry and forgiving. The films have their own code, their own ritual, and their vulgarity, their crudity, is their strength. In films such as *Kid Auto Races at Venice*, *Tango Tangles*, *A Busy Day*, and *The Masquerader*, we see Chaplin and his fellow clowns taking it to the street and making comedy up out of thin air, improvising on the fly, and the free, wild spontaneity and vitality of their "go-for-broke" shenanigans communicates itself vividly through the ages. As well, films like *Between Showers*, *Twenty Minutes of Love*, *Mabel's Married Life*, *Those Love Pangs*, *The New Janitor*, *Dough and Dynamite*, and *Tillie's Punctured Romance* hold their own as bright, lively, clever, rude entertainments. The drunken, adulterous husbands, the flirtatious young vixens, the sullen crones and angry cops of the Keystones existed as a warped mirror for America, reflecting back its anarchic nature in a whirring hurricane vision of apocalyptic buffoonery — the hypocritical nature of Victorian mores and morals was blown wide open for all to see, in the very same year that the first "war to end all wars" erupted across the face of Europe, ending an era, destroying the old world order and creating a new one, changing civilization forever. Chaplin himself would never be quite so raw and unhinged and punk-like as he was in these early inroads into the public consciousness, in the frenzied, almost desperate performances he gives in these primitive, unpretentious, compelling films.

3

Essanay

Chaplin traveled to Niles, California, to the studio of his new employers. Finding the facilities unsuitable, he moved on to Chicago, where Essanay owned another studio. He found his salary and bonus slow in coming, and the company's methods to be bureaucratic and creatively stifling. Irked by his new employers' seeming insensitivity and carelessness, Chaplin began his first comedy, using a method seen at Keystone, one easy to put in motion with little preparation—basing a film on the idea of working in a film studio.[1]

At Keystone, Chaplin was surrounded by a ready-made stock company. Now he had to assemble his own team. For his first two films, Chaplin made extensive use of an Essanay comic named Ben Turpin. Well known for his crossed eyes, which he would later famously insure, Turpin's scrawny physique and undersized head gave him the look of a malnourished rooster. Chaplin used him as a sort of less lugubrious Chester Conklin. There was also the large, cherubic Bud Jamison, whom Chaplin used as a "heavy" in place of Mack Swain—though Jamison was notably less menacing and expressive than Swain. Leo White, another actor at Essanay, whose specialty was playing an effete, overwrought "Frenchman" with goatee and top hat, was also pressed into service as a foil for the Tramp.

Chaplin enters the waiting room of the studio—which is named, interestingly, "Lodestone"—in his first film for Essanay, appropriately titled *His New Job*. He performs his usual eccentric interactions with banal reality—resting his arm on the backside of a woman who's knelt to fix her stocking, being oblivious of the fact that the stern man at the desk pointing in his direction is signaling him to remove his hat, instead assuming he's ordering him to appreciate the hat of the woman next to him, glancing at the hat and back to the man, smiling, as if to say "Yes, it is quite nice, isn't it?" before the man is forced, as always, to stride over and physically remove the hat from his head.

Then Ben Turpin enters, and he and Charlie are instantly, simply, manifestly and primally at odds with each other—they immediately fall into nasty, spiteful, painful war. For every blow Turpin is able to deliver, Chaplin, naturally, delivers five or more with cruel grace to meaner effect. He hooks his cane around

Turpin's ankles and pulls the smaller, gelatinous form thumping to the ground. There is a gag in both this and the next film in which Charlie, having pummeled Turpin into apparent unconsciousness, stands over him as Turpin tries to revive himself in a series of jerky, spasmic movements, his head struggling up like a blind mole's—until Charlie mercifully whacks him into oblivion again.

Chaplin is given a position as a carpenter in the studio. Later he fills in for the missing lead actor in the period drama that's being filmed—in a soldier's uniform and brandishing a sword, he is able to do some business in the "melodramatic pastiche" mode that seems to come so easy to him. Most of the last part of the film is a series of gags based on sets and props found in the Essanay studio—a column, a staircase. The film, at two reels, double the length of most of the Keystones, flags in its second half.

This is true as well of his next effort, *A Night Out*. Presumably recognizing that his interactions with Turpin provided most of the best parts of *His New Job*, Chaplin now consciously teams himself with him in the same manner he teamed himself with Roscoe Arbuckle in *The Rounders*. This film owes a fair amount to that earlier entry, in that Chaplin and Turpin are boozehounds out for a night of drinking. It is a film which gives us one of the longest renditions of Chaplin as the drunk. It is ironic that a man who came to prominence impersonating a drunk, who was billed on the vaudeville stage as "The World's Greatest Impersonator of Inebriates," and who would return to the theme of comic drunkenness throughout his career, was the son of a man who died of alcoholism at age 37.

Chaplin and Turpin are old friends who meet on the street and start out sober. But they soon repair to the nearest saloon and come out reeling, lurching, careening—it is only through leaning unsteadily on each other that they can remain erect at all. Chaplin's drunk is vacant-eyed and agape, all the while attempting to effect nonchalance as he stumbles and weaves. At times his eyes become impossibly empty as he attains complete detachment from his immediate surroundings, hovering in that blissful mental space of utter alcoholic indifference.

They stagger into a café and encounter Leo White in his guise as the dandyish, vaguely aristocratic "Frenchman," whom they'd antagonized earlier. Seated near to White, Charlie provocatively throws his leg over White's lap. White angrily pushes his leg away—Chaplin lifts his cane and with a swift swing of it through the air knocks White's sizable top hat flying. Furious, White leaps up and is ready to attack Charlie when Turpin intervenes, defending his friend. Turpin slaps Charlie a few too many times on the chest, however, as he's evidently explaining to White that "This is my pal!" so that the Tramp becomes angry with his would-be protector, grabbing him by the face and throwing him to the floor. When Turpin clambers to his feet, Chaplin grabs him by the face and throws him down again. Later, after Charlie kicks White into the next room, the massive, burly waiter (Bud Jamison) comes to have a word with him.

Turpin intervenes once more in a display of friendship only to have the waiter throw him to the floor twice, then cuff him repeatedly across the face, as Charlie sits by in complete unconcern.

Ultimately, Turpin and Chaplin are both thrown out of the café— Chaplin, at a fountain, dazedly plucks a palm frond, using it to brush his teeth. Evidently he has suddenly been overtaken by the delusion that he is completing his morning ablutions at his washbasin. Yet the gag is not outlandish and silly in Chaplin's hands— the Tramp with painful sincerity truly believes he is brushing his teeth, that the palm frond is a toothbrush, the fountain a sink.

There is also the often-cited moment when Turpin is dragging the supine Chaplin down the street, and Charlie reaches out, casually picking himself a flower from where they sprout at the edge of the sidewalk. But as mentioned, *A Night Out* grows less interesting in its final half, which reworks ideas from *Mabel's Strange Predicament* and *Caught in the Rain*. The drunks retire to their hotel, which happens to be the same hotel where the burly waiter and his wife are staying. There are flirtations and complications between Charlie and the waiter's wife, which end in Charlie leaving to find another hotel. There is chaos and more knockabout, but the best part is the set piece at the beginning of the film, in the café.

Chaplin was learning the difficulty of sustaining a two-reel film without the frenetic activity of the Keystones. But *A Night Out* had among its cast one who would be completely elemental to his artistic development.

As Chaplin hadn't been overly impressed by the studio— or the weather — in Chicago, he'd returned to Niles to shoot the film. Arriving there he cast about, trying to find a female lead for his films. One of his producers suggested a young woman from Lovelock, Nevada, who frequented a café in San Francisco. Chaplin met with her and hired her, not knowing whether she could act. At a party they both attended, however, she played the good sport by going along with a hypnotist routine he was doing for the guests, so he became convinced of her good humor and acting abilities.[2] Her name was Edna Purviance, and her radiant beauty, composed of a mixture of the sensual, the maternal and the ethereal, would be near the center of Chaplin's films over the next eight years. As well, she became Chaplin's lover soon after they met.

In *A Night Out* she is given little to do. She is given a little more in *The Champion*, a film which takes boxing as its subject in a manner not dissimilar to *The Knockout*, the Roscoe Arbuckle film in which Chaplin did a cameo the year before. The film opens with a vignette of the kind which would soon be called "Chaplinesque." Charlie sits disconsolately in a doorway, looking more like a tramp than ever before. He has a mangy-looking frankfurter which he pulls out of his pocket and tries to share with his pet bulldog beside him, who is evidently as hungry as the Tramp himself. The dog still is possessed of gastronomic discernment, however, and will not deign to eat the wiener until Charlie seasons it appropriately.

The hunger he shares with his pet inspires the Tramp to seek work as a sparring partner at a nearby training center. He seizes upon a horseshoe and places it in his boxing glove, in order to give himself a greater advantage. So injurious are his blows as a result that his prospective sparring partner streaks out of the center and jumps the next train out of town. Charlie is hired by the trainer to face the champion at the big fight—gags follow with Chaplin and the expected props as he trains: barbells, skipping rope, and the like.

Already, changes are afoot in the Chaplin technique. The destitution and hunger of the Tramp in the first scene provide motive for his seeking the sparring partner job—he doesn't just enter into it out of a perverse need to commit mayhem. As well, he meets the trainer's daughter, played by Purviance. As the trainer puts Charlie through his paces, Edna cheers him on, enthusiastically throwing her arms around him when he returns from his run. At one point they embrace, and their lips are about to come together—Charlie looks into the camera at us, and lifts up the jug he's holding to block our view of the kiss that follows.

Such a gag had been done before by others, and throughout his films Chaplin has frequently registered his reactions directly into the camera, as have most of his co-stars. It is simply part of the acting technique of these films, part of their code, and there is no attempt to broaden the relationship as Oliver Hardy would later in the Laurel and Hardy films. What is important here is the very real sensuality, and sexuality, of the Tramp which is revealed. It is a playful sexuality, and is brought out by Edna's obvious joy in Charlie, and the fact that she accepts him as a romantic partner. This allows the Tramp to become more human. As pleasant as the chemistry shared by Chaplin and Mabel Normand was in their cheerful camaraderie there was not the light, teasing sensuality and the sympathetic tenderness which is immediately apparent in the first moments Charlie and Edna share in this very brief romantic scene. It is this sense of romance, more than anything else, which Edna will awaken in the Tramp, kindling in him the aspirations towards ideals which will eventually come to define him.

Charlie trains for the fight, and a lengthy choreographed fight scene follows—it's as though Chaplin had been stimulated by the fight scene in *The Knockout*, and wanted to revisit it, work in some of the gags he hadn't been able to shove into the Arbuckle film. The extensiveness and the complexity of the fight scene attests to the fascination Chaplin had with boxing—reportedly, attending boxing matches after-hours with the rest of the crew was one of the constant extracurricular pursuits Chaplin had during these years.[3] One has to presume a certain sense of kinship was shared between the clowns in the stands, relaxing after a long day of pretending to kick, punch, and fight each other all day long—and their pugilistic brethren, punching and fighting in front of them for real.

Certainly, Chaplin has fought and won so many skirmishes in his films thus far that he can be called a sort of comic athlete, a physical master of the comic fight, so skillfully does he pummel his opponents—and, as importantly, nimbly evade their blows.

Charlie in the end wins his fight, with the help of his bulldog, who sinks his teeth into the behind of the opponent as the Tramp knocks him unconscious. *The Champion*, like its immediate predecessors, sags a bit in its last half. But beyond the revelation of Edna, it also offers another vision of Charlie as hero, the little man who wins, as at the conclusion of *The New Janitor*: in the end he triumphs in his battle, sans horseshoe.

His next film, like the preceding Essanays, takes its cue from one of the Keystone films of the previous year. Perhaps Chaplin was still settling in, still assessing his new stock company and getting used to his new situation, and wasn't sufficiently relaxed enough to originate new ideas. *In the Park* is essentially a remake of his (probable) first film as a director, *Twenty Minutes of Love*. As before, Charlie is an obnoxious loner in the park, aggravating a couple of lovers—the male played by the histrionic "Frenchman," Leo White. Elsewhere in the park, Edna is the partner of the rotund and infantile Bud Jamison. Instead of the reciprocal pickpocketing conducted by Charlie and his foil in the earlier film, there is a thief here who commits the dastardly act. Instead of a watch being the coveted object as it was in *Twenty Minutes of Love*, it is here a woman's purse which passes from hand to hand.

At the standard one-reel (ten-minute) Keystone length, *In the Park* passes as quickly and as spiritedly as did its progenitor. Edna adds a sparkle—when she flirts with Charlie, he dances off wildly among the trees, a joyful, lovestruck sprite. And Chaplin has some fun with the Leo White character when, with overwrought melodrama, White reacts to his lover's rebuffing him by vowing to commit suicide. Charlie is only too happy to help him, planting the kick on his ass which will transport him into the waters of his doom. In addition, there is also a gag which strikes a note we've heard before: coming upon a man robbing a hot dog vendor, Charlie puts his cane and foot into action, dispensing with the thief, saving the vendor's business. The vendor thanks Charlie a bit too effusively, though, so Chaplin then attacks him, making off with some wieners.

In the Park is a pleasant throwback to the Keystone "park" comedies. With the next film, *A Jitney Elopement*, Chaplin returns to the sense of romance touched upon in *The Champion*. Here, Edna figures more prominently; her father has promised her to the wealthy Count Chloride de Lime. Edna, though, pines for Charlie, and their first scene, with her on her balcony and him down below, nervously clutching a flower, provides, like the beginning of *The Champion*, a tableau which defines the term "Chaplinesque." We note also the use of the flower, which will become a powerful symbol throughout Chaplin's work, one of his trademarks. We had seen the flower earlier, when Ben Turpin pulled him along the sidewalk in *A Night Out*, and Charlie had stirred himself from drunken somnolence to pluck some dainty posies passing him by as he dragged along. There, as here, the flower is the frail, fading beauty of existence itself. Charlie's possession of it signifies his profession as, above all else, poet — one moved beyond the concerns of the ordinary into a transcendent communion with infinite beauty as approached through the heightened appreciation of the finite and dying beauty all around — as seen in the flower. He is removed from the rest of the world by his passionate romanticism, by the swoon of his heart towards the sacred mystery of beauty, and is swept up by all the other noble ideals such a commitment entails.

Charlie visits Edna's home, passing himself off as the Count to her father. The Tramp has some battles with the butler, and is quick to grab a larger glass than the one he's assigned when offered a drink, but the most notable aspect of the first part of the film is a lengthy dinner-table sequence with Charlie, Edna and her father. It's the type of leisurely, human sequence, with the three of them simply interacting around the table, that's difficult to imagine taking place in a Keystone comedy. Included here is a gag which Chaplin is said to have performed onstage in a Karno production[4] — while talking animatedly, Charlie slices a loaf of bread. When he's done, his dexterous movements have turned the loaf into an unfolding "accordion," which he charmingly "plays" for a moment. In his hands, palm fronds become toothbrushes, doughnuts become bracelets, a boxing mannequin becomes a man, a loaf of bread becomes an accordion — all because he wills it to be so. His ingenious inventiveness demands our respect, our awe. Like his peer Picasso did in his sculptures, using found objects to display new, unexpected connections — as in the bicycle seat and handlebars he made into a bull's head and horns — Chaplin rearranges reality before our eyes to create something new, something we could not have thought of before, but which, once seen, seems as though it was inevitable, pre-ordained all along. And while we get the idea that Charlie does it as he does here, to charm and ingratiate with his cleverness, and we admire him for doing so, on another level Charlie does it simply to participate with existence, with the creation of existence going on all around him at all times — he does it in order to live, as all should live, creatively.

The real Count Chloride de Lime appears, at which point the Tramp is kicked out of the house. In the second half of the film the Count takes Edna and her father out for a ride in his car, the "jitney" of the title. Charlie comes upon them in the park, and a battle is fought between Charlie and the Count — and the father as well, as the Tramp gets some kicks in at him, too. The film ends with a car chase, Chaplin's first experiment with that comedy standby — and the last, for good reason. As Chaplin himself had noted when speaking of his leeriness of the Keystone technique, he knew instinctively that character — the hallmark of his art — was lost in chase scenes. For whatever reason, Chaplin included a chase here, to not much effect, before wrapping it up with Edna and Charlie united again.

The burgeoning sense of romance, the increasing investiture of the Tramp with real, sympathetic emotions and ideals, come to the fore in the next film, one of the most decisive of Chaplin's career. It is appropriately titled *The Tramp*—for this is the film in which he is defined most clearly as the Tramp, and the film as a whole is the most focused study and exploration of the essential character of that tramp we have seen so far — its subject is the Tramp. It is his first masterpiece.

The film opens, cosmically, on an iconic image of the Tramp which in an instant explains him. He really is a hobo now, hobbling down a country road, his cane in one hand, his belongings tied in a handkerchief in the other. He is coming out of nowhere, materializing in front of us from the ether of our subconscious; he is an outsider from the vast plains of isolation coming into the community of humans.

He makes acquaintance with Edna, who is being bothered by what appears to be a nastier bunch of hobos, some loathsome bums who steal her money. Charlie, in another display of unlikely heroism, trashes the bad guys and returns the money to Edna. There is only the slightest hesitation as he ponders whether he should keep the money himself after he's recovered it. Again, there is the courtliness, the gallantry, which Edna awakens in him.

He is taken home by Edna, and Edna's father gives him a job as a farm-hand. Here, Chaplin reverts to his mischief-making ways. Virtually all he does as a farmhand is to repeatedly plunge his pitchfork into the posterior of his co-worker. There are times in some of the early films when Chaplin seems to indulge in baseless, gratuitous, often painful slapstick when he is at a loss for any other ideas. There is no reason for the Tramp to continually shove his pitchfork into the other guy's backside in this sequence — it's just repetitive, monotonous sadism, performed because he doesn't have anything better to do.

It all leaves us that much less prepared for the great shift in his art which Chaplin effects in the final third of *The Tramp*. The vile thieves of the first act return to rob the farm. They accost Charlie, trying to get him to join in their robbery; he appears to acquiesce, but only does so, as we find, to foil the robbery, to protect the farmer who's taken him in. The Tramp joins the farmer in repelling the thieves, and as the farmer shoots at them, Charlie chases after them. As Charlie climbs a fence, the farmer mistakenly shoots him in the leg, and the Tramp falls to the earth.

The manner in which he falls is not the manner in which he fell in the Keystones, nor even in the recent Essanays — he does not fall on the small of his back with his posterior shoved upwards and his legs splaying wide open. He falls like a real man would fall after being shot. And as the farmer and Edna run to him, his seizes his leg like a real man in pain would.

We fade out and fade into a scene presumably some weeks later. Edna is nursing him to health, mixing a drink for him as he lies back and smokes a cigar — he's sitting pretty. But then there is the arrival of a handsome young man, welcomed effusively by Edna and her father. Evidently the visitor is of some significance to the household — particularly to Edna. Charlie gets the idea pretty quickly, and, gathering his things, he sits down to write a note, turning from our sight every so often to cry a few tears. He leaves the note, which Edna and her father read in surprised alarm later: "I thort your kindness was love but I seen him so I know it ain't — Charlie." And then we see the image the whole film has led to — the solitary figure of the Tramp hobbling down the road, away from us, away from the community of humans, back into the isolation of nowhere. The road curves into infinity, we see only his back, we see his frame consigning itself to its solitary future, leaving his heartbreak behind. Then, with a hitching step and a sudden shaking off of the pain of his past, he makes his way gamely, courageously, alone, down the never-ending road.

It's quite possible to observe, in Chaplin's first conscious attempt at pathos, that the sudden realistic acting style in the wake of the gunshot wound is jarringly out of key with the pitchfork jabbing that had gone on only minutes before. It is entirely arguable that his tears as he writes the note are maudlin, that his weeping is a shameless, unsubtle ploy for sympathy, and that the note with its misspelling is merely pathetic. One could make the case that all these things are missteps, though Chaplin's miserable expression and gestures as he tries to write the note bespeak the nauseating horror of being in such a situation, rather than just portraying the sadness and grief. Whatever the weaknesses of these details, however, they are all entirely redeemed by the film's final, classic image, the image which would become a defining one of Chaplin's entire career. The Tramp, once again freshly ejected from society, saunters into oblivion and he is as he has always been, from his very first appearance on film in *Mabel's Strange Predicament* and *Kid Auto Races at Venice* — alone. This is and has always been the one most constant and notable characteristic of Charlie, that he is completely, impossibly solitary. He passes through situations, he interacts with people, but all the time he is alone. It is doubtful that there has ever been portrayed a character so isolated and solitary as the Tramp.

As well, the image provides a unity to the film — he enters alone, coming up the road; he departs alone, disappearing down the road. There is the image of Edna, her father, and her suitor all standing at the kitchen table reading his note, with puzzled alarm, all wondering about this strange figure who came to them, like an exotic bird, then passed on, leaving them all abashed for a moment in their cozy house — as he fades into the distance, into oblivion. It is the idealistic, romantic hope aroused by Edna in him which gives pathos, even tragedy, to the irrevocable estrangement from the rest of humanity contained in this image — a pathos which would not have been possible without the yearning Edna evokes.

After this heady evolution of his art — easily the most accomplished film he'd produced thus far — Chaplin returned to the Keystone method and the standard Keystone length (one reel) for *By the Sea*, a trifle which looks to have been improvised entirely at the oceanside on a particularly windy day. The wind has necessitated that Charlie and his foil (Billy Armstrong) have strings attached to their hats to keep them from blowing away — the strings become entwined and this causes a fight between the two men. Chaplin has fun with an inventive gag in which the two men, tied together, kick and punch in the standard knockabout manner, each unable to knock the other down without being pulled down himself. Later, Chaplin pummels his nemesis severely as he stands holding him in a headlock — when Edna passes by, he sunnily pretends to be searching the man's head for fleas (or lice?) — several of them evidently jumping ship and making their way up Charlie's arm.

In their fight, Chaplin and Armstrong accidentally deck a cop. They dash away from his unconscious body and agree to be friends; they get ice cream cones, but then argue about who's to pay for them, mushing the cones into each others' face. The comedians cavort and gambol on the sandy beach, wrestle and somersault, while the mammoth waves rush in and crash on the shore behind them, and we can see anonymous bathers in the distance, none of them giving any sign that they are aware their images are being recorded and will be viewed one hundred years in the future. Bud Jamison is also present as a foil, and his make-up would seem to attest to how much Chaplin was missing Mack Swain. At the end, all of the vacationers the Tramp has managed to enrage during his day at the beach converge on him, much like the conclusion of many of the Keystones, bringing an end to this light, (literally) breezy comedy.

It's quite possible that *By the Sea* was shot quickly on location because Chaplin was in the midst of another studio move — from the Essanay studio in Niles to the one in Los Angeles. This had the added benefit of allowing Chaplin to be near his brother Sydney, whom he'd recently gotten hired at Keystone.[5] Chaplin then commenced work on a production which had in its opening scenes an image as arresting as those which closed and opened *The Tramp*, and which possibly owed much to a music hall sketch he had performed with his brother when he was seventeen, entitled "Repairs."[6]

The tersely-named *Work* is the story of a middle-class family engaging some decorators to redo their house. We see the fussy, pretentious, snobbish wife airily describing her "vision" of the house. We see her petulant, ineffectual, short-tempered husband, sulking and stamping his feet because his breakfast isn't ready. We see the lazy, bored, half-contemptuous maid.

Then we see the decorators en route — the larger boss sitting in a cart crowded with ladders and paint cans and an array of Dickensian paraphernalia, and Charlie out front of him, groaning as he pulls the cart along. The guy hits him on the back with a stick, and at times the cart tilts back, and Charlie between the shafts of the cart is pulled up into the air in a manner similar to the donkey in *His Musical Career*. As if this were not enough, we then see the astounding image of Charlie struggling with the cart up a hill in silhouette, the hill bisecting the screen diagonally at a 45-degree angle, Charlie staggering ahead, falling back, on the seemingly impossible incline like some woodcut image representing eternal toil.

Up to this time, Chaplin's method as a director has been mostly to utilize the camera as a device to record performances—scenes are shot at medium range, close-ups are rare, the technique is functional and utilitarian. Here, as with the composition of his entrance and exit in *The Tramp*, he creates an iconic image, a tableau which is a sort of urgent poetry, encapsulating a world of meaning in a striking visual metaphor. As one who could express so much in a simple gesture of his finger, or a movement of his eyes, Chaplin now creates images with the camera which are seemingly as simple as any of his movements in performance, but which are heavy with significance, which burn indelibly into our mind's eye.

For the image of the Tramp laboring in front of the cart, struggling up the perpendicular hill, is stark and shocking, as well as being eerily beautiful, in its evocation of work, of exploitation, of slavery, of humanity's inhumanity to humanity. It isn't just another good-time, brutal gag put on for laughs as in the films before it. It's a bitter, remorseless comment on society, on the system in which we live. Social satire was implicit in the Keystone comedies—the anarchic tales of husbands run amuck and disorderly police forces were inherently subversive. But Chaplin here makes it explicit—and Chaplin the social satirist comes to the fore.

The intent of the cart imagery is further built on for the rest of the film. At the house, the woman instructs Charlie's boss as to all she wants done, gesturing extravagantly, immersed in her self-importance. The boss just stands grimly rolling his cigarette, staring dimly into the distance. With the imperturbably wry calmness known to all tradesmen throughout history, competent as well as incompetent, he stands hearing without listening to the grandiose expectations the woman has for her home. He's heard it all before—he slowly puts his cigarette into his mouth, lights it, as she goes on and on.

Charlie and his boss set in to work. But the woman, having left the room, suddenly exclaims "My silver!," rushes in and picks up her valuables, placing them in her vault as she scowls distrustfully at the men. The men, taking umbrage at her suspicion, make sure that all their valuables are locked up in their pockets.

There will be a continuing obsession in Chaplin's work about survival, money, the rulers and the ruled. Chaplin knows that the reality of the mutual distrust between the working and the ruling classes is as stark as the image of slave pulling an impossible weight up the side of a hill. Chaplin knew that it is a war in which there are no truces—merely relationships of monetary need. The woman's frilly, idiotic pretensions about decorating her house, her husband's asinine whining about his late breakfast—these aren't reality. The guy straining like an insect up the side of the hill, pulling his master, who's beating him with a stick—that's reality.

Chaplin often said that he wouldn't have been able to attain the success he had if he'd stayed in England, if he hadn't come to America[7]—the British class system simply wouldn't have allowed it. But America, like any society, does have a class system, which is no less real or negative simply because it is not consciously recognized as such. And in this system, as in finally all systems, there are only two classes: workers and bosses. Chaplin will never cease to be aware, to make us aware, of the stark difference between the two, of the vast gulf which separates them. He is alive to the basic and undeniable injustice at the heart of existence — and much of his humor and art come from the fact that he refuses to excuse it, to paper it over, to deny its existence. Having felt the harsh sting of inequity himself, knowing the ruthlessness required to attain even bare survival in a world ruled by merciless commerce, Chaplin will again and again draw attention to the elemental injustice upon which society is based.

He was a man concerned with money and its power in a way that only one born in extreme poverty could be. Having spent part of his childhood confined to workhouses, part of it abandoned on the mean streets of London, and knowing wealth and fame beyond that which had been known before by virtually anyone in human history, he was in a unique position to observe and comment upon the nature and the effects of materialism's all-pervasive rule over humanity. He was a man who stated, "I went into the movie business for money. Art just sort of grew out of it,"[8] and "In my pursuit of bread and cheese, honour was seldom trafficked in."[9] He stated in his autobiography, "The saddest thing I can imagine is to get used to luxury,"[10] and chose his good friend William Randolph Hearst, the omnipotent multimillionaire newspaper baron and the model for *Citizen Kane*, as "the one man who influenced me the most."[11] Even in his earliest contracts, Chaplin, with the assistance of his brother Sydney, showed a canny determination to exact every cent he was worth — though movie producer Sam Goldwyn would observe, "Chaplin's no negotiator — he just knows he can't take anything less."[12]

At the same time, Chaplin's vehicle of expression was the portrayal of one who is a societal nullity, one whose very existence was an expression of want, need, deprivation. Chaplin believed unequivocally that poverty was evil, that capitalism was doomed to self-destruction by the weight of its guilt.[13] His art depicted the life of the ultimate underdog and was emphatically, explicitly on the side of all underdogs. He was ultimately banned from America on suspicions he was a Communist — undoubtedly one of the wealthiest individuals to ever suffer that fate.

The ruthless mercenary sense which allowed Chaplin to triumph over his early poverty coexisted with the scarred victim of deprivation within him. Similarly, the bitter cynicism which gave rise to so many wry, satirical observations coexisted with his idealism, his sentimentality and romanticism. Chaplin's art was composed out of the friction between these opposing tensions, and the

Chaplin vision, as we are beginning to see it asserting itself in these films, is the result of this constant war within him.

The rest of *Work* is composed of the standard wallpapering and painting gags. Charlie commiserates and makes time with the maid (Edna), spending some tender moments with her which again allow their sweet romantic chemistry to light up the screen. The lady of the house's lover makes an appearance — he's improbably passed off as one of the workmen as the useless husband rages, and in the end the stove that's been recalcitrant throughout the film explodes, shattering the inside of the house.

We see Chaplin gaining control over his art, developing his style, filmically, thematically. *The Tramp* and *Work* are both very personal films — they express a sensibility, a way of looking at life. They contain bold, risky statements. With these works he's gotten past relying on using old Keystone plots for the films. He's originating ideas and beginning to articulate his philosophy, fashioning a new and deeper, more groundbreaking art.

For each leap forward there is a period of rest required, and so his next film, at first glance, might seem like a backsliding. *A Woman* begins in the same manner as many of the Keystone "park" films — Edna and her parents are out for a walk; when they rest on a bench, Edna and her mother fall asleep, leaving the father, dirty old skirt chaser that he is, to take off and start making time with another woman in the park. When the father leaves his new paramour to procure refreshments, Charlie ambles by and gets involved. In the ensuing brouhaha Charlie ably deposits the father into a pond — and when another fellow he's antagonized steps up to complain, the Chaplin cane hooks around the guy's neck and that fellow is handily flipped into the pond as well.

Charlie happens upon Edna and her mother and ingratiates himself with them. He ends up accompanying them back to their house where he soon encounters the father and the other fellow, who express their desire to pulverize him. With Edna's help, Charlie must disguise himself as a woman to escape the house, and his female impersonation here is even more convincing and alluring than his turn in *The Masquerader*. Both of his foils become immediately erotically transfixed with him — he bats his eyes flirtatiously, leading them on, entirely, eerily female in his vivacious sensuousness. The two men are so charged up by the hot little number that they play along with the sadistic little game Charlie cooks up — placing his pretty face between them, he orders them to shut their eyes and kiss on the count of three — at which point he withdraws, enabling the two men to kiss each other on the lips. In the end, he is found out and thrown from the house — the father emphatically kicking the body he had so recently been sexually aroused by.

A Woman's greatest merit is that it preserves the still confounding, still amazing Chaplin female impersonation in its fullest flight — the implications of which were found to be so disturbing by Scandinavian censors at the time that the film was banned in that region for 15 years.[14] In his next film, Chaplin returns to the progression he had initiated with *The Tramp* and *Work*. *The Bank* begins with Charlie ambling along and entering that venerable institution. He makes his way to the safe and enters the combination, twirling the large dials and gears of two of its massive doors. He enters the safe and emerges in his janitor's uniform, with his mop and bucket.

After this, one of his finest opening gags ever, Chaplin makes with many of the expected gags of hitting people with his mop, engaging in skirmishes with his fellow janitor (Billy Armstrong), exacerbating messes rather than cleaning them up — there are echoes of *The New Janitor*, the Keystone film in which the first intimations of the possible nobility of the Tramp began to make themselves known. But then there is Edna, a secretary in the bank. She has arrived at work all atwitter, with a tie she plans to give to her beloved for his birthday. Her beloved is the bank's cashier, and she leaves her present on her desk with the inscription "To Charles, with Love, Edna."

Naturally, Charlie comes upon the present and assumes it is for him. Overjoyed, he departs and returns with flowers for Edna, accompanied by a reciprocal note. She is happy to find the flowers and note on her desk, and rushes to thank her lover, Charles, for them. He laughingly informs her that the flowers are not from him, but from "the janitor, Charlie." She returns to her desk and angrily throws the flowers in the wastebasket — Charlie, looking on unbeknownst to her, stands with his fingers in his mouth, his face a tragic mask of hurt and dismay.

We see the pathos element establishing itself again, and note the new emotional complexity Chaplin is establishing. The Tramp shuffles in and retrieves the flowers from the garbage pail. Walking through the office, he stares in morose abjection at the cashier's new tie — he even takes offense at his fellow janitor's tie. He sits down leaning against the wall, fingering the flowers. The scene dissolves and we see a robbery taking place in the bank. The thieves advance to the safe where Edna and her heartthrob are making a deposit — her dapper boyfriend scrambles away at the sight of them, leaving Edna to be thrown to the floor by the robbers.

Charlie comes on the scene and saves Edna, battling the thieves and saving the bank. The boss rewards Charlie, and pulls the other Charles from his hiding place, firing him for cowardice. Edna embraces Charlie — after pulling his flowers out the wastebasket.

The scenes dissolves. Instead of having his arms wrapped around the beautiful Edna, Charlie is embracing his mop. He has not been vindicated, not saved. He is still the lowly janitor, an object of ridicule and contempt. The flowers, discarded and now beginning to wilt, have not been accepted by Edna. He shuffles dazedly across the bank and sees Edna and her lover embracing — and with a sudden skip he turns away from them, tossing the flowers into the air and kicking them away with his by now well-known back-kick.

We see the significance of flowers again — and of that back-kick, which

forms the same function as did the sudden hitching-up and shaking-off of wor-
ries gesture at the end of *The Tramp*. It affirms Charlie's defiance of fate — the
same defiance as was directed to policemen and bosses is now directed to life
itself, to the tragic fate always being pushed upon him. Artistically, the sudden
philosophical shift of the Tramp from despondency to defiance stops the film
from becoming unbearably downbeat.

As important as these is the use of the dream, a fixation Chaplin will return
to in his work again and again. The flowers are connected to the dream, and
pull him into that wonderful realm in which he triumphs, in which his heroism wins love, in which his rival is disgraced. The dream sequence in which
his ideals are realized and his paradisiacal visions of happiness come true will
become a regular feature in Chaplin's work, serving to delineate all the implications of the nobility of his spirit, while at the same time providing more of
a tragic undertone when the inevitable awakening comes, and the brutal starkness of his situation is all the more grim in contrast. The Tramp is admirable,
more human, more like us because of his aspirations, yet at the same time he
suffers more, is disappointed and downcast because of them. Luckily, he can
still rouse himself from his torpor to meet his next adventure; he reclaims his
dignity in the face of fate in the same way he maintains his dignity before society — by thumbing his nose at it, by defying its seemingly intransigent laws.

Chaplin's next film is, from the technical standpoint, his most ambitious
so far, if it isn't particularly noteworthy in any other way. In *Shanghaied*, Charlie is hired to shanghai a crew for a boat — and so most of the film takes place
on that boat, the exteriors of which were filmed on a ship engaged for the purpose, the rollicking interior shots of which were filmed in a specially constructed set built on rockers. Many of the gags center on the movement of the
boat, and in a lengthy sequence the Chaplin fascination with digestion comes
to the fore again, as the Tramp sits queasy with seasickness, the oblivious diner
next to him waving his nausea-inducing meal in poor Charlie's face, causing
him to convulse with barely suppressed retches. As for the rest of the film, it is
mostly knockabout; Edna stows away on the boat and her father rushes to rescue her. It is an action-packed effort, but not particularly memorable.

At this point, Chaplin was inspired to revisit his past, for whatever reason, and decided to film his performance as the Drunk in Karno's "Mumming
Birds." We know enough of the action in that famed sketch to know that *A Night
in the Show* is not a direct reconstruction of it. But certainly the premise of the
film — an insouciant drunk stumbles into a vaudeville show and creates
havoc — suggests that it was inspired by the great Karno hit. Chaplin abandons
his Tramp character to inhabit once again the outrageously nonchalant — and
combative — drunk with whom he had had his first great success. He enters
with his hair smoothed down, in evening dress; told to wait at the end of the
line to buy a ticket, he positions himself behind a statue in the lobby, blithely
awaiting his turn at the booth. When an usher points his mistake out to him,

the Drunk rushes into the theatre, after kicking the usher swiftly in the rump for his troubles.

Seated near the orchestra pit, he strikes a match on the tuba player's bald head, lights his cigarette, and deposits the match desultorily down the tuba's horn. An array of acts graces the stage, including a snake charmer whose snakes infest the entire theater. The fire eater causes a yahoo up in the balcony to grab a fire hose and douse the entire house. The yahoo is played by Chaplin as well, wearing a bushy mustache and smoking a pipe, bearing a strange resemblance to Stan Jefferson (later Laurel), his old roommate from the Karno days. On this deluge, the film ends.

It is Chaplin's next, second-to-last Essanay film which is perhaps the greatest of them. *Police* opens with the title: "Out into the cruel, cruel world..." Charlie is being let out of prison. He trudges out of the gates, to uncertain freedom. He is accosted by a minister with Bible in hand, who begins preaching to him, imploring him to go straight. Charlie is moved by the preacher's oratory and he begins to break down a little. He strides off, determined to do better, and encounters a swaying drunk whose dangling pocketwatch tempts him mightily. He restrains himself, walking on, and it is only later, when he sees the minister preaching to the drunk and appropriating the watch for himself, that he realizes his own paltry funds have been purloined by that man of the cloth as well.

It is indeed a cruel world which Chaplin depicts in this film, a world of need and desperation which is seen to be only more dire in the coming scenes, in which the Tramp seeks shelter in a flophouse. Shuffling in at the end of a long line of derelicts, drunks and vagabonds, Charlie finds himself unable to pay even the pittance which would guarantee him a bed in the fleahole—he feigns a cough to appeal to the manager's empathy, but is kicked out mercilessly. At this point he runs into his old cellmate from jail and agrees to take part in a robbery the fellow is planning to carry out. They break into a house, ransacking the place and gathering the valuables. They are interrupted by Edna, an inhabitant of the house—instead of being alarmed by the gun of Charlie's partner, she implores the men not to wake up her mother, who's ill. She even fixes them a meal, and later speaks soulfully with Charlie, who unburdens himself to her—though when she begins encouraging him to "go straight" he suspiciously checks the pockets of his vest, remembering his encounter with the minister before.

It is when the two thieves are leaving the house with their booty in tow that Charlie's partner declares his intention to go upstairs in search of more riches. Edna asks him not to, saying the shock might kill her poor mother. The thug starts to go up anyway, and when Edna tries to stop him, he throws her to the ground. Charlie springs into action, and in full chest-kicking mode defeats his former partner, defending Edna and her mother. In the end—and after the arrival of the police of the title, who have spent the film in cutaway

shots genteelly sipping tea and meandering leisurely to the site of the bur-
glary — he departs, leaving behind the sacks of stolen goods with Edna. Edna
gives him a coin as he leaves, and clasps his hand for a moment. Profoundly
moved by her kindness, and by the touch of her hand, the Tramp departs the
house, still gazing back in a sort of ecstatic delirium at her. He turns his back
to us to walk down a hill before which unfolds a vast vista. He stands, facing
the horizon, and he stretches his arms out to the sky in a grand, all-embracing
gesture of acceptance. The film ends.

The Tramp is changed at the conclusion of the film — once again, Edna
has awakened in him the sense of virtue, of heroism. The final shot is no less
astounding than that of *The Tramp*, yet here there is not merely the blunt statement of Charlie's solitude, but his capacity for transcendence, for an epiphanic
awakening, his always renewable ability to be born again to life. Chaplin has
spared us no detail in his depiction of grim, gritty poverty and the vile, venal
nature of humanity in the scenes of the flophouse, and the chicanery of the
man of God. Yet he also insists upon the power of the inspiration of mercy, of
goodness — love — to save one from the corrupt world, to redeem oneself of its
ugliness. Like much of his work will be, the film is a morality play, though it
is in no way dogmatic or predictable. We do not know if Charlie will steal again
or not as he greets his future, and certainly we would not blame him if he did.
Likely, he does not know himself, as he heads on down the road again, alone
in a world of wolves. But in this momentary open-armed welcoming of the universe he attains a kind of beautiful spiritual heroism, a mastery over his destiny and all space and time as he stands opening himself to it entirely. The
image is alive with the wistful poetry Chaplin was able to bring to the best of
his work. As always, romance and simple kindness are inextricably wedded to
spirituality and its highest virtues.

At this point, to complete his contract with Essanay, Chaplin decided to
assay a type of film he had never done before, and would never attempt again —
a direct parody of another film. In 1915, there was a mania in Hollywood for
the opera *Carmen*; the Metropolitan Opera star Geraldine Farrar had been lured
to California to star in an opulent Cecil B. DeMille version of the story, while
Raoul Walsh followed close behind with his interpretation, starring Theda Bara,
the foremost sex symbol of the time. Perhaps it only seemed natural that there
should be *Charlie Chaplin's Burlesque on Carmen*, as the film came to be known.

For Chaplin, the film's greatest merit likely was its function as a caution-
ary event, since after its completion and his departure from Essanay, it was
expanded to double its length by the mercenary company with the addition of
out-takes and new footage. Their bastardization of his work so distressed him
that he took to his bed for two days,[15] but undoubtedly this interference — along
with the embarrassment another film, *Triple Trouble*, which Essanay compiled
from out-takes and released after his departure — made him aware of the importance of having the final cut on his films, and of the necessity of artistic free-

dom in the creative work which was increasingly consuming him. These points would be non-negotiable in all future contracts.

Today it is possible to view the film in a version very close to what Chaplin intended. A restoration has been created by David Shepard utilizing notes from the unsuccessful lawsuit Chaplin filed upon the film's release. Viewing it, especially after consulting the DeMille film on which it's based, we see what a loyal parodist Chaplin is—he recreates the entire film comedically, virtually scene by scene, even using the same intertitles. Carmen the Gypsy, who seduces Don Jose, the border guard, so that her band can smuggle their goods into the city, is played by Edna in a full-blown temptress mode utterly unlike anything she's done before. As Don Jose, here known as Darn Hosiery, Charlie gets to dress in a soldier's costume and fumble with a long sword sheath — in which he keeps a tiny bowie knife. The film is an amusing series of gags like that, and is best appreciated with knowledge of the DeMille work. The most memorable aspect here — beyond Edna's comely appearance — is the Chaplin version of Carmen's climactic scene, in which the spurned Don Jose wreaks revenge on Carmen by stabbing her, then killing himself. The scene is played by Chaplin and Edna in entire seriousness—with striking realism, she is murdered and dies, and with striking realism and gravity he kills himself, and lies slain over her body. The sudden shift is similar to the Tramp falling to the ground and clutching his leg like a real man who's been shot in *The Tramp*. It is as though Chaplin was expressing his desire to include more reality, more solemnity and meaning — more tragedy — into his films, yet at the same time wasn't sure of the way in which to do it, or even if it was appropriate at all.

Here he retreats from seriousness by having both Edna and Charlie jump up laughing, displaying the trick knife by which their recent apparent demise was accomplished, showing how the blade retracts into the handle. They step outside of the opera, outside their parody of it and outside the film in order to giggle charmingly at the silliness of it all, confirming the film as a good-natured diversion from the more serious work Chaplin had begun to embark on in several of his other films of the time.

With *Carmen*, Chaplin completed his Essanay contract. Over the fourteen films he made with Essanay, released between February 1915 and May 1916, he was able to develop his own method as a filmmaker, and with each film he took progressively longer to create — in over roughly the same amount of time at Keystone, he had starred in 35 films. He was beginning to embark upon a mission in his work which some would call a search for illusory perfection, but which was, as it is for all artists, merely a quest for effective expression. At Keystone, he had completed the transition from music hall comic to film comic, from comic to writer-director. At Essanay, he became a total filmmaker, what the French would later term an "auteur," a filmic poet, an artist whose medium was this new storytelling device, which was his to define and master.

Concurrently with these developments was the rising tide of his popularity, the staggering success these films were having. If he had become famous through his films for Keystone, with the Essanays he now became a full-blown international phenomenon — without being quite aware of it himself, so wrapped up in his work as he was, as he would later recall. The waddling figure in the capacious trousers was inspiring songs, comic strips, poems, animated cartoons, dolls, toys, books and dances throughout 1915. With each of the Essanays his films increased in value, until the company was collecting $50,000 in advance of each release. In view of this fact, Chaplin demanded new creative incentive, and received a bonus of $10,000 for each film. His brother Sydney, now finished at Keystone, devoted himself to managing the new success — and began shopping for a new contract as the Essanay agreement came to its conclusion.

The Essanay period is a transitional one for Chaplin. The early films reprise storylines and themes of his Keytsone films without improving on them in any substantial way. Undoubtedly, he was hampered and annoyed by the short-sightedness and carelessness of his employers, by the unsuitability of the studios he was filming in, by the necessity of assembling a new stock company and the upheaval of moving from one studio to another as he did over the first seven films. As has been noted, many of these films have difficulty sustaining themselves over the new two-reel length. Once he became acclimated to his new situation, and particularly when he got settled in at the Los Angeles studio, he was able to develop his art, to bring forth new shades and textures and to underscore his comedy with a greater depth and humanity in such films as *The Tramp*, *Work* and *Police*. There is no question that much of the depth brought forth from the Tramp, inspired in Chaplin and pervading the films owes itself to the presence of Edna Purviance, whose sturdy, wholesome beauty is a planet around which the manic, energetic Tramp orbits, whose virtue and decency increasingly redeems the former thief, sadist and perverse anarchist Charlie had been. Her sensuality adds luster and glamor to the films, her amiable likability grounds the Tramp, humanizes him.

For each step forward, there are several stumbles backward. There are audacious gambles that work, and others, like *Carmen*, *Shanghaied*, and the film of the Karno sketch, which are mainly curiosities. There is a sense of increasing ambition in Chaplin's art — as seen in his concerted attempts at solemnity and pathos, and in his reported attempt to make a feature around this time — which sometimes outstrips his ability to achieve the effects he's trying for, or to realize their inappropriateness. A breathtaking image such as Charlie's lone departure in *The Tramp*, or his backbreaking toil in *Work*, is often followed by a blur of crude, unimaginative slapstick. The most notable characteristic of the Essanays is their unevenness — the most consistent factor about them is their inconsistency. But there are moments and episodes of richness in each of them which are unlike anything in his work before, and which presage the richness of his work to come. There are intensely serious, intensely personal moments which would have been unthinkable in his comedies of only a short time ago. At their highest points, these films— made a scant year after his entry into film — signal his arrival as a master artist in a medium he was helping to create and refine, to evolve and to expand.

4

Mutual

The success attained by his brother with the films at Keystone and Essanay enabled Sydney Chaplin to negotiate a contract for him with the Mutual Film Corporation for twelve two-reel comedies to be produced over the next year. For these, the comedian would be paid $10,000 per week, with a bonus upon signing of $150,000, making his entire contract worth $670,000, the largest salary ever paid to anyone in the film industry — and pretty much any other industry — up to that time.

Chaplin would later call the fulfilling of his contract with Mutual the happiest time of his career.[1] The monetary triumph of his contract undoubtedly was a factor in that happiness. As well, his work was likely made more joyful by the decency of his new employers in contrast to the appalling insensitivity of Essanay. Most of all, Chaplin was at the point of his artistic development when his unique vision, gaining force in the final Essanays, was ready to manifest itself in full flower — and was able to do so in the freedom offered by Mutual. It is with these films that Chaplin fulfills the promise he had shown in the earlier films and comes to his maturation as an artist. It is arguable that much of his best work is contained in these two-reelers, untainted by the self-consciousness or pretentiousness which, some would say, increasingly infected his later work. Certainly, the Mutuals stand with his greatest accomplishments, and of the twelve films, at least six rank as masterpieces. Virtually all of them are classics.

Elemental once again to the success of these comedies is Edna Purviance, whom Chaplin brought with him from Essanay. He also brought the aristocratic esthete, Leo White, and from his old Karno days, the lean, perpetually aggravated Albert Austin.

But perhaps more decisive than any of these to the success of the Mutuals is the presence of Eric Campbell as Charlie's nemesis. In his Essanays, Chaplin seemed to miss the burly contrast which Mack Swain provided at Keystone — the plump Bud Jamison had been a less menacing, less expressive substitute. At Mutual, Chaplin engaged the six-foot-four hulking behemoth Eric Campbell, a massive whale of a man around whom Charlie could frolic, dance and pirouette like a dolphin. Campbell, in real life a gentle and amiable Scot, invariably wore ludicrous beards or goatees and absurdly large windshield wiper–like eyebrows in his roles, and vacillated between teeth-gnashing fury, apoplectic outrage, and sociopathic sadism — all within the same film, if not the same scene, and all provoked by the perverse proddings and tauntings of Charlie. Campbell provided an irresistibly extreme contrast to the diminutive Tramp, and was undoubtedly the best foil Chaplin ever had.

Two other associates new to the fold were Henry Bergman and Rollie Totheroh. Bergman, who would make his debut in the sixth Mutual, was a rotund stooge who possessed the invaluable ability to take on a wide variety of roles, of both sexes, which he occasionally did in the same film. Chaplin would continue to use him in every one of his films for the next twenty years. Totheroh was a photographer Chaplin had known at Essanay, and would likewise become invaluable — he would work as trusted photographer for every Hollywood-made Chaplin film thereafter.

As Chaplin worked with the talented artists he surrounded himself with, he created the template he would use to form the most important works of his career. In his days at Essanay, he had been starting to take longer and longer to make each film. At Mutual, which required him to complete a two-reeler every month, his pace would slow until his final four films there would consume eight months. Chaplin was beginning to focus in on the particularities of his vision, to hone the all-important nuances and subtleties of his comedy of attitude and personality; he was searching for the same precision of emotion and movement in his filmmaking as was present in his acting. Chaplin was ruthless and unyielding in his search, refusing to be satisfied until he reached the closest approximation to perfection he and everyone else was capable of. Actors in his films told of taking and retaking scenes over and over again, until they were quite certain there could be no difference between one variation and the next. Retakes in films up to this time were mostly reserved for mistakes, for times when things went horribly wrong in a scene. For Chaplin, they were the means by which he sought the indefinable magic of emotion communicated potently and poetically through motion and gesture. He himself possibly could not have explained precisely what it was he was seeking as he retook the scenes over and over — except, perhaps, to say that it fell under the category of truth — but he certainly would have felt it, joltingly and undeniably, when it occurred, as we do watching it.

In addition to the many retakes his quest for perfection demanded of him, it is likely there were times he shot a scene over and over simply because he couldn't think of what to do next, as several of his actors suspected. As noted, Chaplin films had no proper scripts until the sound period. Though he would usually begin with a general idea, he would largely make the films up as he went along. He confessed that at times he began a film with no idea — he'd order his carpenters to build a set and hope that it would inspire something in him.[2]

Sometimes even then he would be stuck, or would get stuck in the playing of a scene, and stall for time by asking the carpenters to arbitrarily move a window over here, switch the door over there.[3] Chaplin would shoot entire scenes, entire weeks of work, and then discard them, something unheard of in the industry at the time, and largely at this time as well. He would create in front of the camera, originating with his actors their purely physical pieces of business. Something would catch his interest, something which might determine the thrust of the entire film, and he would elaborate on it, perfect and polish it, all the while on celluloid. He would create these routines, these comic revelations of human frailty and absurdity — and only when they were perfectly executed down to the least gesture and eye-blink and kick in the pants, would he set them in the context of his larger story, painstakingly uniting all his comic gems in a chain of narrative which he worked to make as inevitable and natural as the first moment of truth glimpsed and attained in performance before the camera. Even his later feature, the epic-themed *The Gold Rush*, made ten years after the Mutuals, was begun without a definite plot — he started it by improvising a series of scenes based around the Arctic motif, hoping a narrative would suggest itself as he did so.

In this sense, Chaplin remained first and foremost a performer, as he was on the vaudeville stage under Fred Karno — he drew the stories of the films from moments of inspiration in his repetitive extemporaneous performances on the set, from the subtleties of silent gesture and movement which yielded the essence of his art, and which sound film later made inaccessible to him. For this reason the advent of the talking picture would be a disaster for his art, ending his quest for perfection and the method by which he attempted to achieve it.

As Chaplin "thought" and "wrote" with his camera — with the increasingly time-consuming methods which were tolerated by his employers only because of his great popularity and success — it is notable that what that camera was recording was essentially a series of brilliant, exemplary British music hall sketches, performed by perhaps the greatest music hall comedian who ever lived. Chaplin's genius was to make out of the comedic tradition of his youth a new art, drawing from the fleeting sketches of the stage all their tragic undertones, all the implicit observations they made about humanity, life, society and the cosmos, and elaborating and expanding upon them. His Tramp embodied the surreal anarchism, always flirting with madness, at the heart of this cruel yet infinitely tender comedy. Chaplin created set pieces, doing them over and over to get them just right, knitting them together and enlarging upon them to make them into an art whose precision and exquisiteness — and on occasion, whose profundity — are not contradictions to their lowly, often vulgar antecedents, but are the logical, if revolutionary, development and evolution of them — an expression of the highest and greatest attributes comedy, or any genre, is capable of expressing.

We can see Chaplin's filmmaking technique as an outgrowth of his brilliance as a performer in the very camera set-ups he used. With notable exceptions, such as the overloaded cart going up the hill at the beginning of *Work*, the camera is placed at medium range, in order to facilitate the frame becoming a "stage" on which he and his colleagues performed their routines. Every so often Chaplin would do something "showy" with the camera, as if to display that he was capable of doing so, but mostly it was for him an instrument to record performances— and with his constant retaking, to construct and perfect them. As for his directorial technique concerning other actors, Chaplin would act out their parts for them, requiring them only to replicate his movements— several of the actors attested that he played their parts better than they ever could anyway, and this served to make the films even more of a personal, singular expression of the sensibility of one man. Of all performances documented, the one continuing performance to which all others are subsidiary, Chaplin's own performance as the Tramp, is featured and focused upon with laser-beam concentration in the Mutuals. The nuance and subtlety hinted at before now becomes more pronounced, and the whimsical absurdity at the heart of the character is allowed to flow more freely. If before the Tramp was more violent, we see that his violence now is less motivated by hostility than by an energetic, desperate sense of self-preservation, executed in a manner which must always be beautiful and imaginative. If he was more lascivious in the past, we see more of a romantic, gallant approach to women as the Mutuals progress— though he is still certainly inspired by a sexual desire which is at times surprising in its frankness.

More than these, it is the behavioral surrealism of the Tramp which comes to the fore in the Mutuals, examined in all its preposterous vivacity in the slower pace and longer takes of the new two-reelers. By now, the predilection of the Tramp to tip his hat to a tree after bumping into it, or to do the same to an uneven section of pavement after tripping over it, had become one of his most defining and beloved pieces of business. We have seen him give life to the inanimate before, to conjure new uses and meanings for objects and beings; we have seen him transform the universe through acts of the imagination — such as his use of a hat rack as a pair of tongs to remove his co-worker's odious boots in *The Tramp*, or his animation of the statuette in *Work*. The Tramp's motive for all of these, as much as it can be discerned, would seem to emerge from a sense of play, somewhere in the region where the world of childhood and the world of madness meet, where all is creativity and to live is itself an act of the imagination, where nothing can be fully what it is without simultaneously being reconceived gracefully, with impossible élan, as something else — as, perhaps, all things. When Charlie tips his hat apologetically to an object for having stumbled over it, it is in the nature of an infant who talks earnestly to a cat, or a child to whom a toy car is, if only for a moment, the real thing. For the Tramp, as for the child, as for the mad, the universe is alive with meanings and possibilities largely beyond the scope of the adult and the sane. It isn't that Charlie rejects the conventional meanings given to reality, or that he rejects the limits imposed upon existence, because for him they don't exist in the first place. In his acting as though these limits don't exist, he arouses the fury and violence of his foils, for whom these meanings and limits most assuredly do exist — and for whom it is very important that they exist. Again, the Tramp isn't motivated by hostility—for him there are too many possible meanings to ever be relegated to one, and it is the very nature of his being to "play," to dance with all the burgeoning, life-giving creative energy of the universe, and by doing so to find communion with his own creativity. For the Tramp is an artist, who joins with reality to reconfigure it, to make it new again, and his transpositions of objects, in which he renames the world, are metaphors in the ongoing poem he composes to existence.

From his entrance in *The Floorwalker*, the first Mutual, it is clear that this is, for whatever reason, a more liberated Tramp. As the persnickety Albert Austin watches balefully, Charlie enters a department store and saunters up to a counter display of toiletries. In an extended scene, Charlie picks up a shaving cup, and procuring a bit of water from a nearby fountain, avails himself of some soap, lathering up his face and proceeding to shave himself as if it were the most natural thing in the world — as though he was an aristocratic gentleman performing his daily ablutions in his own private lavatory, rather than in the midst of a department store. As Austin glowers, Charlie completes his hygienic duties, adding a dash of cologne as a final touch — then he tosses each of the used objects back onto the counter with a bored and disdainful flourish. There's certainly a strain of mischief here, but more than this is that spirit of play; sighting the toiletries arranged on the counter, the Tramp would surely be remiss, and surely not himself, if he were not to put them to good use as quickly as possible — in as elegant and dexterous a manner as possible.

The Floorwalker is a film constructed around one prop — a functioning escalator, or "moving staircase" as it was called, which Chaplin had constructed on the set, conceiving of it as a surefire inspirer of gags. There are many gags and lots of inventive action around the escalator, and all of it is beautifully choreographed. But like Charlie's adventure at the toiletry counter, the most memorable aspects of this film — a retelling of the basic embezzlement theme as seen in *The New Janitor* and *The Bank*—do not concern the escalator hijinks.

One is when the store's floorwalker, who is trying to make off with the embezzled loot, comes face to face with Charlie. He bears somewhat of a resemblance to the Tramp, which is important to the plot later on, when he bribes Charlie to trade clothes so that he can escape. Before that, the two men meet in the floorwalker's office — each is convinced that the other is his reflection, and they stand before each other magically mimicking the other's gestures. It's a version of a routine done by the French comedian Max Linder, and before that in the music hall, and likely somewhere before that — and of course the Marx Brothers would perform it most famously in *Duck Soup* (1933). Here, Charlie and his doppelganger mirror each other's movements and gestures until the floorwalker reaches forth and, laying a hand on either side of the Tramp's face, studies it intently. Obligingly, Charlie darts his head forward and kisses the man on the lips.

There is no homosexual overtone here — if anything, the Tramp is omnisexual, encompassing the genders we know and one or two others besides. We have seen him kiss his nemeses before, as when he kissed Mack Swain on the forehead after knocking him unconscious in *The Fatal Mallet*, and here he sweetly kisses the decrepit white-bearded elevator boy as well, in thanks for a safe ride. As we have seen in his female impersonations, Charlie is able to take on various sexual identities without vulgarity, without scornfully mocking the characteristics of these identities — he simply inhabits them, becomes them with a totality which is as mesmerizing as it is unsettling. The Tramp kisses the man's mouth simply because the man's movements seem to invite him to, in the same manner by which the toiletries of the department store invited him to shave, to freshen himself up. He is unrestrained in his momentary inspiration by the bonds of gender division, by the bonds of social acceptability, because he does not recognize the reality of their existence.

Later, the Tramp has his first encounter with the mammoth, marvelous Eric Campbell, who takes him for the floorwalker — from the first, it is obvious that Chaplin the comedian is inspired by their glorious contrast, and the dynamic is set up which will govern all their future relations: Campbell strikes madly out at the Tramp, his mountainous form towering over the puny figure; Charlie darts, weaves, frolics, and pivots around the increasingly befuddled and stationary Campbell, until in the end, as he always must be, Campbell is dispatched, vanquished miraculously, by his insect-like tormentor. The nature of their relationship really is identical to that of David and Goliath, and Charlie's spriteliness and dexterity are emphasized by the monumental stolidity of his opponent. We have seen evidence of the Tramp's grace before, but here, when Campbell smashes him to the ground, Charlie leaps up and performs an astounding dance, leaping and pirouetting about the room, amazing Campbell no less than ourselves — all of a sudden we are transported out of the two-reel comedy into the midst of a balletic performance. With joyful elegance Charlie cavorts daintily around his tormentor, ending with a flourish and arms outstretched as if to welcome applause. Without hesitation, Campbell smashes him to the ground once again.

We have seen Chaplin pull this maneuver before — in *Making a Living*, his very first film, he had suddenly punctuated a scene by executing an admirable curtsey. But in the Mutuals there will be more of this sense of the Tramp as a performer, as an artist practicing his obscure vocation before the eyes of a stunned and infuriated world — and before us, who are no less stunned, but awed and transported as well by his seemingly limitless invention and energy in the cause of entertaining us. We are left asking: why does the Tramp suddenly begin dancing as if on stage, and just who is this strange creature, anyway? It is as if Chaplin is acknowledging the real attraction of the Tramp — that he is a wonder to behold, and by giving him these little set pieces, after which he unabashedly solicits our applause and approval for his efforts, he makes Charlie into an even more surreal character, even more alive and creative than the flummoxed drudges which surround him. It is as though Chaplin is acknowledging the real purpose of his filmmaking technique — to record his own ongoing performance. But if we are transported by Charlie's terpsichorean finesse, elevated for a moment from the mundane, dingy concerns of everyday life, so is he: there can be no question as Charlie dances before his nemesis that he is, for that instant, in a world of ecstasy. Similarly, when the Tramp, in his guise as the floorwalker, later takes over as shoe salesman when he sees an attractive woman heading in that direction, the touch of her foot so arouses him that he leaps up, kicks his fellow salesman to the floor, boards the moving ladder and sails across the room with angelic grace — it's a frenzy of erotic excitement which, like his balletic exuberance of before, is uncontainable, must be expressed despite, and because of, all the laws of gravity and reality which are broken in the process. More and more, the Tramp's dynamic creativity, his exuberance, dominates reality.

The next Mutual film, like *The Floorwalker*, is essentially based around one prop. *The Fireman* is an "occupation" comedy using a real firehouse as its backdrop. Charlie is a firefighter with a tendency to sleep through the alarms, unlike his fellow brethren who, Keystone Kop–like, immediately go into a bizarre exercise of zealous, if manifestly incompetent, readiness. *The Fireman* is the least interesting of the Mutuals, mainly because it is a reversion to the Keystone style — Eric Campbell is the fire chief and he spends most of the first half of the film repeatedly kicking Charlie in the ass. So intensive is his abuse that at one point he belts the Tramp to the ground and becomes rather worried when Charlie doesn't arise again — he evinces concern that he's gone too far this time, and helps Charlie solicitously to his feet. The Tramp shakes off his languor and kicks Campbell in the chest, knocking him into a tub of water.

This type of roughhousing dominates the film, along with a few mechanical gags using backwards photography, in which the horse-drawn fire engine is made to retreat to the firehouse in reverse, but it's important to note that *The Fireman* is a well-constructed exercise in slapstick. In the Essanays we had seen that Chaplin had trouble at times sustaining the two-reel length, that some of his efforts and flagged in their final half. By this time Chaplin had improved as a craftsman, and had no trouble in any of the Mutuals creating a story arc which captivates for the entire running time. Here, a man promises Eric Campbell the hand of his daughter, the lovely Edna, if he'll let his house burn down for the insurance. The climax comes when Charlie rescues Edna from the fire by scaling the wall without a ladder, in a seemingly superhuman feat, triumphing and walking off with the girl in his best mock-heroic mode.

If *The Fireman* is largely an exercise in full-on, non-stop slapstick, the romantic, heroic aspect of Charlie, touched upon in the Essanay shorts *The Tramp*, *The Bank*, and *Police*, is purposefully revisited in *The Vagabond*. Charlie is a traveling troubadour, equipped with his trusty violin (Chaplin played the violin and cello in real life). He busks outside a tavern — which gives him the chance to reach down and pick up what appears to be a coin on the pavement, only to hastily straighten up and wipe his fingers on his pants as he discovers it's a gob of spit. He has competition in the form of a loud German band — so he stops playing and ventures into the tavern, holding out his hat and collecting money for the band's music. The other musicians become wise to this and chase him through the tavern — he escapes, and we next see him ambling down a country road.

He comes upon a Gypsy caravan — Edna is slaving away at the washing outside and he begins to serenade her. She is abused by a repulsive old Gypsy crone — played by Leo White in drag — and by Eric Campbell, as a Gypsy chief who whips her. Charlie rescues her, first dispatching the band of Gypsies by shimmying out on a branch and slamming them on the heads with a thick stick, then stealing off in their caravan, making his getaway with Edna. After an intertitle which tells us "Next morning," we see Charlie waking on the grass outside the caravan — Chaplin is careful to inform us of the chaste nature of the Tramp's relationship with the girl. But Charlie's dreams of romance with Edna are shattered when an artist comes upon the scene and paints her picture. The artist departs, but she has been captivated by him. When the painting is exhibited, her mother recognizes her and the artist brings the mother to the caravan to claim Edna. Edna leaves with the artist and her mother in a big limousine, and Charlie watches the car disappear down the road. But Edna has a twinge of conscience — the car returns, they beckon Charlie to join them, he jumps in with his violin and they all take off together.

The Vagabond is a return to the dramatically ambitious Chaplin of his later Essanays— and he is successful here in telling a story based on the old archetype of the child stolen by Gypsies later restored to their parents through the trusted device of the birthmark. Around this he explores once again the theme of the Tramp as frustrated lover, as the eternally alone one who again tries to build a bridge to another, to join with another, and fails. The relationship of the Tramp with the girl has begun with him taking the role of rescuer, protector, and then caretaker — there is a charming scene when he notices her scratching herself, and after seeing her dabbing her face with water in a paltry attempt at washing it, grabs her and scrubs her down energetically. When the artist comes on the scene, Charlie is jealous, but more than this, he is distraught — he knows that this is the end, and as they watch him depart he observes Edna's obvious smittenness with the tragic mask we had last seen in *The Bank*, when he saw her throw his flowers into the garbage.

He becomes even more tragic when she sits mooning over the artist and Charlie tries to draw pictures himself on the side of the caravan. As the Tramp tries to appeal to her, she weeps helplessly, unable to put aside her feelings for the artist. When the artist and her mother come to claim her, Charlie greets them with wounded dignity, and nobly bids good-bye to Edna, surrendering her to her new destiny. Chaplin's acting here is exemplary, and the incredibly effective use of his remarkably expressive eyes really does prompt one to marvel at the profound meaning he is able to put into the smallest looks and gestures. As they travel off, the Tramp tries to do his little skip-step, to affect a revivifying display of spunk and a casting off of cruel fate, as is, by now, customary—but he can't do it. He stops and leans against the caravan, burying his head in his arms. This is all convincing and moving and, as many have pointed out, has much in common with the pathos Chaplin will use in the features ten years down the road. But it is a bit daunting to realize that for the last third of the film, the Tramp is largely a tragic figure. There is humor, but *The Vagabond* essentially tells a serious story—it is a drama artfully constructed within the confines of a two-reeler, and it is because of this that the ending is so faulty and unsatisfying. Chaplin hasn't been able to reconcile his creation of what is supposed to be a slapstick comedy with his dramatic ambitions, so that the true ending of the film, and the only really possible one—the Tramp left alone again, callously abandoned after his momentary bliss—couldn't be used. Chaplin has asked us to invest ourselves emotionally in the film far too deeply than to leave Charlie in his infinite solitude once more. And yet the filmed ending, with him going off with the two lovers and Edna's mother, is unsuitable as well—what living arrangement are we to imagine they will fall into?

There have existed reports that Chaplin filmed an alternative ending to the film in which the Tramp committed suicide by leaping into a pond—rescued by a hatchet-faced old crone, he took a look at her and jumped back into the water.[4] This ending would have reintroduced some rude comedy to the film yet it, too, would have been unsatisfactory. Chaplin had turned the focus of the film away from comedy to drama and had given himself no suitable way to end it. *The Vagabond* is skillfully done, and has several great moments, but it shows the dangers of introducing pathos into his comedy—it was something, as he would learn, that was always more successful when done more judiciously, with a lighter touch.

Undoubtedly, the imperfect ending annoyed Chaplin, and may have been the reason he abandoned romance and sentiment entirely in his next film and headed in the opposite direction. *One A.M.* is a pure comedy in which he resurrects his Drunk from the "Mumming Birds," last seen in *A Night in the Show*. The film is a tour de force, virtually a one-man show in which Chaplin delivers a bravura performance the like of which it's difficult to imagine any comedian, past or present, being able to come close to. The film consists of the efforts of a drunk to go upstairs to bed after a night of drinking. That's all—the unending variations on that theme, with Chaplin wrestling a variety of outlandish props in nightmarish house which seems to have been designed by the architectural partnership of Salvador Dalí and Hieronymous Bosch make *One A.M.* a masterpiece of gag construction as well as a showcase for one of the ultimate Chaplin performances—and, in its conscious focus and starkness, a virtuoso artistic exercise. It is his most consciously artistic film, in a conceptual sense, and his most overall successful film, up to that time.

It really is the logical and ultimate expression of Chaplin's conception of film as the documentation of himself as performer—here, aside from Albert Austin's typically laconic, brief performance as the cab driver at the beginning, it is all Chaplin and the world of inanimate objects. Unlike the Tramp's imaginative, transformative relationship with objects, however, the Drunk is bedeviled and tortured by objects—it is they who "play" with him, is they who are "magical" with a bright and grotesque malevolence. Chaplin has abandoned the open, childlike wonder of the Tramp, taking on the stunned, yet eternally nonplussed and unruffled demeanor of the Drunk, whose benumbed assumption of control means that he is punished by reality again and again. Like the Tramp, the Drunk does makes unliving things "live" and take on personalities of their own—but he does it through his befogged and stuporific misapprehension of reality rather than through the Tramp's quick and wily manipulations of the material world. He is the victim of objects, rather than their master.

He enters his home—a garish nightmare burning in some eternal dark night of the soul—through the window, unable to find his key. Then he discovers he has the key after all, so climbs back out through the window to reenter the house properly. He slips repeatedly on an impossibly slippery carpet on an impossibly slippery floor. He finds himself on the floor surrounded by a small herd of manifestly unlikely stuffed animals; he is quite convinced that they are real, and shows some concern about their ferocity—through his movement he does indeed make them "live" and attack him, to the degree that he must kick them away when they seek to maul his legs. Spying a table laden with booze, he considers himself in need of nightcap, so he moves towards the alcohol. The table's circular top, however, spins round each time he tries to reach for the booze, so that he finds himself caught in an unending pursuit of alcohol, running around and around the table with the bottles spinning just out of reach as if in some previously unknown circle of Hell.

The Drunk does not become notably angered, nor even that frustrated, by these indignities inflicted on him by the universe. He is simply trying to make his way, and shows that he is quite willing to change his goals if reality is that stubborn about refusing to comply with his wishes—when he tries to hang up his coat on a hook which is perversely tilted downwards, he shrugs and dons his coat again; when he is unable to climb the stairs to his bedroom, he gives up the effort in order to have another drink; when the fold-out bed refuses to take any form which might allow him to get some sleep on it, he gives up and is quite content to take his rest on the floor. But the things are unimpressed with his accommodation of their unreasonability, and they merely pile on more abuse — in the case of the bed, it leaps out of the wall and slams down on him where he has meekly settled himself.

Artistically, *One A.M.* is a statement of audacity, not only in its one-man show, but in its gag variations — Chaplin is showing off his skills as a gag creator as much as he is showing off his peerless performance skills. Each attempt by the Drunk to perform a mundane task gives birth to a series of gags as inventive as they are unexpected. He attempts to light a cigarette — he throws the cigarette away and tries to smoke the match. Later, he tries to light it again, this time striking the match and blowing it out without applying it to the cigarette, wondering why he can't get a decent drag. Now out of matches, he endeavors to ignite his cigarette on an electric light — a gag he performed as the Drunk in "Mumming Birds." To do so, he climbs onto the table of the spinning top, on which he scurries frenetically until he is dashed to the floor.

Likewise, he is confounded in his attempts to mount the stairs — his drunkenness causes him to lurch and stumble backwards down the entire flight. His second attempt, clutching desperately to the railing, ends in his being beaned by the ludicrously huge pendulum of the clock at the top, doing a backwards somersault and careening down the stairs again in surely one of the most spectacular and potentially neck-breaking falls Chaplin ever took. He tries again, and this time he is beaned by the pendulum and goes down the stairs, the carpet detaching itself and wrapping around him as he tumbles, ending at the bottom all rolled up in it — his camera-look to us betrays a rising perturbation. He then does away with the stairs altogether, shinnying up the hat rack to the second level of his home.

The coup de grace, though, is his tangle with the fold-away bed, which begins by falling down on him as it springs from the wall, then folding up with him in it, pinning him against the wall. Chaplin rides on top of the bed, then is crushed to the floor by it over and over, wringing a dizzying succession of gag variations out of it, engaging with the demonic device in a sequence which is, again, both impeccably constructed and admirably performed. The film as a whole, with Chaplin bearing the entire burden of the two-reel short, drives home just what a remarkable performer he was, and *One A.M.* is one of his alltime greatest achievements.

It was also a film he couldn't have done in the character of the Tramp — or perhaps the Drunk is an accentuated aspect of the Tramp. He returned to the rather more dynamic character in *The Count*, which begins with Charlie working under boss Eric Campbell as a tailor. He displays some of his eccentric method of taking measurements, but is quickly fired by Campbell when he burns through a stack of clothes with an iron. The Tramp totters off to hook up with a rather matronly cook at the mansion where she works. When he has to run to avoid the detection of the butler, he stumbles into the party of Mrs. Moneybags, at which Campbell has arrived, passing himself off as the Count whose invitation he'd found in a pair of pants at the tailor shop. Campbell whispers to the Tramp not to give him away, that Charlie can be the secretary to his Count — Charlie introduces himself to Edna (playing Mrs. Moneybag's wealthy daughter) as the Count, denoting Campbell as the secretary. The rest of the film is composed of the two battling for Edna's attentions, until the real Count shows up, and the police enter the scene.

Based on the same "impersonating a Count" theme of *Caught in a Cabaret* and *A Jitney Elopement*, *The Count* is better than both earlier works, and is light, frothy entertainment. The most memorable scenes are a sustained eating routine at the party, at which Charlie most shush the clamorous soup-slurping of Eric Campbell in order to carry on a decent conversation with Edna, and a dancing scene, in which the Tramp brushes off some of the most ungainly, unlikely, and utterly bizarre dancing moves ever seen — including hooking his cane around the chandelier to pull himself to his feet when he goes down too far doing the splits. Later, Charlie and Eric surreptitiously kick each other in the ass as they dance with their partners around the floor, Charlie performing the neat trick of swiftly turning Edna's behind into the line of fire just at the time Campbell's about to let go with another kick.

There is a strange sexual energy which runs through *The Count*, glimpsed when Charlie's matronly girlfriend in the kitchen is seen entertaining a policeman as well; also when Charlie, who has begun pursuing Edna, much to the chagrin of his girlfriend, then becomes attracted to yet another woman at the party, and starts following her around. At one point the Tramp becomes so excited at being in the proximity of the latter woman that he erupts into a sort of fit of sexual exhilaration, somewhat like his episode when he touched the woman's foot in *The Floorwalker*, but more violent. In a shockingly suggestive movement, he lifts his cane and thrusts it through a roast chicken on the buffet table, flinging it away. He then begins smashing things on the table with his cane in a strange mania, batting pastries at the assembled guests. In the end, the cops arrive and a chase ensues, with Charlie speeding away from the chaos he's created as in so many earlier films.

The mischievous aspect of the Tramp also comes to the fore in his next film, which is one of the greatest he ever created. In *The Pawnshop* he is one of the assistants in the eponymous establishment, and in this role he is a whirling dervish of transformational energy. From the beginning moments when he tries to make up for his tardiness by synching up his pocket watch to the calendar on the wall, to the moment when he is engaged in his perpetual fight with his co-worker (played by John Rand), his prizefighter shuffle magically mutating into a graceful dance — again — when he becomes aware of the cop standing by watching him, Charlie is alive with a comic exuberance, he is a fountain of overflowing creativity in every frame. There is an obsessive, compulsive need in Chaplin to see things other than they are, to recreate them in a new way, to bring about a new order, that is almost a kind of madness. *The Pawnshop* is the companion piece to *One A.M.*, in that it gives full rein to Chaplin's relationship with material reality — and what is a pawnshop but a storage place for the plethora of props Charlie puts into use throughout the film? In his hands the rungs of a ladder momentarily become the bars of a monkey cage, a piece of dough and a spoon become a lei and a ukulele, and in the most celebrated scene, an alarm clock becomes a doctor's patient, a can of tuna, and a host of other intricate devices and organisms we can only dare to imagine.

The Tramp, manning the counter, is brought the alarm clock by the ever-doleful Albert Austin, who dares to entertain the modest hope of getting a few bucks for it. Charlie eyes him and the timepiece suspiciously — he pulls out a stethoscope and expertly listens for the alarm clock's heartbeat. He takes its pulse. Still eyeing Austin doubtfully, Charlie holds the clock up to his ear, pinging it with his finger to check its resonance. With fierce, decisive solemnity, Charlie makes the decision to corkscrew into the alarm clock with a drill. Finding the results of this inconclusive, he tries to chisel in, then pulls out a can opener and opens it that way — sniffing the contents most disapprovingly. He examines them, using the mouthpiece of a telephone as a jeweler's glass, with the intense concentration of a diamond aficionado. He pulls the mechanical innards out with a pair of pliers — the mainspring begins wriggling on the counter as it uncoils, so he attacks it with a hammer, finally "killing" it by dousing it with an oil can. All the while, Austin looks on in mute horror, and all the while Charlie regards him with the most dubious skepticism imaginable, as if to say: "Just what is it that you think you're trying to pull here, anyway?" Finally he takes Austin's hat from his head, sweeps the remains of the decimated timepiece into it, and returns it to him, shaking his head. "Nope, no go, sorry."

This is the longest set piece, or routine, Chaplin has injected into one of his films so far, and it's an exemplary one, examining at great length that most essential aspect of his art: the impulse to reimagine the universe, the absurd but wildly ingenious compulsion on the part of the Tramp, of Chaplin, to change the meaning of objects, to invent new meanings. Nowhere is it seen more than in this film, and this scene is a virtuoso display of it like the virtuoso display in *One A.M.* He takes it as far as it can go — and it is a form of divine madness. It is so wildly imaginative that it is a threat to the way things are, to the agreed-upon realities on which our common sanity is founded.

It is not just objects which Chaplin can transform — he can also, in an instant, transform himself. We see this in the fighting shuffle which becomes a ballet recital when he becomes aware of the cop, and also in the ongoing fight with his co-worker — they're wrestling savagely, and when the boss enters they take up their positions at work lightning-swift. Later, the boss's daughter comes in when she hears them fighting, and Charlie, who'd been viciously pummeling his opponent, immediately collapses to the ground with a wounded, "hurt" expression on his face. Edna comforts him, patting his face as he stands staring in innocent forlornness—when she moves her hand away, he places her hand on his cheek again. She tells off his nemesis for picking on Charlie, as he furtively sneaks glances at her posterior.

When his boss fires him, Chaplin sadly appeals to him for sympathy, miming with his hands the immense family of children — some of them taller than he — that he has to feed. The boss turns away brusquely. Charlie takes this opportunity to kick his scornful co-worker in the face, then presses on with his crestfallen plea for pity from his boss. The boss remains intransigent — Charlie sorrowfully moves to the door. Then the boss relents, calling to him. Charlie leaps upon him, embracing him; he kisses his hands, so beamingly, tearfully grateful is he. When the boss leaves, Charlie spits the taste of the boss's hand out of his mouth, and turns to begin pummeling his co-worker once again.

These rapid changes in mood, these split-second shifts in emotion follow one upon the other so quickly that one is left wondering which one of them is authentic. Just as Charlie's supplying of new meanings for the world around us leads us to question whether his definition of things might be the right one after all, we are led to wonder what is at the core of the character, or if there is a core at all. The answer is that the core of the Tramp — the essence common both to the anarchic hell-raiser and the romantic sentimentalist aspects of him — is this very flame of transformationalism. He is the artist, the creator, the performer who must always be creating, performing, transforming in order to exist. In fact, it his way of existing — his only way — as it was for Chaplin.

The dance the Tramp performs is followed by his doing a tightrope act, when he sweeps up a long piece of string and essays the feat, leaping off with a triumphant curtsey when he finishes, even though there's no one in the room to witness it. At the end of the film, the bad guy trying to rob the shop, played by Eric Campbell, is foiled when Charlie pops up out of the trunk he's been hiding in to bop Campbell on the head with a rolling pin. After executing this move, Charlie leaps up and does an upraised arm flourish towards us in the audience, inviting applause for his bravura performance before he goes to embrace Edna. It is a gesture which fittingly acknowledges the essence of his character, and, as well, the fact that Chaplin has just completed one of the most remarkable performances he — or anyone — has given in a film.

After such an essential film, Chaplin shows that he's not above falling back on the tried and true method of generating a new project by using the same gambit of *A Film Johnnie* and *His New Job* — making a film about the making of a film, and using the studio itself as a backdrop. Charlie is stagehand and Eric Campbell is his monumentally lazy boss in *Behind the Screen*, a film which entertains on the same level as *The Count*. Transformation appears here when Charlie, ordered to gather up a bunch of chairs, slings them over his arms onto his back until he takes on the appearance of a porcupine. Later, we are given another episode in the Chaplin obsession with digestion, when Albert Austin eats a fist full of green onions for lunch, disgusting Charlie mightily. Austin masticates his onions repellently, and belches so authentically that we can almost smell his fetid, noxious breath — Charlie understandably dons an iron helmet to stave off the stench. Yet when Austin next pulls out a long meat bone for his next course, the Tramp is only too happy to enclose the end of it in two pieces of bread and surreptitiously make a sandwich of it when Austin isn't looking — and when discovered, he gamely barks and begs like a dog.

The other notable aspect of *Behind the Screen* is Edna's performance as an aspiring actress trying to make it onto the lot. She outfits herself fetchingly in overalls and workshirt to pass herself off as a stage hand, a young boy — a transformation of her own. When Charlie comes upon her powdering her face, he grinningly assumes she is a gay male, winking and laughing at her knowingly. When her cap comes off and her long hair is seen, she replaces the cap and pleads for him not to give her away. In exchange for his promise not to, Charlie exacts a few kisses — Eric Campbell passes by and comes upon what appears to be two men kissing. Far from being outraged and infuriated as we might expect, Campbell responds with a fey "You naughty boys!" gesture, and begins leaping about with abandon in some sort of dance of sexual excitement — we again note how extraordinarily light on his feet Campbell could be — before Charlie kicks him on the posterior which has been thrust towards him. Homosexuality had been depicted before in films, as it had been in every other art form since the beginning of human history. But to have it alluded to so undeniably, so overtly as it is here, makes this scene startling even today, nearly a century later. And the gag of the ultra-masculine, bullying Campbell being revealed as gay suggests a happy acceptance of this natural aspect of human sexuality which is absent in some quarters even today.

The knockabout comedy of *Behind the Screen* continues in *The Rink*, a film which is classic simply because it contains the most extended sequences of Chaplin displaying his almost supernatural roller skating abilities. There had been a Karno sketch called "Skating"[5] — undoubtedly Chaplin was making use of that inspiration here. The film opens with Charlie as a waiter, with all the expected mayhem such an occupation would seem to guarantee for him. Chaplin once again has fun parodying middle-age infidelities when a couple named Mr. and Mr. Stout — the Mr. played by Eric Campbell with Henry Bergman as the burly Mrs. — come to the restaurant separately, both soon evincing the desire to be unfaithful to the other. Various confusions and pratfalls occur until they all come to a head at a skating party held by Edna, the daughter of the comparatively puny object of Mrs. Stout's affections — and the woman Mr. Stout and Charlie have been fighting over. Most of the memorable action consists of

Charlie whooshing around Campbell like an unbelievably graceful insect — he speeds around on the skates with mesmerizing elegance. We see a series of routines with Campbell and the others stumbling around on the skates while Charlie moves amongst them with effortless ease — the slapstick collapses and falls are executed flawlessly by the entire cast. But it is the Tramp's feats which cause the mind to doubt what the eye sees, as he leans tilting over the supine Campbell at a forty-five degree angle, his feet pumping feverishly to keep himself from falling, and later, when Charlie hooks his cane around Campbell's neck, pulling him around the rink, then sending him spinning into the adjacent café, upsetting patrons and tables and chairs. At the end of this perfectly constructed comedy, a group of men skate after Charlie, chasing him from the place after the chaos he's caused — he hitches a ride on the back of a car, smiling and waving as he leaves his tormentors behind. In many of the films of this period he seems to be a supernatural, magical creature, triumphing effortlessly over the common mass of humanity.

If *The Count*, *Behind the Screen*, and *The Rink* reconnected Chaplin back to his purely mischievous, knockabout roots, *Easy Street* marks a return to the more ambitious Chaplin, pointing the way ahead to the next evolution of his art. There are elements in *Easy Street* which have not been seen in any of his films so far, and it is a statement of purpose, a manifesto for the future — without intending to be in any conscious manner, of course; but there is a sureness of narrative in *Easy Street*, a mixture of gritty realism and hopeful idealism, of brutal violence and tender romanticism, that ranks it as an essential masterpiece. It is with *Easy Street* that we enter into the final four films he completed for Mutual — it was with these films that he fell most definitively behind his schedule of one two-reeler per month, the time between films increasing until it took him eight months to complete these last four entries. If we can surmise that the greater time was due to the relentless search for perfection, the quest to stretch out into a more serious type of art, we can say that in *Easy Street* a new emotional complexity and richness announces itself most forcefully.

A midnight choir of vagabonds and ragamuffins sings in a charity mission. Charlie, sleeping in a crevice between some steps and a building, looking more genuinely bum-like than we have seen him since *Police*, awakens to the singing — he is hopeless, cast off from society. He stumblingly follows the sound of the hymn into the Hope Mission. He joins the motley assembly gathered there, mostly, it seems, to get in out of the weather. The hymn ends, and there is a sermon — as the crowd disperses, Charlie finds himself nearly cornered by the preacher. When mission worker Edna approaches to give him the Good News, however, the Tramp is considerably more interested, his eyes taking in her luminous presence with a beatific gaze. Once more, romantic love for Charlie is tied to the higher virtues, to a spiritual rebirth — for as Edna and the preacher speak to him, he shakes off his misery, becomes inspired by determination, plans to make a new start of things. He even returns the collection box he'd planned to steal from them.

So rejuvenated is he that he applies for a job as a police officer when he passes a "Help Wanted" sign. He is assigned to Easy Street which, far from being the millionaire's row of popular song, or the carefree, pleasure-filled state of being known from the dialogue of a thousand movies and paperback novels, is a dismal, haunted ghetto of want and need, where a monstrous bully controls the street through brute force. It is a hell of poverty, drug addiction and wife abuse.

Easy Street introduces a landscape which will be seen in the films again and again — a dumpy street setting which is more like an alleyway, advancing from the screen, ending in another street at right angles to it, its buildings forming a backdrop, the buildings at either side forming a proscenium. Evidently a recreation of the London street Chaplin had once lived on with Hannah and Sydney, the basic set appears in such later films as *The Kid* and *City Lights* — it is Chaplin's ideal stage, his "world."

His world here is a badly broken one. The street bully, Eric Campbell, spends all his time thrashing entire groups of men for their pocket change. The police station sends cop after cop out to Easy Street. They return on gurneys, beaten to within an inch of their lives — Campbell mockingly wears one of their policeman helmets, declaring his brute force to be the only law. Charlie arrives, and never has Campbell towered over him so monstrously, so menacingly. The Tramp finds in short order that his billy club will be of little use to him in this contretemps — his hardest blows upon the cranium of his suspect have less effect than the landing of flies, and Campbell even offers his skull for further pounding, to demonstrate the futility of trying to rein in his rule. It is when Campbell decides to further display his power, bending a streetlamp nearly double, that the Tramp leaps on him, pulling the lamp over his head and gassing him. He turns the knob on the side of the lamp, administering the gas with the air of practiced anesthesiologist, felling the giant. His ingenuity, his gift for transformation, is here decisively heroic — itself transformed into a practical, triumphant tool. Some of his fellow cops take the vanquished thug away, and Charlie nonchalantly patrols the street, the citizens now scurrying fearfully away from him.

He catches a woman stealing food from a store. He is softened in his law enforcement duties by her tale of woe, which moves him to tears, and when she begins to faint from hunger, he goes and procures more food for her. With Edna, he brings food to the poor, arriving at a cramped apartment filled with uncountable children — on the floor, on the bed, on chairs. Charlie encounters the frail, diminutive father — he looks from the children to the little man and back again in disbelief, and after certifying the wan old fellow's patrimony, takes off his medal and presents it to him.

The giant has by this time awakened, snapping his handcuffs in two at the station, sending Charlie's fellow cops flying. He returns furiously to Easy Street and pursues Charlie — who defeats him this time by dropping a stove on his head from a window. Edna, however, is taken away by a lowlife to his lair. The lowlife shoots himself up with a hypodermic needle and prepares to subject the helpless Edna to unknown perversities. Meanwhile, Charlie is dropped through a hole in the street by a hostile crowd — into the drug addict's den. The Tramp lands on the needle, which is evidently filled with high grade Benzedrine, as it inspires him to bash the addict into insensibility, and then to take on all the other thugs and ruffians of Easy Street in hyped-up Superman manner. Vanquishing them all, he embraces Edna.

"Love backed by force/Forgiveness sweet/Brings hope and peace /To Easy Street," an intertitle tells us. We then see Easy Street redeemed — the denizens make their way to a ministry down the street, appropriately named New Mission. Even Campbell is now reformed, nodding to Officer Charlie as he makes his way piously along with his wife. Charlie is joined by Edna and they too make their way to church as the film fades out.

It is as eloquent a marriage between gritty realism and slapstick comedy as Chaplin ever accomplished. When, earlier in the film, Eric Campbell comes back from the jailhouse, he returns to his apartment and lays a beating on his long-suffering wife which is more unpleasant and vivid than all the other violence in the film — he is the picture of a vicious, amoral lout. Likewise, Chaplin spares us little detail in his depiction of the tawdriness and pain of poverty, from the dim ugliness of Easy Street to its cramped apartments, from the woman fainting from hunger, and the crowded floor of screaming infants, to the repellent evil of the drug addict and his dismal lair. Chaplin depicts a world of miserable chaos, where only brute force rules and all else is crushed.

In Chaplin's vision of redemption at the end, of a Paradise he returns to occasionally in his works, he reveals his Utopian aspect, the dream always hovering at the periphery of his world in which a corrupt, cruel order is washed away by the forces of forgiveness and mercy. But like all Utopians, particularly comic ones such as he, the dream, however passionately sincere, is not entirely innocent or without its tinge of irony. For Chaplin knew better than anyone that the hungry often are driven to steal food, that the forces of worldly justice offer no free passes on account of empty stomachs; that the hungry do suffer hunger pains, that they faint, and worse, and no ingenious, acrobatic little man with a mustache comes to save them; he knew the world of wife-beaters, despairing addicts, and thugs who rule through terror and violence — and that in the real world they are rarely called to account, rarely defeated, rarely reformed.

Easy Street may mimic the street of Chaplin's youth, but in a larger sense, it is not a street at all — it is the world. In this remarkable film, Chaplin creates his own universe, his own cosmology. Against the forces of darkness and destruction, we are given the ingenuity, energy and athleticism of the Tramp, these qualities within him now raised to levels which confer upon him the title of hero as never before. Charlie's battle with Campbell, coming after the Tramp's spiritual awakening, makes explicit the David and Goliath relationship between the two which had been hinted at in previous films—their battle is spiritual, Biblical, and the film's ending, with goodness decisively remaking the world, shows that what we've been watching is an archetypal, eschatological tale of a world redeemed. *Easy Street* isn't just a great comedy two-reeler — it is a great film.

As if to further display his versatility both as performer and creator, his next film is as far-off from *Easy Street* as it is possible to get. *The Cure* mines the humor to be gotten from the story of an alcoholic repairing to a sanitarium in order to dry out — not exactly a subject that would seem to guarantee surefire laughs, but then neither would the theme of urban decay as found in the previous film. The setting is a retreat for dipsomaniacs who gather around a fountain of restorative spring water, and is perhaps based on a Karno sketch that Chaplin's brother Sydney had performed in.[6] Chaplin comes staggering into the sanitarium grounds, his incarnation this time seeming to be a hybrid of the Tramp and the Drunk characters— he possesses the enlarged trousers and boots of the Tramp, but sports a smart white sports jacket and a boater. His intoxicated arrival at the "rehab center" would not seem to bode well for the purpose of his visit, nor does the wardrobe trunk full of liquor he is later seen to have brought with him.

The Cure is one of the most relaxed, and the most deeply comic of the Mutual films. Here, the Drunk's drunkenness, persisting as it does in a place where sallow-faced teetotalers keep trying to goad him into turning over a new life and getting sober, is both perverse and subversive — he gives the lie to all the good intentions of those around him. Like *The Floorwalker* with its escalator, much of *The Cure* revolves around a single prop — a revolving door which births a host of inventive and perfectly choreographed gags. In addition, there is also the circular little pond displayed in the first scene, which we (rightly) spend most of the film anticipating will be the site of a dunking. But it is not these which supply the most memorable moments of the film — again, the nuances and flights of whimsy Chaplin invests in his portrayal of the Drunk are responsible for those. When the Drunk is taken to the swimming pool to begin his regimen he goes into an elaborate mime routine, going through the motions of diving and swimming and drying himself off without ever leaving the edge of the pool — all the others gathered there just stare at him in dumbfounded wonderment. When he is to be massaged, he turns that into wrestling match with the masseur, fighting skillfully, dexterously, with controlled savagery. We are back in the realm of Charlie as surrealist mischief maker, a vessel of absurd anarchy — Charlie as the performer before an audience of awestruck dullards, the only truly alive person in a landscape of grim, grey, dead boredom.

Eric Campbell is again the nemesis here in one of his all-time great performances. He and another man are undressing in a locker room — a shoe comes sailing over the curtain behind them, hitting one of them, who turns and blames the other. Then the other gets hit ... a fight between them gets rolling before they realize where the shoes are coming from, and they open the curtain. Charlie stands posing before them like a photograph in an ancient Sears & Roebuck calendar, with cane and hat — he smiles and pulls the curtain closed. They pull it back, and now he's in the coquettishly mincing pose of a cheesecake model, coyly smiling up at the two men in turn. The curtain's closed, then opened again, and we are greeted by a prima ballerina, nimbly prancing out to greet us before retreating and closing the curtains again. Campbell and the other man simply stand gaping with puzzlement, like the observers by the pool. They are as transfixed as we by the vivid transformations. We get the idea that the men could stand closing and opening the curtain forever, and that each time there would be some new unexpected transformation, that the possibilities of Chaplin's magical shapeshifting ability are as infinite in variation and imagination as they seem to be — as infinite in creativity as the universe itself.

The transformative aspect, the fluidity of identity, is also seen later when Campbell is flirting with Edna, and Charlie comes to sit between them. He assumes Campbell is coming on to him, so he agreeably — and quite enthusiastically — flirts back.

At another point in the film, a maneuver by Charlie causes Campbell to take a spill to the floor. At the behest of Campbell, the manager comes and orders Charlie out — but Edna, whom the creepy Campbell has been harassing, comes to stick up for Charlie, insisting he stay. Vindicated, Charlie turns to the camera and executes a triumphant curtsey. He is again a performer for whom all of life is a performance — the artist who dignifies each twist of fate with a concluding flourish.

The Cure continues with all of Charlie's liquor being thrown, mistakenly, into the "well" of the restorative spring water. All of the inhabitants of the retreat become drunk — including Charlie, after he finally accedes to Edna's pleas for him to try the water. The next day, with a tremendous hangover, he asks Edna's forgiveness and pledges to go on the wagon, so that the film surprisingly ends on the same romantic, spiritual note as *Easy Street* — the Tramp and the Drunk have become one.

Though attitudes towards alcoholism have changed in the ninety years since *The Cure* was made, there is no need to lump the film in with other films which are "of their time," and insensitive in terms of their attitudes towards certain subjects. The man who was once billed as "The World's Greatest Impersonator of Inebriates" does not use the situation as an occasion for frivolous "drunk" humor, but as a backdrop for his anarchic, life-affirming transformations, in the same way that he has used deadly serious, grimly realistic situations in his other comedy films. For Chaplin, there is no other world — the pain of poverty, drug addiction and alcoholism do not exist in a universe separate from his slapstick fooling, but rather tragic circumstances create and shape his comedy as they do for no other comedian. All of Charlie's magical abilities are a defiant rebuke of tragedy — not a denial of it, but a mad fight against it, a staving off of it, and a triumph over it, if only for a fleeting moment. The more serious and tragic a subject, the more energetic and deeply humorous does Chaplin's comedy become, for, as Chaplin has begun to discover first unconsciously, now consciously, his comedy is unseverably linked to tragedy, even in its most whimsical moments — particularly in its most whimsical moments. The Tramp is a being whose purpose is the defiance of tragedy and sadness — think of his trademark half-skipping step as he wanders down the road — and so must always be placed in situations of great seriousness and suffering.

This is proven in the setting for his next film, *The Immigrant*, in which the Tramp is one of many poor immigrants, of many ethnicities, all crowded together on a violently pitching boat headed across the ocean to what they hope will be a better life. The motley crowd huddles on the swaying deck, all contending to varying degrees with the waves of nausea the merciless sea has visited upon them — one unfortunate man in a fez seems particularly prone to an imminent upheaval, and is sagely avoided by Charlie, who's dealing with his own gastric unrest. With this extended gag, rather nauseating in itself, we once again see the Chaplin obsession with the digestive processes of the stomach.

As well, the nautical setting gives Chaplin to opportunity to return to the "rocking boat" gag he'd used in *Shanghaied*, using a set built on rockers so that it can swing from side to side. The eating scene in the mess from the earlier film is repeated, but is much funnier here, with Henry Bergman in drag as a portly old matron sliding helplessly across the floor with Charlie — as well, there are Charlie and Albert Austin alternately taking spoonfuls of soup from the bowl which sails back and forth between them on the table. The Tramp soon makes the acquaintance of Edna, traveling on the ship with her soulful mother — the radiance of Charlie's customary instantaneous lovestruck demeanor upon seeing Edna is only mildly dimmed by another attack of seasickness. As always, her presence inspires gallantry in him, and he gives up his seat for her. Later, the Tramp whiles away the time by gambling with some other men on deck — a poor loser departs the game furiously and steals the money from the small purse hanging around Edna's mother's neck as she sleeps. The loser then loses this money to Charlie, and when the Tramp comes upon the weeping Edna later, he is moved to give her money. He becomes a friend to her and her mother, and they are together when the ship comes to port. They all gaze hopefully, timidly, up at the Statue of Liberty as she becomes visible on the horizon. No sooner are they able to catch a glimpse of the monument at whose base is a welcoming call to all the "poor ... huddled masses yearning to breathe free" than immigration officials roughly pull a restraining rope across their chests and all the other immigrants, pushing and forcing them back as if they are all a bunch of cattle.

Here Chaplin the social satirist and critic makes his appearance again — though the degree to which his target is his standard one of brute authority (the Tramp manages to score a retaliatory kick at the behind of one of the officials), the promise of America in particular, or the concept of "liberty" in general, and the manner in which societies fall short of this ideal, is purposefully and artfully left ambiguous by Chaplin. The sequence is a wry comment on all three aspects, and such is the power of his mastery over the images he employs that the vignette quite easily accommodates all the interpretations noted. Far from being a crass attack on hypocrisy or a didactic exercise in social criticism, the interlude is simply another swift, ironic, sharply observed comment on human nature — rich with a variety of meanings and implications.

The Tramp bids a heartfelt good-bye to Edna and her mother at the dock. In the next scene, Charlie is alone, walking down a dismal street. He is in the Land of Liberty, but he has not been liberated from hunger. He is quite happy to find a coin on the street — he hastens into a café to put it to use, not knowing, as we do, that the coin has slipped through a hole in his pocket and remains on the sidewalk.

He enters the café and enters into a sequence which might be described as a mini-masterpiece within a masterpiece. In the following scene, all that Chaplin has striven to do in films since his first entry at Keystone, all that he has attempted in his quest to bring the comedy of personality and attitude, of psychological nuance and subtlety to film, comes to fruition. In his growing awareness at Mutual that his technique consisted of a series of routines linked to a dramatic, serious story, Chaplin took this one routine — the Tramp's archetypal dilemma of being without money in a restaurant — and stretched it out, sustaining it with such richness of psychological detail and with such a dizzyingly imaginative series of variations that it becomes one of the finest scenes he ever created — and one which exemplifies his vision of film as a means of recording performance, of documenting a routine which follows, with unrelieved doggedness, the at times infinitesimal yet always very human shifts and gradations of the Tramp's anxiety, his concerns all centering around one coin.

He begins by having the Tramp seated at a table and ordering a plate of beans, which he consumes with such idiosyncratic unlikeliness that this time it is his tablemate, Albert Austin (in a different role from the one he played on the ship), who is appalled by Charlie's unsavory manners, rather than the other way around. Just as we are wondering what this scene has to do with the earlier part of the film on the boat, Charlie takes notice of Edna at a nearby table. Elated, he beckons her over — but their reunion is dampened when he spies her black-rimmed handkerchief: her mother has died. Charlie offers to treat Edna to a meal of beans, and soon all is well again.

The waiter is Eric Campbell, in full menacing bruiser mode. A drunk at
another table is ten cents short on his bill. For this infraction Campbell beats
him to a pulp, the entire staff of the café gather to kick and pummel him, and
his remains are hoisted from the scene as Charlie and Edna look on in horror.
The Tramp cautiously checks for his coin and finds it isn't there. Panicked, he
looks about for help, ordering more coffee in order to stall for time. He sees a
man counting out some change at a nearby table, tries to signal to him, to go
over and see what he can get from him, but all the time he must do this without arousing the suspicions of Campbell — who seems somehow to surmise
that Charlie has no way to pay the bill, and is only waiting for that presump-
tion to be validated so he can joyfully pound him into nonexistence.

The Tramp sees a coin drop from Campbell's pants onto the floor. He
must now find a way to secure that coin without Campbell noticing — he throws
his foot out onto the floor, slamming it down over the coin. In all of these
interactions we notice the quick shifts of movement and attitude, the split-
second actions and reactions of both Charlie and Campbell, and we marvel at
the rapport they have established as performers by this time, at the intricate
choreography that goes into these routines. Charlie secures the coin and handily pays his bill with it. But Campbell picks the coin up and bends it disdainfully between his teeth — it's a fake. At this, Charlie collapses to the floor. He
orders more coffee to stall for time.

An artist observes Edna from a nearby table — he's played by Henry
Bergman, who was seen earlier as an immigrant woman on board the ship.
Inspired by the thought of Edna as a subject, he comes to their table and begins
talking to them. When his bill is delivered to him, he picks up Charlie's bill
as well, offering to pay it for him. In a variation on a gag from Chaplin's first
film, *Making a Living*, Charlie makes a show of pride, gesturing that it isn't
necessary for the artist to pay his bill. The artist takes it back, insisting — the
Tramp continues in his show, the bill goes back and forth, till finally the artist
shrugs, relenting, giving the appalled Charlie back his bill. He's back where he
started.

The artist pays his own bill, laying a tip on the plate. Charlie places his
bill over the tip, presenting it to Campbell. Campbell takes it, tendering the
change to him. Charlie dismissively waves the change back to Campbell, presenting it to him as a tip. Then he nonchalantly yawns, stretching out his
arms, every inch the satiated, blasé diner as he prepares to depart the café with
Edna.

The two immigrants emerge onto the rainy street with the artist — he
promises them a position with him, starting the next week. Charlie asks for an
advance, and receiving it, walks with Edna around the corner to a marriage
license office. He directs her in, but she resists with an insistence which quickly
becomes less emphatic, more flirtatious. The office registrar observes them
balefully as the two lovers come to happy terms, Charlie finally lifting Edna and

carrying her into the marriage license office from the rainy street as the film fades out.

Chaplin would write that *The Immigrant* touched him more than any film he ever made, and would remain proud of the poetic feeling of the ending. The film unites two sections which are at first glance seemingly disparate, yet each revolves around money, food, sustenance and survival in a harsh, ruthless world. The quest of the immigrants coming to the land of an elusive liberty gives the film a tenuously hopeful, bittersweet tone which persists and finds culmination in the final frames. Only Chaplin would choose immigration, and the squalid conditions thereof, as a backdrop for a comedy, and only he could portray the death of a character in a two-reel comedy with such delicacy and deftness as he does here. The entire sequence of the coin, where everything is brought right down to its essentials, is a tour de force — Chaplin's art at its finest, on full display, given the space necessary to expand to its ultimate and defining dimensions. He has succeeded in transforming the music hall comedy sketch — and the two-reel comedy — into high art.

His next film and his final film for Mutual, *The Adventurer*, is the tale of an escaped convict — Charlie, replete in striped prison uniform and cap, on the run from a group of police. The film opens as they hunt for him along the California coast, and with its shots of the Tramp cavorting on the rugged, mountainous shoreline, and amongst the smashing ocean waves, *The Adventurer* benefits more than any other Mutual from some stunning location work.

Charlie's head appears out of the sand near where one of the policemen sits resting. When he realizes his predicament — his face inches from the barrel of the policeman's gun — the Tramp hurriedly tries to bury himself again. A chase ensues over the rocks and the rolling landscape. At one point a cop shoots at him and he falls to the ground — the cop runs to him, and as he bows over the prone form, Charlie raises his leg and kicks him over the side of the cliff. He finally escapes into the ocean, switching into a bathing suit he steals from a nearby rowboat. He resurfaces near an amusement park and bathing area; Edna and Eric Campbell are seated nearby, and are alarmed to hear the sound of a woman calling for help from the waves. The cowardly Campbell stays behind as Edna runs to rescue her, only to succumb to the current herself. Charlie comes upon the scene, and in one of his most strenuous displays of heroism, rescues the two women — through the first woman is left to struggle a little longer than Edna, once Charlie adjudges her as less attractive.

Eric Campbell, too, falls into the ocean, and the Tramp gamely rescues him as well. When he drops Campbell back in again by accident, he retrieves him once more. As Campbell climbs up on the dock he kicks Charlie in the face, sending him sprawling unconscious into the water. He is taken by Edna back to her home. He awakes the next morning with no idea where he is— and is panicked to find himself in horizontally striped pajamas, his hands groping the frighteningly bar-like columns of the headboard of his bed.

The butler comes in and lays down some clothes for him — Charlie changes into evening dress and descends the stairs to the elegant soirée the household's hosting. From here, the film is a restatement of the theme seen in several films so far, with the Tramp as an impostor in high society, passing himself off as one who belongs in such surroundings, all the while striving to escape detection, confronted at every side by circumstances which threaten to expose him. Nowhere has this been executed better than in *The Adventurer*. Here, as in *The Count*, the jealous Eric Campbell is his enemy, the agent determined to blow the Tramp's tenuous cover.

At the same time, none of these concerns stop Charlie from enjoying his fleeting fling in high society with his usual flair and panache. He's more than convincing as a charming bon vivant, chatting up Edna debonairly, even if all the while he is concerned with nothing of greater import than cadging all the drinks possible. Left alone for a moment, he summons the butler — who could it be but Albert Austin? — who impassively watches as Charlie pours the remains of several drinks left on Austin's tray into one glass, then downs it. As Edna approaches he quickly hides the glass in his pocket and resumes his elegant, aristocratic demeanor of before.

They sit near where a large, matronly woman dances, shaking her sizable behind in Charlie's face. The Tramp is quite nonplussed by such a spectacle, and pulling a pin from his pocket, is fully intent on putting it to use — until he sees Edna's surprised and puzzled expression, at which point he grins and chuckles cutely, replacing the pin in his pocket.

Campbell, however, knows him for what he is, and they exchange rapid rounds of surreptitious ass-kicking as they make their convivial way around the party. Campbell sees Charlie's "wanted" picture in the paper and in short order the inevitable chase ensues with the police bursting upon the party and the frenzied, dexterous evasions of the Tramp as he leaps from balconies, and stands stock-still beneath a lampshade in a shape-shifting impersonation of the light fixture. In the end he is caught, and gallantly bids farewell to Edna. As a seeming afterthought, he politely introduces his apprehending officer to her — as the cop releases his grip on Charlie to shake Edna's hand, Charlie takes off, and the film ends. The end is perfect because although it seems inevitable that he will be caught again, we are left with the image of Charlie setting himself loose, breaking free with the imaginative ingenuity which has defined him throughout the film. He is the hunted one, and we are vouchsafed with no knowledge of his ultimate destination, but know him always as the one ever escaping, ever endeavoring to free himself from the forces of confinement, of the ruthlessly harsh reality and dull unimaginativeness which pursue him.

The Adventurer is a "chase" picture, and one which displays the master craftsman Chaplin had become by this time, for it flows from one incident to another with rapid yet fluid grace. Like the other films preceding it, it contains now familiar elements of wistfulness and an underlying, nameless poignancy —

in these comedies a sudden shift to seriousness will take us by surprise in midst of the laughter, as when we see the image of Charlie's body drifting, apparently lifeless, in the waves after he's been kicked unconscious by Campbell. Chaplin was now able to intertwine serious emotions and subjects with outrageous physical comedy deftly—both worlds were now available to him, and were united in the world he created in his films. In *The Adventurer* his art is able to imply these other depths without unduly calling attention to itself for doing so, and as such it is a fitting conclusion to the Mutual films. With each of the twelve shorts, Chaplin has steadily raised the ante until he has constructed the base for all his films of the future; they constitute such an explosion of creativity and invention that one can only be amazed at their richness and originality. After finding his footing with *The Floorwalker*, *The Fireman* and *The Vagabond*, he had moved from the virtuoso performances in *One A.M.* and *The Pawnshop*, to the audacity and emotional intensity of *Easy Street* and *The Immigrant*—which fulfill the promise of *The Vagabond*—to the pure comedy delight of *The Rink*, *The Count*, *Behind the Screen*, *The Cure*, and *The Adventurer*, which are as good as slapstick hijinks get. The Mutuals are an inexhaustible fount of comic innovation and imagination. They are the inspired, ambitious creations of Chaplin just as he gained control over his art, just as the anarchic primitiveness of his style came under the guiding hand of his burgeoning craftsmanship as a writer, director and actor, and his vision presented itself more strongly—focused, with clarity and certainty. His conception of the universe was laid bare for all to see.

As well, the Tramp, if he has lost some of his vulgarity and rough edges, if he has been found to rely less on brutish violence and more on cunning and a supernatural ingenuity, has become more defined as a hero of transformation, a more poetic, artistic entity who triumphs over the dread realities always swarming forth to engulf him, not through force but through imagination, gallantry, poise, through his performance skills and his ever tireless ability to recreate himself and the world anew.

It is a sad irony that the one person outside of Chaplin himself responsible for the excellence of many of these films, whose talents help to ensure their classic status, and in which his own immortality is guaranteed—Eric Campbell—was killed tragically in a car accident two months after completing *The Adventurer*. He was thirty-seven.

The Mutual films would set a bar of achievement for all other comedians working in the two-reel format. Having mastered the form, Chaplin was now typically looking beyond it, towards his next evolution.

5

First National:
A Dog's Life, Shoulder Arms,
Sunnyside, A Day's Pleasure

The Mutual company had been a sympathetic and patient employer with whom Chaplin had realized almost total artistic freedom. Although they offered him a contract to make more films, Chaplin's artistic ambitions were such that he decided he needed more freedom, more independence—the kind he could only attain by becoming his own producer. His brother Sydney negotiated a contract with a new company, First National Exhibitor's Circuit, for the production of eight two-reelers over one year for the fee of one million dollars. In his new capacity as producer, Chaplin built his own studio, and in January 1918 settled in to create the next stage of his artistic development, newly unfettered—but with a new burden of responsibility as well.

His ability to successfully weave serious storylines and issues into his comedies had greatly developed at Mutual, as evidenced especially in *Easy Street* and *The Immigrant*. He would refine this ability in his new films. His First National shorts would mostly be three reels long (thirty minutes) as opposed to the two-reel shorts he had made at Mutual. This enlargement of his canvas was as decisive as the shift from the predominantly one-reelers made at Keystone to the predominantly two-reelers made at Essanay had been. Now he had more time—and greater necessity—to fashion a fully structured plot. Most of the Mutuals had needed only premises—the Tramp in a pawnshop, the Tramp at a skating rink, as a cop, the Drunk trying to get to bed. He remembered that at this time he began to think of comedy architecturally—of one episode proceeding naturally from another. His new filmmaking would be more story-driven, less gag-oriented, less based around improvised routines. These were natural developments on the way to what was Chaplin's real, increasingly obvious ambition—to progress directly to features. The First National shorts, with their increased length, were the stepping stones toward the longer form which Chaplin was restively anticipating.

Counterpart to the new expansiveness of form, and the new discipline, is, as Chaplin himself noted, an inevitable restriction on his "comic freedom."[1] This is evident from his first First National film. For the Tramp here is neither the violent anarchist of his Keystone/Essanay films nor the transformational performance artist of his Mutual comedies. In *A Dog's Life*— noted in its publicity as his "first million dollar film"— the Tramp is a real tramp, in a more recognizably "real" world than ever before. He is still a figure of energy and ingenuity, but more and more these qualities are directed towards specific tasks— there isn't the sense of gratuitous whimsy that there was before. This is a price to pay, but it is a necessary trade-off for the sustained development of plot, the more prestigious, "larger" works of art which Chaplin is driven to create.

We find the Tramp lying in a vacant, garbage-strewn lot, beside a rickety, dilapidated fence. The broken fence seems to be all that protects Charlie from the wind as he lies on the bare ground — he uses his handkerchief to plug one of the holes. We have seen him languishing in poverty before, but even in Easy Street he had a building to cower against as he slept. Here is a barren, ugly, dismal poverty which in its starkness is more depressing and disturbing than the comparatively stylized slum of *Easy Street*. The Tramp steals a wiener from a hot dog vendor and nimbly evades the police. He then goes to an employment office to seek work— and goes into a routine with the motley assemblage of other down-at-the-heels men seeking sustenance: each time he tries to sidle up to the employment booth, the other men shove in front of him, sending him flying. He runs from booth to booth, the men appearing in front of him each time. The Tramp of before would have dispatched these competitors with a few deft thrusts of his bamboo cane — but the Tramp here is more of an Everyman, the "Little Fellow." He's simply trying to do the honest thing, but finds himself victimized by the rough aggressiveness of his fellow bums.

Charlie's hardscrabble battle for survival also feeds into the structure of *A Dog's Life*, which is based on the parallel between his precarious existence and that of a stray cur. We meet Scraps, a mongrel pup as mangy, hungry and homeless as the Tramp. As the Tramp has been belted around by coarse lunks in his attempt to gain employment, so Scraps is set upon by a coalition of street dogs who try to wrest away from him a tiny scrap of food. Charlie runs into the melee and rescues Scraps, perhaps recognizing a kindred spirit. In a charming vignette, he tries to provide some nourishment for the dog —finding a half-empty milk bottle, he lets Scrap drink it, and in order for him to get the last few drops at the bottom, Charlie dips the end of Scraps' tail in them, encouraging the dog to lick the milk from it.

The Tramp and his dog walk up to lunch wagon, and Scraps filches some sausages from the counter. The owner of the counter is less angered by that theft than by Charlie's pilfering of pastries throughout the scene. The owner is played by Sydney Chaplin, who follows up on his triumph in negotiating the million-dollar contract for his brother by playing roles in nearly every First National production. The two brothers play out a vaudeville routine, Charlie grabbing the pastries, shoving them in his mouth, and swallowing them frenziedly the moment Syd's back is turned, effecting innocent nonchalance the moment Syd turns again. Syd knows that Charlie is eating the pastries, but believes he must catch him in the act — he doesn't know who he's dealing with.

The Tramp repairs to a disreputable dive, the Green Lantern, a local hangout for assorted drunks and pickpockets; since dogs aren't allowed, he takes Scraps in his pants, the canine's tail wagging out a hole in the back. There, Edna is singing a heart-rending song from the stage — her emoting causes all the clientele of the café to weep copiously. In one of Chaplin's more idiosyncratic gags, a man seated near the Tramp turns to him, weeping. The man's expression, though, might easily be mistaken for one in the grips of laughter, so the Tramp agreeably begins chuckling along with him; the man becomes angry, pointing to his tears, causing Charlie to resume his former downcast manner.

Edna's duties, we soon see, extend beyond the simple singing of songs, at least as far as the manager is concerned. He informs her that she is to flirt with the male customers, get them to dance with her. Charlie is bemused by her uncomfortable attempts at seduction, but he is soon thrown out of the café once his lack of funds is detected. Meanwhile, on the street, two thieves roll a drunk man and steal his wallet. They hide the ill-gotten currency by burying it, and when Scraps digs it up the next day, the Tramp is overjoyed. He speeds with the money to the Green Lantern to greet Edna; having rejected the sexual advances of a customer, she has been fired and is on her way out. The Tramp speaks romantically to her of starting over in the country with the money he and Scraps have found. Unfortunately the two thieves who stole the money are eavesdropping — in short order, they have reclaimed their loot and Charlie is thrown out again.

The resourceful tramp sneaks back into the café. Hiding behind a curtain, he approaches the table where the two men sit — and when the one nearest him (Albert Austin) leans back, Charlie knocks him unconscious through the curtain. Unbeknownst to the other thief, Charlie thrusts his arms beneath the arms of the unconscious thief and begins animating him, gesturing wildly, his hands "becoming" the thief's hands. In one long take, this routine is performed — and it is very much a music hall routine similar to the muffin-eating routine of before — Charlie straightening the thief's tie, raising the thief's glass when a toast is proposed (and surreptitiously taking a drink for himself), and when the criminal shows signs of coming to, the Tramp cuffs him smartly across the jaw and sends him into oblivion once more. In the end, Charlie has the thief beckon his compatriot closer, closer, at which point he smashes him over the head with the bottle and makes off with the money. The Tramp takes off with the cash — a fight and a chase ensue, and Scraps saves the day by making off with the wallet.

The final scene is another of Chaplin's visions of Paradise. They have made it to the country, out of the urban slum in which they were all so oppressed — Edna by the exploitation of her employer, Charlie and Scraps by their merciless, knockabout fight for bare survival. The Tramp is now a man of the soil, planting an entire field one seed at a time by hand. He retires to his pastoral home to find Edna waiting happily for him within. They look adoringly into the crib by the fire — to find Scraps and his— her — offspring nestled snugly.

A Dog's Life is a very well-crafted, well-structured film — its ambitions reach beyond the simple excuse for slapstick antics that the earlier films had been, and it succeeds in attaining those ambitions. Chaplin presents a convincing vision of a world in which there seems no honorable way to live, and the brilliant juxtaposition of the Tramp's plight with that of the stray dog drives home the sense of unsettled, frenetic desperation which poverty bequeaths to its sufferers. In the Tramp's rescue of the dog from the fight, in his subsequent care for Scraps, and in his rescue of Edna from the corrupt, dirty city, we see the Tramp's altruistic, self-sacrificing side, which will come to the fore in later films.

Directly after completing the editing of *A Dog's Life*, Chaplin left to go on a personal appearance tour to support the Liberty Bond Drive for the war. World War I, or simply the Great War as it was called then, had been in progress at that time for three and a half years. Spurred by the assassination of the Archduke of Austria, which unleashed a tidal wave of tribal hatreds which had been brewing since the last century, it had begun during the time of Chaplin's Keystone films and spiraled into the bloodiest war in recorded history — by the end of it, more than nine million people would be killed. America entered the war in August 1917 and began to contribute to those casualties. Fighting was done by bayonet, rifle, cannon and poison gas, and fighting conditions were brutal, with troops dug into mud-filled trenches, living in flooded dugouts for months at a time as they waited their orders to go "over the top" and kill or be killed.

Perhaps it was the Bond Drive which helped Chaplin decide on the subject matter for his next film when he returned to the studio. People suggested that the war was not something to be used in a comedy film, that the atrocities occurring overseas were not to be made light of. But Chaplin, as usual, did just as he wanted to. He began filming an account of the Tramp as a soldier on the front lines of the Great War.

Shoulder Arms was Chaplin's most ambitious film to date and his most successful one. It has all the dimension and sweep of a feature film, and was in fact planned as one for a time. Chaplin's boldness in taking on the defining conflagration of the time and daring to wring laughter from it solidified his standing as the preeminent star of his day. The film is a display of the great skill and sensitivity he showed in doing just that.

Charlie is a recruit who has trouble keeping his feet facing the same way when he marches — they continually splay out into their customary opposite positions. He is dispatched overseas, directed to a trench, assigned a dugout. One of his fellow soldiers— Syd — is bemused by the Tramp's inclusion of a mousetrap among the tools he has attached to his uniform. Packages from home are distributed and all the soldiers enjoy the letters and treats they've received — except for Charlie, who receives nothing. He contents himself by looking over the shoulder of another solider as he reads his letter from home, and laughing when the soldier laughs, frowning when he frowns, sighing sentimentally when he sighs ... until the soldier becomes aware of his presence and turns on him irritatedly. Charlie is again the alone one, set apart from others in his utter solitude as though he inhabits a thoroughly different reality.

He does end up receiving a package from home, though — a slab of limburger cheese, that odious slapstick standby. Charlie dons his gas mask, not to protect himself from a lethal mustard gas attack but to spare himself the noxious smell of the fromage. He tosses it out of the trench and it ends up plastered across the face of the German captain across the way.

Another horror of the war is referred to when it comes time for the Tramp to bed down in the dugout which has become flooded chest-high with water. Charlie wades to his submerged bunk, as three other soldiers sleep clustered together in the bunk above his. The Tramp reaches beneath the black water, retrieves his pillow, plumps it up delicately, then replaces it, watching as it sinks out of sight. Syd, nearby, miraculously sleeps with his head and feet poking out of the water. Charlie settles in by procuring the horn from a nearby phonograph to breathe through as he relaxes beneath the waves.

The order comes to go "over the top" and Charlie is much concerned by the unfortunate implications of his serial number —13 — and sundry other bad omens. However, as an intertitle informs us, the number 13 proves not to be so unlucky after all as the Tramp nonchalantly returns from his mission with exactly 13 German soldiers he has managed to capture singlehandedly, in one of Chaplin's neatest and most unexpected gags. When asked how he managed such a feat, Charlie replies: "I surrounded them."

The Tramp is sent on a mission behind enemy lines, disguised as a tree. A German soldier ordered to cut some wood for a fire finds his efforts repelled by the swiftly moving, violent tree, and there are some surreal shots as the German chases the tree across a field, and then through a grove of other trees, the "Charlie tree" posing and passing itself off as the real thing repeatedly. Syd is captured by the German soldiers and is about to be shot before a firing squad when Charlie dispatches his would-be executioners with a clonk of his branch.

Shedding the tree costume, the Tramp escapes and comes upon the devastated home of a French girl (Edna). Unable to speak French, Charlie conveys his identity by miming the flight of an eagle, hitting himself on the head with a brick, counting the "stars" and miming some stripes. The house is soon taken over by German soldiers, who capture Edna. Charlie is able to rescue her by knocking a German officer out, then disguising himself in his clothes. He is still dressed in the German uniform when the Kaiser himself visits, and by disguising himself and Edna as the Kaiser's chauffeurs, they are able to capture him and his retinue and bring them back as prisoners of war. Charlie inflicts the ultimate and inevitable indignity upon the Kaiser when he kicks him in the ass as a final gesture. The troops all celebrate — but suddenly we are back with the Tramp in training camp, and we find it has all been a dream.

Aside from the fantastical elements of the ending, we see that Chaplin throughout the film has not turned away from the misery and brutal conditions of the war, but rather has delved into them and mined his comedy from them. Charlie's fear in the trench at the explosions going on around him is palpable and evocative — millions likely found communion in the humanity of its portrayal. Likewise human is Chaplin's portrayal of the German enemy. The diminutive German commandant is seen to be the enemy not only of the Allied forces, but of his own soldiers: when he pours a glass of champagne to celebrate the imminent capture of Paris, Chaplin shows him refusing to allow any of his men to have a drink. Later, when the Tramp has captured his thirteen prisoners of war, he offers them all cigarettes. They all take one, but the officer disdainfully throws his to the ground. As punishment for this rude conduct, Charlie takes him over his knee and spanks him — and all the Germans cheer and applaud excitedly. Chaplin displays the solidarity of common men which transcends nationalism or war. He affirms the reality of a humanity united beyond all arbitrary notions of country and politics — a concept he will return to later.

This is also seen in the final frames of Charlie's dream, in which the Tramp effectively ends the Great War — as he and Edna and Syd and the troops all laugh and cheer into the camera, the intertitle reads "Peace on Earth — goodwill to all mankind." Undoubtedly the wish contained in these words resonated with many who watched the film in 1918. Understandably, *Shoulder Arms* took longer to make than any other Chaplin film to date, so that it was released only twenty-two days before Armistice was declared. But perhaps this was fortuitous — no one seems to have appreciated the film more than the returning soldiers from the War to End All Wars. The film succeeds because of its masterful construction, its unspoken but enduring empathy for all those who suffer in war, and Chaplin's sheer inventiveness at drawing on its horrors and fashioning comic episodes from them.

During the making of *Shoulder Arms* Chaplin made a ten-minute short in support of Liberty Bonds, entitled *The Bond*. Consisting of a series of vignettes about various types of bonds — the bonds of love, of matrimony, and finally the War Bonds, the purchase of which will defeat the Kaiser — the film is most notable today for its experimental quality. It is shot against a black background, with props and sets which are highly stylized.

Experimental as well is *Sunnyside*, the next short Chaplin made after the triumphant success of *Shoulder Arms*, and perhaps his oddest film. The film is set in Sunnyside, a placid little hamlet in the country. Charlie is a "jack of all trades" at a hotel — he is awakened each morning by his boss kicking him in the ass to get him out of bed. The boss thoughtfully pulls his boot on over his foot before enacting this ritual. The Tramp is a harried handyman, making breakfast for his master, or cleaning the hotel, or leading his herd of cattle around. Charlie's life is somewhat sweetened by his girlfriend Edna, to whom he gives a ring. A city slicker comes to the placid little village, however, and steals Edna's heart away. Charlie tries to win her back by emulating the city fellow's ways — he wears a pair of socks over his shoes to imitate his rival's spats, he attaches a match to the end of his cane to simulate the other fellow's cigarette lighter. All his efforts only serve to make him more pathetic, however, and he leaves in despair. He walks to the middle of the road and crouches before an oncoming car. Just before the car is about to mow him down we are suddenly back at the hotel, at the moment the city slicker is checking out. Edna walks in and Charlie embraces her, glad to have her back — they wave as the city slicker departs the village.

Where *A Dog's Life* and *Shoulder Arms* were impeccably constructed and focused, *Sunnyside* seems like a sloppy jumble of ideas, none of them followed up on properly — nothing in the film really works. The basic premise would seem to be to take the Tramp from his usual urban setting and plunk him down in a rustic, pastoral scene. This is nodded to when Charlie, following his herd of cattle down the road, suddenly slips on something we can't see. We anticipate that it's likely a cowpie deposited by his bovine friends, and are surprised when he bends and picks up the old urban slapstick standby, the banana peel. But there are other things going on in the film as well.

The film begins by irising from the cross of a steeple. It irises back in and then out again on the words "Love Thy Neighbor" on the bedroom wall of Charlie's boss who is seen here, and again later in the film, studiously reading his Bible — this is just before he ambles into the next room to kick the Tramp out of his bed. Edna's father is shown to be Jewish, wearing a yarmulke and reading a Hebrew newspaper. We are shown the townspeople flocking to church on Sunday morning — all except Charlie, who walks placidly out in nature, with the cows — "His church, the sky," the intertitle reads, "his altar, the landscape." Chaplin is playing with the idea of Charlie being a pantheist, one who finds God in all of nature, far from the borders imposed by the monotheistic religions he refers to and — in one case — gently satirizes. We have seen him kid Christianity before, or perhaps the hypocrisy of humanity in general, with the pickpocket minister in *Police* — here, he sharpens the satire: his cows escape from him and stampede through the church, disrupting the villagers' service.

The pantheistic note is sounded strongly when Charlie is bucked from a cow and falls unconscious beneath a bridge. He is roused by the sudden appearance of white-robed nymphs who dance about him. He rises and joins in with their joyful prancing, creating a transcendent moment and the most memorable scene of the film. Liberated by their otherworldly acceptance, he returns to the balletic performance mode of his Mutuals and throws himself with abandon into an eccentric dance. He is now Pan himself — the Greek mythological figure was a herdsman as Charlie is here. Where he was a flickering flame of absurd beauty against the background of grey normality in his dancing interludes of the Mutual pictures, he is now subsumed and in complete harmony with a dream world, another fantastical vision of Paradise. Subsumed, that is, until he falls beneath the bridge again and is pulled up by some townfolk, his Christian boss kicking his ass all the way home — pausing a moment to chat with one of his neighbors as Charlie waits patiently, then resuming the ass-kicking trek home.

There is an undercurrent of feverish sadness and violence, like a springtime dream, within the pastoral images of the film, culminating in Charlie's rather shocking suicide attempt. When the Tramp visits Edna at her home, the village fool hangs about, interfering with his courting of her. The old demonic Charlie makes a return, proposing a game of blind man's bluff with the fool, blindfolding him, and sending him to wander gropingly off into the middle of the road, where cars whiz by. As well, it is a car accident which brings the city slicker to the hotel, and the Tramp bends before a car to commit suicide — a gruesome image which makes one really wonder what Chaplin was thinking. Perhaps he was commenting on the incursion on small village ways by the arrival of the automobile.

As bizarre as *Sunnyside* is, many of the routines within it are halfhearted and uncertain — the Tramp has a cleaning scene in which he fools with a mop, and later he plays around with the doctor as he examines the city slicker, but his actions seem unmotivated and uninspired. The attempt here to achieve pathos for the Tramp is obvious and inept. Chaplin would later describe his unhappiness with the film, noting its creation was "like pulling teeth."[2] For all its faults, however, there is a basic strangeness to *Sunnyside* which allows one to designate it as a failed experiment. The same can't be said for his next film, which is the worst of Chaplin's maturity.

A Day's Pleasure is bad in the ghastly manner in which only the bad works of a genius can be. Charlie is domesticated here, setting off on a day's outing with his wife (Edna) and their three children — symptomatic of the film's haphazard construction, little is done with the wife and children as characters, or with the rarely used concept of the Tramp as father and husband. They pile into their Model T, which shakes and rattles frightfully as they start off, and they make their way to the docks, where they set off on a pleasure cruise. Henry Bergman makes an appearance as a large woman who runs to board the boat as it departs, misses, and ends up hanging suspended between the boat and dock, providing a bridge for Charlie to nimbly scamper over. The boat ride is the lurching, nausea-inducing, seesawing trip we have seen earlier in *Shanghaied* and *The Immigrant*, with an even greater quotient of stomach-clutching and retching than had been in the earlier films—it really is remarkable how often this gag appears in Chaplin's work. Here it drags on for an interminably long time, with Charlie's queasiness not helped by the jazz combo on board, playing energetically as the Tramp and his wife dance their nauseous dance. Even the musicians become ill, and Chaplin includes, for good measure, the dubious gag of having one of the black players turn "white" with his sickness. Charlie ends up collapsing against a woman (played by Babe London) whose husband has just left to vomit over the side of the boat. The husband returns, finds the Tramp there, and they square off to battle, both fighting off waves of illness as they pummel each other on the rocking deck. At one point the man must leave to upchuck over the side of the boat — the Tramp rushes over and deplorably kicks him in the seat of the pants again and again as the man vomits. They start to fight once more, and the man collapses feverishly against Charlie, who takes the opportunity to deliver a rapid series of blows to his stomach.

The simulations of nausea are convincing and unsparing, the rocking of the boat achieved here by the camera rolling from side to side. Even this is done shoddily, for in several shots the jazz musicians are seen sitting in stolidly stationary position, followed by a shot of the dancers slanting wildly from side to side, though they're supposed to be on the same boat.

As drawn out as the seasick scene is, so the Tramp's befuddled inability to open a deck chair is elongated past the point of amusement. After this, we see Charlie and the family heading home in the car, getting into traffic difficulties with a cop. There are misunderstandings and collisions, and tar is poured on the street, providing the one memorably amusing gag in the film — the Tramp with his feet stuck in the tar, leaning at a forty-five degree angle as he argues with the cop. In the end, Charlie and his family trundle off in their quivering car as it billows clouds of smoke in to the air — "The end of a perfect day," the final title reads.

One of the problems with A Day's Pleasure, and, to a lesser degree, Sunnyside, is that the new style Chaplin has forged in his First National shorts only works if the film as a whole is focused on a solid storyline, with, at least, serious undertones. Whereas the Mutuals were largely based around Charlie's energetic and improvised flights of whimsy in banal situations, the First Nationals are about the Tramp as a more realistic, practical character acting within dramatic situations, advancing a plot — as in A Dog's Life and Shoulder Arms. When there is no strong plot, we are left with only the limitations of the new style and none of the strengths of the old style.

As well, A Day's Pleasure contains so much that's unpleasant and its comedy is of such a sour disposition that Chaplin almost seems to have made his satire of middle-class family outings purposely objectionable. Its inadequacies are understandable, even forgivable, when one considers that the first part of it was filmed, then shoved aside when Chaplin became diverted by another project. He then became so immersed in the other project, and spent so much time on it, that First National began to demand some new product. Chaplin went back, hastily completed *A Day's Pleasure* to fulfill their demand, and got back to his new project. He likely knew the film was not up to his usual standards, but didn't care. The project he was immersed in was his first feature-length masterpiece.

6

The Kid

From the opening scenes, we are made aware that *The Kid* is unlike any Chaplin film previously seen, for a full five minutes of serious storyline goes by before the Tramp makes his first appearance. A new mother, played by Edna, is leaving a charity hospital with her infant in her arms. She is a woman "whose only sin is motherhood," we are told, and her plight is compared, via an inserted image, with Christ's bearing of His cross. By contrast, we are shown the father of the child, an artist who carelessly knocks Edna's picture from the mantle in his studio. The mother deposits her baby in the back seat of a fancy car in front of a mansion, leaving him with a note. She later has second thoughts and comes back to reclaim the child; but two thieves have stolen the car, driving it back to their slum area. They hear the baby crying and decide to get rid of it, dumping it behind some garbage in an alleyway. Down the alleyway comes a diminutive hobo in large pants, with a small mustache and a derby hat.

Chaplin conceived of *The Kid* during the creative crisis he experienced during *Sunnyside* and *A Day's Pleasure*. He had gone to a vaudeville show and seen a young boy named Jackie Coogan dancing as part of his parents' act. So impressed was he by the boy's dancing and charisma onstage that shortly thereafter he engaged him for his company.[1] He began shooting a new film, his artistic logjam now broken as he filmed scene after scene, newly inspired by the child. Certainly the idea of the Tramp saddled with a child was a creatively fertile one, and one which would allow him the scope to venture more into the serious, dramatic territory he was drawn to. As well, he discovered to his delight that he simply couldn't have found a better child to play the part — undoubtedly Jackie's instinctive brilliance reminded Chaplin of his own success as a child actor.

The Tramp, after helping himself to another cigarette butt from his sardine can cigarette case, looks down and sees the baby lying amongst the trash. He looks up, thinking someone threw it from a window along with the rest of the trash. He picks it up — then tries to deposit it back on the pavement, but a nearby cop forestalls that. Charlie scampers off and tries to dump it in a baby carriage with another baby. The baby's mother, an angry little harridan, objects to that. The Tramp waddles off and hails a man walking along the street — he asks the guy to hold the baby while he ties his bootlace. When the man takes the infant, Charlie runs off. The man runs after him, and passing by the harridan's baby carriage, tosses the baby in there. Later the mother returns, seeing the other infant in there again as Charlie happens to be ambling by. She chases him down and fells him with her umbrella, demanding he get the baby out. With his usual audacity, Chaplin creates a perfectly executed slapstick routine about the attempted abandonment of an infant.

Resigned to his possession of the child, the Tramp sits on the curb with his charge — toying only for a minute with the idea of tossing it down the sewer. He carries the infant to his tenement and a group of blowsy neighborhood women standing about ask him: "Is that yours?" He nods yes, and when they ask "What's its name?" he disappears inside for a moment with the baby, before returning and stating confidently, "John."

We are again in the slum of *Easy Street*, of *A Dog's Life*, Chaplin's "world" of claustrophobic, seedy streets, their grim and poverty-numbed residents, their hard, brutish policemen. We see again the "stage" of the grey, broken buildings at each side, a backdrop of another building across the back, a panorama of trash and hard times, the human spirit wounded nearly fatally, with all the sad, melancholy poeticism of a fallen world. Into this setting, needy, broken-down and love-starved as the Tramp himself is, Chaplin introduces a child who comes to a consciousness of this world's being the universe as much as Chaplin himself did in his correlative slum, in his childhood of poverty and uncertainty. Yet here his alter ego, his own inner eternal child, the Tramp, is present to guide the child, to be his companion and to save him.

The Tramp takes the child back to his dingy garret, and puts him in an improvised hammock that hangs from the ceiling — he uses the spout of a tea kettle as a makeshift baby bottle and fashions a potty for the baby by cutting a hole in the seat of a chair. His transformational gifts are now directed towards specific, practical tasks, are harnessed by his devotion to the child in the self-sacrificing mode which is now more typical of him — we have seen him show solicitous concern for Scraps in *A Dog's Life*, and now we see him making faces and gazing with lovestruck eyes upon his new son.

He is still a rogue and a rascal, however, for we see, after an intertitle informs us "Five years later," the use to which Charlie puts the now five year old child (now played by Jackie Coogan). Jackie runs ahead through the dreary streets, energetically throwing bricks through windows. The Tramp appears on the several minutes later, a glazier with his window-mending tools, just "happening" upon the scene and more than amenable to doing the needed repairs. A cop becomes suspicious, observing the Tramp nonchalantly going about his work after he's seen Jackie's pitching abilities. Here Chaplin manages to work in one of his finest comic routines. The Tramp completes work on a window, standing back and displaying his handiwork to his customer, a housewife — as he points out some of the finer details, he casually puts his arm around her waist. She removes the arm indignantly, he reacts with false innocence, and as she stands with her arm lying across the windowsill behind them, he positions himself so that her arm is around his shoulder, and rebukes her for her familiarity. They chuckle and flirt — as we see her husband entering the house. Her husband appears in the window behind them, and his hand resting on Charlie's shoulder seems to be the woman's hand — the Tramp is rather disturbed when that hand tightens, starts shaking him, and finally throttles him. He makes his escape with the kid, the cop chasing him.

The mother of the child, now a successful actress, comes to the slum to do charity work, and at one point holds one of the neighborhood women's babies, going into a reverie as she remembers her own child — as that child, Jackie, sits quietly nearby on a stoop. Chaplin plays with the irony of coincidence which is so much a part of the melodramatic tradition he passionately embraces. As well, the manner by which he keeps bringing Edna as the mother back into the film stresses that as the Tramp's relationship with the child develops and strengthens, it is and can only be a temporary one, that it is doomed to be terminated.

This relationship is responsible for the most charming scenes of the film. We see Charlie sternly inspecting the boy, cleaning his ears, eyes and nose with his handkerchief. But we also see them with the father-son roles reversed, when Jackie makes pancakes for breakfast and must shout and pull at the Tramp to get him out of bed. As well, when Jackie gets in a fight with the neighborhood bully, Charlie is quite disapproving — until he sees that Jackie is winning, at which point he takes on the role of being the boy's manager. The bully's mammoth big brother comes along, informing Charlie that if his little brother is beaten in the fight, he will smash Charlie. The big brother chases down the Tramp until they are forestalled by Edna who remonstrates with them for fighting, quoting the Christian edict: "If one should smite you, turn the other cheek." The big brother, unexpectedly moved by this, offers his other cheek to Charlie, whose response is not only to slug him, but to take vicious delight in kicking him, slamming him on the head with a brick, and otherwise assaulting him until he is reduced to dazed incoherence.

Typical of the finely crafted melding of comedy and sentiment of which *The Kid* is composed, this raucous slapstick is immediately followed by Edna approaching the Tramp with Jackie in her arms — he is ill. He retreats with the child to his garret and a doctor is summoned. In the course of treating Jackie, the doctor asks Charlie whether he's the boy's father. In replying, the Tramp hands him the note that came with the child when he'd found him. The doctor takes the note with him when he leaves, saying, "This child needs proper care." The Tramp keeps worried vigil by the sick boy's bedside.

We are seeing the Tramp involved in a relationship unlike any he's been involved in before, in its intensity, in its commitment. His extreme "aloneness" is here vaporized by the kid, who is Charlie's equal in ingenuity, mischievousness, cuteness — in a sense he really is Charlie, or a projection of one aspect of his personality — he is his son, in a true sense. At the same time, we know that, with the doctor's retaining of the note, the noose is drawing tighter around the Tramp's neck, that this relationship must end, that the respite from his aloneness is temporary.

In an astounding scene set five days later, after Jackie's convalescence, the wagon from the County Orphan Asylum pulls up in front of the dingy garret. The Asylum official barges importantly into Charlie's dump with his flunky, and what's interesting is the way Chaplin portrays the two men. The official refuses to look at the Tramp or the child, or to speak with them — he directs his orders to his assistant to relay to them. When the Tramp finally so infuriates the official that he does begin to scream directly at him, the Tramp feigns that he can't hear him, and asks the flunky what his boss said. In short order the flunky has grabbed the kid, and is pulling him from the room. The child cries, and stretches his arms out to Charlie, who becomes a wild man, attacking the two men. Jackie at one point strikes the two orphanage employees with a large hammer. But the flunky runs to get the cop on the corner to help them, and the cop — the same one the Tramp had antagonized earlier — comes to help the flunky restrain the Tramp. The child is pulled screaming from the room, is taken downstairs and thrown into the wagon by the orphanage official. The child is screaming, standing in the wagon with his arms outstretched. This shot is followed by a shot of Charlie being held by the cop, helpless, powerless, his eyes looking with anguish into the camera. We see the child again, then Charlie, like two halves of a torn photograph. The child looks up to heaven, prays pleadingly — then to the official, begging him. The official pushes the child roughly back into the wagon.

They drive off — the Tramp escapes from the cop, climbs through the skylight of his garret and races over the rooftops, following the wagon in its circuitous journey. He is able to leap from a rooftop into the wagon and kick the official out. When the wagon is stopped, he embraces the child, the child's terror melting into delight, and their tear-stained faces kiss.

The entire sequence is brilliantly conceived and brilliantly executed. The interplay with the Tramp and the officials is sharply observed, and it is significant that they enlist the help of a policeman in restraining Charlie and making off with the child. If Chaplin's filmic style has, to this point, mostly consisted of stationary medium shots in order to record performances, we see here a bravura piece of filmmaking in which quick shots and editing give emotional and dramatic intensity to the chase — and the unique idea of having the Tramp pursue the wagon by running from rooftop to rooftop is stunningly, stirringly realized. As he leaps from a rooftop into the wagon and vanquishes the official we see again the Tramp's athletic heroism, saving the child from the fate Chaplin himself had known as a child. The entire sequence builds in intensity to the point where the Tramp and the sobbing child kiss, and the screen radiates the psychic pain and sad beauty of being human — it is the starkest, most harrowingly emotional point in all of Chaplin's work, and its extremity of feeling is shockingly profound, though everything in *The Kid*, and in all of Chaplin's career to date has led to this moment. As pure film, it is perhaps the most artfully realized scene in all of Chaplin, at the same time as it glows with a frightening necessity, both primal and passionate.

The Tramp and the child gaze from their embrace to see the flunky still at the wheel of the wagon. Charlie now swaggers forth to dismiss him as well, but he needs only to venture towards him and the flunky scurries away in fear. The Tramp and the child are now on the run, and must bed down in a flophouse for the night — the hostel scene recalls the hostel in *Police*, and is another scene in which Chaplin is compelled to portray the transient, dismal accommodations of the poor. There is a neat gag in which a man lying on the next bed, supposedly asleep, deftly attempts to pick the Tramp's pockets. Charlie catches the man (who is played by Jackie Coogan's real-life father), but is pleasantly surprised to see that the thief has palmed a coin from his trousers that he didn't know he had. He puts the pickpocket's hand in his other pockets to see what else he might find.

We have seen the doctor return to Charlie's deserted garret, meet Edna there, and show her the note — we know that she now realizes Jackie is her son. As the Tramp and the child sleep in the flophouse, the hostel owner (Henry Bergman) reads in the paper of the missing boy, and of the reward for his return. He makes off with the sleeping child. The child and the mother are reunited at the police station. The Tramp awakes, runs panic-stricken, calling for the boy. He returns back to his garret, slumps disconsolately against the front door, and exhausted, goes to sleep.

Here, incredibly, a dream sequence opens up, in which the dingy slum surrounding the Tramp becomes a flower-garlanded Paradise, and all the inhabitants of the world Chaplin has created become angels replete with wings and harps. Charlie is awakened by his beloved Jackie, now an angel too. The boy takes him to get a robe and a set of wings of his own — which, the Tramp finds, tend to itch a little bit — and they fly about the street. The Tramp's vision of Heaven seems to share a bit in common with the Garden of Eden when Charlie becomes enticed by a comely young angel — the Devil appears and cues her to flirt with the Tramp, and also inspires the Tramp to respond. The girl angel turns out to be the girlfriend of the big brother character seen earlier — now in his angelic incarnation he is quite open to sharing her affections with Charlie, until the Devil whispers jealousy into his ear. Charlie and the big brother fight in a flurry of feathers. The neighborhood policeman in his angelic incarnation breaks up the scuffle, and as the Tramp flies away, he shoots him from the sky. The Tramp falls lifeless at the doorway to his garret.

Some have criticized the inclusion of the dream sequence as an unnecessary diversion from all that has come before in *The Kid*. It is a diversion, but it's arguable that it is an entirely necessary one — for we already know that Charlie has lost the child, that he is once again alone. Chaplin presents us with another of his visions of Paradise, one which is contaminated and doomed by sin, rather like Dostoevsky's vision in his "Dream of a Ridiculous Man." The lightness and brightness of this slum-transformed-into–Heaven provide balance to the grim inevitability which has been established, provide relief from the pervasive grayness throughout the film. We are distracted, as the Tramp is, from the sadness of his peril by this mysterious, strange parable. It is a merciful escape, a last trip to Heaven before the task of coming to terms with unyielding reality once again.

For the Tramp is awakened painfully from his dream to cold fact — as in *The Bank*, as in *Sunnyside* — this time by the cop, who does not seize on the moment to clobber him as before, but rather escorts him to a limousine. Charlie is taken to the mother's mansion, and the film ends as Edna comes to the door, and Jackie races out and leaps into the Tramp's arms — they all go into the house together. As in many Chaplin films, the ending is a "happy" one at first glance, and we want to accept it as such. The mother is a successful actress, she can provide a better life for the Tramp and the boy. But we know that the entirely copacetic team of Charlie and the boy can never be again, that the happiness and communion they found with each other is gone, that the child is now part of a world that the Tramp can never really be a part of — we know that for all intents and purposes the Tramp really is alone again. As in the case of the ending of *The Vagabond*, we are given a makeshift conclusion which can be said to be superficially "happy" simply because the alternative is too tragic to contemplate. This is especially true in *The Kid*, and here we are most grateful for it — the distraction of Charlie in Heaven has allowed us to draw back from the emotional demands of the film, so that we are able to hope for the best as he disappears into the mansion.

Chaplin spent an entire year making *The Kid*, much to the trepidation of his colleagues at First National. It is a film which is a natural progression from all the films he did leading up to it and at the same time it contains much that is new, that has not been seen before — the naked, intense emotionality of the wagon scene, with Charlie rescuing the child, is certainly beyond anything which was foreshadowed in his earlier films and remains stunning today. The interweaving of sentiment and humor, of slapstick and drama, is masterful — though the film is his first feature, nearly double the length of his longest (self-directed) films to date, it never lags, but moves smoothly, quickly along. Undoubtedly the time spent on the film, as well as the sheer amount of film Chaplin shot in his quest for perfection — it is estimated he filmed fifty times more footage than was included in the final release[2] — allowed Chaplin to obsessively work at and master all of his abilities to craft a film of such piercing emotional truth, as fully realized as any of his later features.

The concerns of First National were washed away by the great worldwide success which attended *The Kid*. Jackie Coogan, whose wonderfully natural performance makes him perhaps the most impressive of all Chaplin's supporting actors, became an international star. With *The Kid* Chaplin garnered more acclaim than ever before and had graduated into a new stage of his career — his fulfillment in creating a feature ensured that as far as he was concerned, the days of the shorts were numbered.

He had also created an enduring work of art, drawing upon his own trauma and using it to express something truly universal, for the kid is every child in a fallen world, and the Tramp is once again our human surrogate in that world, saving the child we once were, heroically defending innocence in the name of love before the forces of a harsh, violent, ruthlessly malevolent system. We are united in our common humanity, our common childhood, stricken through our layers of protective cynicism and world-weariness by the plight of the Tramp and his child, and in that moment we are again the children we once were, and see the world as we saw it at the very moment before it robbed us of our innocence, at the very moment before it broke our hearts. We are united, again, in our recognition of our common need of tenderness, of love, beyond the grim machinations of survival, as we watch the Tramp tenderly kiss his child. Driven by a feverish emotional necessity more than any of his other works, is a timeless film, which is and always will be capable of delivering its passionate, eternally relevant message to every race and creed of humanity on the planet.

7

First National:
The Idle Class, Payday, The Pilgrim

Chaplin had grown embittered with the First National Exhibitor's Circuit. During the making of *Sunnyside* and *A Day's Pleasure* he had approached them for greater compensation owing to the more ambitious, elaborate — and successful — works he was creating. He was rebuffed, and his irritation at their shortsightedness contributed to the lower quality of those films. His friends, Mary Pickford and Douglas Fairbanks, mentioned to him that they had experienced similar callousness from their employers. Since the three stars were the cinema's greatest draws at the time, they were perplexed — until they heard of a plan for a proposed merging of all the big production companies into a new entity, which would be able to hold the upper hand in any negotiations with actors. In response, Chaplin, Pickford and Fairbanks united and formed their own independent company, the appropriately named United Artists Corporation.[1]

The contract with First National had to be fulfilled before Chaplin could graduate to the total freedom with United Artists. His anger with his employer turned to fury at their initial indifference and stinginess in regards to *The Kid*, and their attempt to attach the film via a difficult divorce proceeding he was going through. It was in this frame of mind that he completed the final shorts for First National — and the final short films of his career.

The Idle Class must rank as one of his most elegant, if not elegantly mounted, short films. Here, Chaplin parallels the life of the Tramp with that of one of the wealthy upper class, in the same way that he had contrasted the Tramp's existence with that of a stray dog's in *A Dog's Life*. We see the hoi polloi disembarking a train with their golf clubs, on their way to their well-earned rest and relaxation — and then we see Charlie emerging from beneath the train with his battered golf bag, off for a vacation from his worldly woes, too. The Tramp's method of playing golf differs from that of the other players, however—finding himself out of balls, he handily appropriates those of the other players by nonchalantly kicking them away from where they land on the course. When he is confronted by a golfer for stealing his ball, Charlie feigns ignorance—then, when another golfer's ball lands nearby, he happily points to it, saying, "There's your ball!" With apologies, the player gratefully pockets the ball, and is subsequently attacked and pounded by its owner, as the Tramp continues blithely on his way.

The wealthy counterpart to the Tramp is Chaplin himself, in his final version of the Drunk, or "rake" character. In keeping with the more subdued nature of the First Nationals, the Drunk here is a more sedate one, perpetually confused and manifestly indifferent towards anything outside the veil of his alcoholic haze. As a result of his failure to meet his wife—Edna—on the train which brought Charlie to town, he receives a letter from her stating that until he quits drinking she'll be "occupying separate rooms." This inspires the oft-cited gag: the Drunk turns away from the camera, shoulders shaking as if the throes of anguish—then turns to us again, revealing that he's merely been preparing himself a martini.

The Drunk is offered another chance by his wife, and she invites him to attend a ball that night. Notably it is a costume ball, so that when Charlie runs in, escaping from the sort of trouble which always seems to dog him, he is accepted as a rich man dressed as a tramp where he could never be accepted as the mere and actual tramp that he is. This is played upon when the Tramp looks warily over at the policeman who's been following him and is now approaching him—only to don a mask, revealing himself as a man in costume as a policeman. Chaplin is commenting on the social roles and uniforms which humans define themselves, and others, with. As always, there is the unbridgeable chasm between the comfortable and the comfortless, the irreconcilable separation of people based on their degrees of material ownership.

The inevitable meeting of the Tramp with the wife, and her mistaking him for her husband, occurs, and is the most memorable moment of the picture. Charlie had seen her out riding earlier, had fallen in love with her from afar, fantasized about her in full romantic flight. Now she sits there before him, saying with grave tenderness: "Come here—You look so strange." Edna's portrayal of the wounded dignity of the long-suffering wife makes her performance here one of her finest. Charlie approaches her wonderingly, sits beside her. She looks at him with intense sadness and love, and gives him her hand. With soulful reverence the Tramp takes her hand in both of his, raises it to his lips, and kisses it.

His passionate romanticism is in stark contrast to the cold, benumbed apathy of the Drunk towards his wife. Again we see these two polar opposite extremes of the Chaplin outlook—the cool and sophisticated, cruel, blasé attitude of the Drunk, and the heartfelt, idealistic dreamer that is the Tramp. The Drunk dons a costume for the party—a suit of armor, whose visor clamps down and gets stuck over his face. His identity thus obscured, he comes upon Charlie and his wife and goes into a rage. The Tramp and the Drunk fight with each other, Charlie hurting his fists on the armor — the two sides of the Chaplin personality at war. Edna's father also gets involved — he is played by Mack Swain, Charlie's old foil from Keystone days and undoubtedly brought back by Chaplin as an admission of his need for a hulking nemesis. Swain admirably brings his considerable talents to a role that Eric Campbell would have played with gusto not so long ago.

All the suitable confusions, embarrassments, ass-kicks and scrambling chases are played out — in many ways, the film is a more sophisticated, more deeply shaded version of the "phony count" stories Chaplin has used in several films to date, in which he's an impostor in high society — and then the visor is pulled up on the Drunk's helmet, and Charlie is revealed to be nothing more than the lowly bum he is. Edna turns resolutely from him and he is banished from the mansion. He gamely offers his hand to Swain, who bellows at him to leave. He waddles off, twirling his cane. Suffering a twinge of remorse, Edna says to her father: "We owe that man an apology." Swain goes out after Charlie, calling to him. The Tramp comes up, and points to something lying on the ground. As Swain bends over to see what he's pointing at, the Tramp kicks him solidly in the behind as a parting gesture and runs away.

There is more opulence, more a sense of elegance in *The Idle Class*, than has been seen in any of his films to date — since Chaplin himself had recently become a millionaire, and had lately been initiated into the company and confidences of his fellow millionaires, it is not difficult to ascertain the inspiration for the central premise of the film: a tramp mistaken for a millionaire, and the subsequent battle that goes on between the two doppelgangers. If there is the standard poignancy in Chaplin's portrayal of the Tramp's plight, however, there is also a disturbing sadness in the emotional vacuity of the Drunk and the genteel distress of his wife. A very conscious, very adult poignance runs through the film, emanating from Edna's portrayal of dignified suffering, which isn't resolved in the end, as she is left with her incorrigibly drunk husband, and the romantic Charlie must be banished. We are very far away from the one-dimensional cartoons which the secondary characters had been in the earlier films, whose style had never required them to be more than broad caricatures. In films like *The Idle Class*, Chaplin was finding that the new style allowed him to dramatize, with a mature, empathetic poetry, the plights of all walks of humanity, with a more far-ranging, more sophisticated worldview.

He makes a conscious reversion to the old style with his next film, *Pay Day*, in which Charlie is a harried construction worker, dominated by his boss (Mack Swain) at work, and bullied by his battleaxe of a wife at home. In its return to uncomplicated knockabout, and in its depiction of the Tramp as an "Everyman" replete with nagging wife, *Pay Day* resembles *A Day's Pleasure*, though it is considerably more agreeable than the earlier film. The Tramp enters the construction area, sheepishly late, proffering a flower for his boss. He then sets to work, shoveling in a pit with Herculean effort, yet only producing a thimbleful of dirt as a result of his toil. Chaplin has fun with a succession of gags which are mostly mechanical in nature: he has the Tramp up on a platform catching the bricks his co-workers throw up to him with impossible dexterity. The spectacle, mesmerizing and strange, was facilitated, we soon realize, by having Chaplin drop the bricks from his hands, feet, and buttocks, then running the film backwards. Part of our amusement at the gag is in realizing how cleverly and simply the effect was achieved. As well, there is the byplay with the elevator, which magically ascends and descends in time for Charlie to sit on its seat and not go plummeting backwards to the earth. As is the case with a later gag, in which the Tramp attempts to board a streetcar and is deterred from doing so by a crowd that rushes in front of him, boarding the car in fast-motion and taking off, these gags rely on photographic effects, and in that they are experimental for Chaplin. There is less of the old free and easy approach to slapstick here, but a more conscious, constructed deployment of ideas.

There is some fine and subtle pantomime in the scene in which Charlie computes that he's been underpaid in his weekly paycheck, and confronts his boss only to realize that he's actually been overpaid. The Tramp makes his way from the work site only to have his horrific wife take control of his money — because of this she is referred to, interestingly enough, as his "First National Bank." Charlie has ferreted some funds away in his derby, however, and makes his escape to go out for a night of drinking with his friends. There is some fun with drunkenness, and with the Tramp's repeated attempts to board a streetcar. At one point Charlie leaps onto a lunch wagon, grabbing onto a sausage as if it were a commuter strap, blandly picking up a newspaper from the counter and musing over it as though he's another routine-deadened nine-to-fiver heading home to the suburbs — as the confounded proprietor looks on.

The Tramp makes it home and the expected confrontation with the wife occurs — he tries to sleep in the tub, but it turns out to be filled with water and laundry. *Pay Day* is mostly interesting to see how the more artistically mature Chaplin consciously tries to return to the simpler, slapstick-oriented approach of earlier films. The whimsy and mayhem of the Mutuals, though only four years in the past, were unsurpassable comedies of their kind, and stand with the best of his work; his new style is more suited to the larger canvases that features allow. This not to say that the newer approach is better artistically, for certainly an argument can be made that Chaplin never reached the level of sheer inspired lunacy that the Mutuals contained. But the newer approach has come about through artistic necessity, resultant of Chaplin's desire to achieve a different kind of greatness, and its strengths are different from but equal to the earlier strengths. *Pay Day* was Chaplin's last two-reeler, and entertains in a light-hearted manner. But Chaplin's heart was with the features now, with the greater latitude they allowed him to portray subtlety of emotion and ideas, and so there is a sense that he's marking time. He has outgrown the form, and is no more convincing in his acceptance of its limitations than the Tramp is in being subjugated by a monstrous wife. That Chaplin's real commitment was now to the longer films became evident when his next short ballooned into a four-reel featurette.

The Pilgrim is the best of this later batch of First National films, and Chaplin was happy that the company accepted it as the equivalent of two shorts, thus freeing him from his contract with them.[2] The premise of the film is set up with admirable efficiency and sophistication: we see a "Wanted" poster being put up with Charlie's picture on it; then we see a man emerging from a swim in a lake, reaching for his clothes and finding a striped prisoner's uniform instead; next, the Tramp at a train station, dressed as a parson. Two elopers see Charlie at the station and run to him, saying, "He can marry us!" He runs away and they chase him around the station — the angry father of the bride arrives and he furiously chases the groom as Charlie runs from both of them. The Tramp boards a train which takes him to a small town in Texas, and it just so happens that a congregation from a local church is at the station, awaiting the arrival of their new pastor.

The rural setting is further evidence of Chaplin's ambition and constant experimentation. The Tramp disembarks the train and sees a policeman — he offers forth his wrists to be handcuffed. He soon is greeted by the congregation, however, and quickly ignoring the older women, evinces a very un–minister-like interest in Edna. Mack Swain as the deacon of the church shepherds the Tramp off, folding his hands piously on his chest as he walks. Charlie mimics the gesture, holding his hands in the same manner, but over his crotch.

It is generally felt that The Pilgrim is a gentle satire on Christian hypocrisy and small town mores in general. We have seen Chaplin comment on Christianity in Police and in Sunnyside, but his attitude towards the congregation here is never disdainful or ridiculing — though The Pilgrim would be attacked in some quarters for "insulting the Gospel."[3] When the Mack Swain character bends to tie his shoe and Charlie sees a bottle of whiskey in his back pocket, Chaplin seems mostly to be commenting on the humanity of the deacon, rather than scornfully exposing him as a religious phony. As well, it allows Charlie to steal the bottle, and to shove it in his own back pocket. This sets up a neat gag when the two men, walking alongside each other, both slip on a banana peel thrown in their path by a kid — a consciously ironic deployment of the old Keystone standby. They fall, the bottle shattering beneath them, the deacon looking nervously over at his new parson, his secret sin revealed. What Chaplin is more interested in here, more than mocking religious feeling, is the central situation of one of the societally-designated least virtuous persons— an escaped convict — being accepted as one of the societally-designated most virtuous persons— a minister. He is interested again in satirizing the absurd roles and uniforms we assume, and in standing them on their head. As always Chaplin is interested in extremes: the convict and the minister, the rich and the poor, the powerful and the powerless.

This is seen when Charlie is taken to the church and is led up to give his first sermon. After fearfully seeing the choir in the box beside him as a jury, he feverishly consults the Bible open before him and starts into telling the story of David and Goliath. It is another set performance piece for Chaplin, and the enthusiasm and showbiz pizzazz he brings to his miming of the tale understandably take the congregation aback somewhat. In the end, after graphically miming the hitherto unknown addendum to the story, in which David follows up on vanquishing his foe by slicing his head off, twirling it around in the air, then giving it a back-kick into the ether, Charlie executes several of his flourishing curtsies—coming back for a few curtain calls into the bargain. A young boy excitedly registers his approval.

The collection is taken, and the Tramp, with furtive absorption, follows the collection box as it travels around the church. Absentmindedly, he begins to light a cigarette, then turns ands sees the choir staring at him puzzledly. The boxes are brought from each side of the church, and Charlie weighs them in his hands, smilingly sweetly at the section of the congregation which has provided the heavier box, glowering with baleful disapproval at the side which hasn't quite come up to expectations.

He is taken to the home of Edna and her mother, where he'll be boarding. On the way, a rough-hewn old cellmate recognizes him — he hails his old pal Charlie as he walks down the street with the deacon and Edna and her mother. The Tramp swiftly steers them away from the reminder of his past. At the house, Charlie socializes with members of the congregation in his role as pastor. One of the guests is a vile little child who repeatedly slaps his father (played by Sydney Chaplin) and Charlie across the face. The Tramp's restraint is remarkable until the final moments of the scene, when he's finally left alone with the boy and kicks him to the floor — the move predating W.C. Fields' celebrated takedown of Baby Leroy by a decade.

The Tramp is enamored of Edna, and talks to her in the evening by the front gate. It is then when his old cellmate happens by and insinuates himself into Charlie's new situation, forcing his way into the house. In the drawing room, introducing himself as the Tramp's pal, he wastes no time in pickpocketing the deacon's wallet. Charlie frenziedly must steal it back from his old friend and replace it in the deacon's pocket without his knowing — this is repeated several times with variations. At one point the Tramp replaces the wallet in a ludicrously inventive manner: summoning the room's attention, he announces a conjuring trick, and with elaborate hand gestures makes as if to magically transport the wallet from the deacon's pocket into his old friend's pocket — with a laugh, the wallet is taken from his friend and good-naturedly returned to the deacon.

Charlie's plight only gets worse when his friend sees Edna's mother deposit her mortgage money in a nearby bureau drawer. The friend announces that he's missed his train, and so of course the good Christian people insist that he stay overnight. As in *The Idle Class*, the supporting characters here are portrayed in three dimensions—they are not caricatures, but empathetically conceived human individuals, signaling a new maturity in Chaplin's work. Throughout the night the thief keeps trying to slink down to the bureau and steal the money and Charlie keeps trying to stop him — at one point he leaps on his old friend's back, and as the thief repeatedly tries to open the drawer, Charlie repeatedly kicks it shut. Finally, the thief succeeds in knocking the Tramp out, and makes off with the money. Edna and her mother awake to find their life savings gone, but Charlie vows to restore it. He goes into the saloon in town, and taking advantage of a holdup in progress, handily regains the stolen money.

In the meantime, the police have come by the house, and Edna tells them of the robbery and of the Tramp's mission to help them. "He'll never come back," the cop tells them, showing them Charlie's "Wanted" poster. And so when the Tramp does return, it is only for a moment, to give Edna the money before the sheriff hauls him off. "Isn't it possible to let him go?" Edna asks, making a plea for mercy. But no—justice must be served, and Charlie is led away in tragic romantic mode. So swift and so inventive have been the gags that we haven't noticed that the Tramp has undergone a transformation. Once more, his romantic love for Edna has turned him from a criminal into one who defends decency and innocence from criminals—his thwarting of his former cellmate's crimes is his redemption, a renunciation of his own criminal past. But his newfound virtue is its own reward as he is led helplessly from Edna, taken by the sheriff out to the Texas-Mexico border.

The sheriff leisurely lights a cigarette, asks Charlie to pick him some of those flowers, "over there," he says, pointing over the border. Puzzled, but obliging, the Tramp goes to get the flowers—those symbols of the higher virtues of beauty and freedom so important to Charlie. When the sheriff takes off on his horse, the Tramp gamely chases after him with the flowers. The sheriff, a trifle frustrated, grabs Charlie by the collar and marches him back to the border, places him emphatically on the other side. After a moment the Tramp realizes what the sheriff is doing. In the full comprehension of his freedom, he raises his arms in delight, his iconic posture recalling his earlier embracing of the universe in *Police*—he is, for an instant, once again in an unfettered Paradise. But suddenly a shoot-out occurs between rival gangs of bandits across the borderline, and our final image is of Charlie running off into the distance, desperately straddling the border, one foot on each side.

It's one of the supreme examples of Chaplin's visual poetry, an image which sums up the Tramp and the human condition better than a thousand words— for the Tramp, who can never belong anywhere, really is on both sides of the border, with one foot in this world and one in another, one we can't see or touch.

Throughout the film have been the reminders of Charlie's past in a variety of clever gags in the nature of the earlier *The Adventurer*: at the train station, the bars at the front of the kiosk remind him of his cell; when presented with the Bible at the church, he raises his hand as if to give an oath in court. The reality is that Charlie doesn't belong anywhere, and this amazingly rich, remarkably sophisticated film — most of the humor is subtle and situational, with very little slapstick — tells us that, like us, the most freedom he will know consists of ducking gunfire while straddling an infinite border. The wistfulness at the end of *The Adventurer*, when Charlie bids adieu to Edna before running from his pursuers, has been expanded into a larger, metaphysical wistfulness. Adopting and shedding identities, citizen of no country, the Tramp rides, like us, the infinite borderline into eternity.

In this, his last film in the pay of someone else, Chaplin was crossing a border, into a new and potentially daunting artistic freedom. He would use this freedom to create a film utterly unlike any he — or anyone else — had created before.

8

A Woman of Paris

Somewhere in France, Marie St. Clair, identified via intertitle as a "woman of fate" and "the victim of an unhappy home," waits at the window for the arrival of her lover, Jean Millet. Her baleful father, however, comes and locks her into her room, so strenuously does he disapprove of their affair. She escapes through the window and rushes to meet Jean. They make plans to take the train that night to Paris, and to marry there. On returning to Marie's home, they find she's unable to enter — her father has locked the window. Jean knocks on the front door, informing Marie's father that she's been locked out. The father suggests that Jean provide a bed for her, then shuts the door.

Jean takes Marie to his parents' house, determined they will leave in the morning. But Jean's father objects to the alliance as well, shouting angrily for Marie to leave. Marie goes to wait for Jean at the station as he packs his things. At his mother's urging, Jean bids a final farewell to his father, now sitting in a chair by the fire. To his horror, he finds that his father has expired. He calls for a doctor. Shortly after, Marie calls from the station: he tells her he can't leave with her, something horrible has happened — and breaks off their conversation, running to open the door for the doctor. Marie leaves for Paris alone.

A year later, we are in Paris, and Marie is in a world far from her humble, homely beginnings. She is the kept woman of a high-living, rich, sophisticated boulevardier, enjoying all the extravagances, luxuries, and delicacies that the Paris of the 1920s can offer.

A Woman of Paris is Chaplin's first serious, non-performing film — and his only serious non-performing film, considering that his next one, forty years later, was essentially a romantic comedy. He was inspired to create it by several factors, the most practical and personal of which was his desire to launch Edna Purviance into a new career as a serious actress. He had found that her appearance had become too mature for her to continue to serve as the romantic lead in his slapstick comedies. It is true that she was no longer the winsome, fresh-faced girl seen in the earlier shorts, the subject of the Tramp's awakening romantic dreams. Her part as the wounded, sophisticated wife in *The Idle Class* seemed now to be more suited to her appearance and demeanor, as did her portrayal of the unwed mother in *The Kid*. Chaplin's romantic relationship with Purviance had ended five years before; in creating for her the leading dramatic role of Marie St. Clair, he hoped to provide her with a means of continuing her career beyond her association with him.[1]

His other inspiration, and just as important, was his fascination with film acting technique, with the qualities of naturalism, nuance, and subtlety which were all the hallmarks, the most revolutionary aspects, of his own performing style. Chaplin's great power as comedian, the details which mark him as the ultimate master of his trade, is in the nuances of emotion, thought, and action which go into his clowning, and always take us by surprise — allowing us to view and experience our own humanity anew in the magical mirror all great art provides. Chaplin envisioned his serious film as a manner by which to tell a simple story using technique which he felt should be the next evolution of filmic language — in the acting as well as in the images employed to tell the story.

"As I have noticed life in its dramatic climaxes, men and women try to hide their emotions, rather than seek to express them," Chaplin noted,[2] by way of explaining the new, psychological (as he termed it), more restrained and naturalistic style of acting he had his performers adopt.

As well, in the telling of the story, nuance is the key to the imagistic language. We have seen the graceful manner by which he has established the death of one of his characters with a black-rimmed handkerchief in *The Immigrant*; we have seen the fluent telling of the exposition of *The Pilgrim* in a quick handful of images. These types of devices are seen throughout *A Woman of Paris*, a large part of whose existence owes itself to Chaplin's need to explore this new sophisticated maturity of technique to its outermost limits — something he could not do in the slapstick comedies of the Tramp. Nor would he have had the freedom to create such a startling departure if he hadn't lately become his own producer.

Sophistication is also the byword in his choice of subject matter, for *A Woman of Paris* is observed from the sophisticated worldly view we had been beginning to get a glimpse of in *The Idle Class* and in *The Pilgrim*. The situation of Marie's being a kept woman, as well as Chaplin's depiction of some raunchy hedonism at a bohemian party later in the film, were quite mature for their time. The man by whom Marie is kept, the charming and amoral Pierre Revel, is the epitome of this sophistication. As the intertitle informs us, he's a "gentleman of leisure" who "makes an art of living." Portrayed consummately by the debonair Adolphe Menjou, Revel is a suave lady's man with a snappy mustache, he's a gourmand and an appreciator of fine wines, impeccably tailored. He is referred to by another character as "the richest bachelor in Paris"; he whiles away his days in silk pajamas in bed, keeping abreast of his stocks by reading from his own ticker-tape machine, his valet at attention nearby. At night he enjoys sumptuous meals in the finest restaurants.

Drawing on his own recent immersion in high society, as well as his own experience in becoming something of a playboy as a result of his success in romancing such high-profile women of the world as Pola Negri and Peggy Hopkins Joyce, Chaplin was driven once again to his fixation with material wealth and the power that it wields. From the moment the film moves to Paris, Chaplin is as extensive and exhausting in his depiction of the opulence and decadence of wealth as he has been in depicting the horror and destitution of poverty in *Easy Street*, *A Dog's Life*, and *The Kid*. From the moment Marie enters in her glittering gown and headdress—she had dressed in dowdy grey, back in her puritanical hometown—with her lover Revel in his immaculate tuxedo, Chaplin delights in the luxurious, amoral hedonism of the scene. Nearby, a young gigolo of indeterminate sexual preference accompanies an old robust woman, described by Revel as "the richest old maid in Paris." When Marie questions him as to the nature of the relationship Revel merely shrugs and smiles winningly—his response summing up an entire world of infinitely subtle nonverbal understanding in which the ever-casual bon vivant exists.

Revel is also one who makes a "study of eating," as the intertitle informs us, and so he is extensively fawned over by the maitre d' of the exclusive restaurant; he even is invited into the kitchen to inspect the tiny bird which is being prepared for his meal. Then, he and Marie are served a truly exquisite delicacy—champagne truffles. We are shown the dish being carefully prepared, and all the service of the waiters as they prepare the table and serve the wine is enacted as a form of nearly sacred ritual—Chaplin draws out and takes great delight in showing this extended pomp and circumstance, this languorous indulging in the pleasures of material wealth and worldly position.

Marie is kept by Pierre in her own well-appointed apartment. If she has any beliefs that their relationship is about more than her making herself available for his pleasure in return for a life of ease and luxury, these are soon dashed. She learns from an announcement in the paper that Revel will soon be marrying another woman—in a joining together of two fortunes, as the paper says. When Marie confronts Revel about his upcoming nuptials, he airily retorts that they needn't have any effect on the present understanding. Marie deigns to dine with him that evening. Later, when she attempts to sever their relationship, Revel mocks her, saying that she's become too accustomed to her luxury to give it up.

Marie is a "fallen woman," a figure which has already appeared in several Chaplin films, and will continue to be a recurring character in his works. Her falling from virtue unites her with the exploited dance hall entertainer in *A Dog's Life*, or especially the unwed mother in *The Kid*: in a time when the latter were figures of shame and were spurned as such, Chaplin compared them to Christ, bearing His cross up the mountain. The characters in *A Dog's Life* and *The Kid* are notably performance artists, as was Chaplin's mother. Her unorthodox and ultimately tragic lifestyle—Chaplin wrote that "to gauge the morals of our family by commonplace standards would be as erroneous as putting a thermometer in boiling water"[3]—must, to some degree, loom behind these figures.

Marie's dilemma is more intricate than that of her forebears. Here, the artist is her one-time fiancé Jean, whom she comes in contact with by chance. He now lives in Paris, too; he's a painter and lives in a studio with his mother. He is still the Spartan, puritanical suitor of his earlier appearance — his drab demeanor and wardrobe attest to his poverty-stricken dedication to his art. Marie, now the grand dame, commissions him to paint her portrait. He does, with her posing in one of her finest gowns. Yet when the portrait is finished and he lets her see it, she sees that he has painted her dressed as she was when they were preparing to leave for the train, back in their hometown.

She has learned the reason Jean left her waiting at the train station that night. He pledges his love to her. They resolve to get married. They do not know, as they make their plans, that Jean's ever-black-cloaked mother is listening from the next room. They cannot see, as we do, that she is anything but pleased by the news of their upcoming nuptials.

Jean, the artist and romantic, is representative of an aspect of the Chaplin character we had seen in the Tramp before: the earnest, romantic, soulful dreamer. Revel, too, represents an aspect we are familiar with — the cad, the rake, the cynical ladies' man. Like the Chaplin character in *Tillie's Punctured Romance*, Revel is a fop who callously uses women for his own ends; like the drunken husband in *The Idle Class*, he is impeccably attired and emotionally empty. Jean is the artist with paint and brush; Revel, as we have been informed, makes an "art of living."

Marie makes an attempt to break with Revel and he chides her, reminding her that she "has everything." In her fury at his glib condescension, she tears off her string of pearls and flings them out the window, to show that she is not imprisoned by the luxurious life. In the only moment of the film which resembles any of Chaplin's previous works, Marie watches from the window as a bum comes upon her pearls and picks them up. She runs out and repossesses them, astounding the bum, breaking the heel off her shoe in the process. All the while, Revel guffaws derisively.

In the end, Marie tells him of her plans for marriage and they part. We then see Jean and his mother. She has confronted him about the marriage and they are arguing. "Of course I won't marry her!" he shouts angrily. During the course of their argument, Marie arrives at the studio and she overhears Jean disavowing their plans. He notices her, too late, and she bitterly takes her leave of him — he has let her down again.

She returns to Revel. Jean, overwhelmed with despair and remorse, arrives with a handgun at the restaurant where Marie and Revel are dining. He sends a note requesting to see Marie "for the last time." Revel takes possession of the note and summons Jean to their table; he uses the note to mock Jean and a tussle ensues. Jean is escorted from the restaurant. In the lobby, the artist shoots himself and falls dead into an ostentatious fountain.

His body is brought to his mother, and when she reads the note in his hand, she picks up the revolver and decides to pay a visit to Mademoiselle St. Clair. Marie has left to come to the studio, however, and as the mother returns, she sees Marie weeping over her son's body. The mother drops the gun, and she and Marie clasp hands over the dead artist's body in their shared grief.

We are given a denouement: a year later, Jean's mother and Marie operate an orphanage out in the country. The local pastor drops by, and then Marie and one of the children walk out to get water from the well. On the way back, she and the boy get a ride on the back of a wagon of cheerful peasants. Coming down the same road is Pierre Revel and his valet in a chauffeured limousine. As they obliviously come abreast of Marie on the wagon, Revel's valet asks him: "Whatever became of Marie St. Clair?" and Revel shrugs indifferently. The limousine passes the wagon and the two vehicles continue on in opposite directions as the film fades out.

At one level the film has been about, as an intertitle has informed us, Marie needing to choose between luxury and marriage. If Revel and Jean are two portraits of two aspects of the Chaplin persona taken to extremes — Revel so Machiavellian and venal that he is emotionally dead, and Jean so mournfully dramatic and romantic that he must kill himself in reaction to lost love — we see that Marie occupies an ambiguous place between the two. We see that she has lost the innocence she had in her hometown, that she has become accustomed to the glitter and privilege of her new life in Paris. When she finds out about Revel's upcoming marriage, which effectively relegates her to the status of a well-compensated prostitute, she tries to break with him in an attempt to redeem her dignity; in the vow she makes to Jean, she is prepared to sacrifice her life of wealth and delicacies for love. As was seen in the incident with the pearl necklace, however, Marie rather does care about material possessions, as Revel is all too quick to remind her; and when she ends their relationship, her demeanor expresses anything but assurance and happiness about her choice. When she overhears Jean's betrayal of her to his mother, she is only too quick to return to her gilded bondage with Revel. Revel is the summation of all the sophisticated world which denies love, which sees all of reality as a series of material transactions. In her attempts to free herself from him, he has mocked and ridiculed her, smug in the knowledge that she'll return to the life he offers. He also delivers the most telling summation of her character: "You don't know what you want!"

The most defining moment of the film is perhaps when Marie makes herself available to Revel again, after she has stalked away from Jean's perceived betrayal. After hanging up the phone, Revel grins and snickers with delight that she has succumbed, that he "owns" her once more. His jubilance is contrasted with a shot of Jean, waiting in the dark, staring mournfully up at Marie's window.

If Jean has been unwavering in his solemn earnestness, Revel has been so in his resolute, amoral nonchalance. He seems to have no genuine feelings aside from those attending his procurement and enjoyment of sensual pleasures—even his marriage has the purpose of consolidating a fortune. The possible reaction of Marie to his marriage is a matter of amusement between himself and his valet. He is playing a game with Marie, toying with her affections for his own amusement. As charming and as chilling as he is—and Adolphe Menjou's portrayal of him is easily the most memorable performance in the film — Chaplin allows us to see that he is also faintly ridiculous in his pampered, superficial life. When he is invited into the kitchen to examine the food, we are treated to a little vignette in which the various workers make clear their repulsion at the odious petite bird so exalted as a delicacy by the chef; and after Revel leaves, the excessively fawning flamboyance of the chef instantly vanishes like the performance it has been. All that Revel values and esteems, all that he lives by and for, is nothing but an empty charade.

The film's final scene is the ultimate statement on the character's emptiness. It is another of Chaplin's visions of redemption, of Paradise; in setting up a home for orphans in the country, far from decadent Paris, Marie and Jean's mother cleanse themselves of the past, dedicate themselves to a more spiritual vision of the future — signified by the presence of the local Father. "Experience tells us that sacrifice is the way to happiness," Chaplin tells us via intertitle, and it is an idea he will return to in his films. When Revel is shown traveling through this vision of Paradise all his luxury and prestige are seen to be small and futile; his self-absorbed materialism is revealed to be absurd and pathetic.

Jean Millet, his counterpart, is no better, however. He is weak, unhealthily dominated by his mother, and his suicide is an act of morose cowardice. Tellingly, it is he who Chaplin has represent "love" and marriage, as opposed to the luxury offered by Revel. The frictions in the Chaplin worldview are obvious—and at the base of them is the main theme which has underlain all his works to date: survival, the need to destroy or be destroyed. Jean is a self-made martyr to his melodramatic notions of romance, while Revel is the manipulative hedonist laying lives to waste for his own amusement — typified by his mocking of what becomes Jean's suicide note.

If all three of the main characters in the film contribute to its climactic tragedy, we see in a larger sense that this "drama of fate," as it is called in its main titles, has been preordained from the start. All of the action has been put into motion by the self-righteous disapproval of Marie's and Jean's parents: Marie was cruelly locked out of her home by her father; Jean's father ordered her from his house, becoming so exercised by his rage that he died; and Jean's mother, always cloaked in black like some mythological figure of death, precipitates the tragedy by her objection to their marriage. "I wouldn't care," she tells Jean, "but it's the type of woman she is." In each case the parents' actions are motivated by their misplaced ideas of virtue. In their sullen attempts to impose morality, they commit a much greater immorality. In their judgment their hearts are closed, and they destroy the lives of their offspring. It isn't simply a vision of parents condemning their children, one generation inevitably, inescapably poisoning the existence of the next. Chaplin's Marie St. Clair, a small-town girl who becomes a woman of Paris, is the victim of prejudice and chauvinism masquerading as virtue. She is the victim of narrow-minded conventional morality.

The film originally featured an introductory title: "The world is not composed of saints and sinners, but of men and women with all the passions God has given them." Chaplin removed the title on the film's rerelease fifty years later, and that is the version most common now. But the original opening epigram makes Chaplin's aim more clear, enabling one to see the film as a plea for tolerance, for acceptance, in a world driven with judgment and false morality. He was pointing out the real danger of social and sexual discrimination, of the domination of the self-proclaimed virtuous—making the point that no human is entirely bad or entirely good.

The fable is told with stark fluency, and the directorial and acting styles pioneered here would influence filmmakers to come. There are many moments of exquisite imagistic communication: Jean's father sits with his back to him in a chair, and Jean knows he has died when he spies the old man's pipe lying on the carpet beside him; when Marie stands stoically at the station, we know the train has come in when we see the lights flash across her face—the train itself is never seen; the casualness with which Pierre Revel replaces his handkerchief with a fresh one from a bureau in Marie's apartment swiftly conveys the intimate nature of their relationship. As well, there are memorable moments of acting: when Marie reads of Revel's impending marriage in the company of her friends, her reaction is to laugh lightheartedly and dismissively—only in the incessant tapping of her cigarette do we see her inner agony. When Jean's mother is told of his death, she does not scream and collapse weeping, as we have been trained to expect by many other films. She stands solemnly, disbelievingly, before the police officer, as the reality sinks in.

A Woman of Paris is rather like the champagne truffles whose preparation is depicted so carefully in the film: it is a rarefied delicacy, in which Chaplin was able to indulge and explore all that he had learned and imagined about film in the previous eleven years. He spent seven months on the film — he certainly wouldn't have been able to make it under the employ of another producer— and, as he observed in a special program note he wrote for its premiere, he "enjoyed every minute of it."[4] He fulfilled his self-proclaimed aim to pioneer a new realism in films, and in this he inspired a generation of directors as well as winning the praise of discriminating critics.

Financially, the film was a failure — the first of Chaplin's career. It was also a failure at establishing Edna Purviance as a serious dramatic actress. Her performance as Marie St. Clair is competent and credible, but it is possible that she lacked a certain spark which would allow her to persist in a career as a lead actress. She would make two more films, then retire from the screen. Undoubtedly aware of how much Purviance had contributed to the evolution and success of his art, Chaplin kept her on payroll for the remainder of her life.

The one person who would seem to have benefited from the film the most was Adolphe Menjou, whose performance as Pierre Revel made him a star and furnished him with the basic character he would portray for the next thirty-seven years of his career.

A purposeful divergence from all that had made Chaplin successful, *A Woman of Paris* seems at first to be anomalous to his career as a whole; it is only when we look closer that we see the same old themes explored in a new, if at times unrecognizable manner: survival, wealth, poverty, sacrifice, redemption. The story, pieced together in the usual intuitive manner by Chaplin, is a parable of human nature, tragic and sympathetic, with all of the characters imbued with complexity in their follies and frailties—ultimately we find that what is most expressed is a tender acceptance of human imperfection. Though he withdrew the film from circulation for fifty years after its poor box office, he would remain proud of the film's sophistication in both technique and content. The last creative act of his life was the rerelease of it, with a new score composed for the occasion, two years before his death. Its elegant, haunted musings on the ideas of virtue and vice, love and necessity still deserve and repay attention.

9

The Gold Rush

In 1896, Skookum Jim Mason, a member of the Tagish nation of indigenous peoples, discovered gold deposits at the mouth of the Klondike River, in the Yukon, Canada. Realizing that a claim made by a native person would arouse the dubiety of the locals, it was arranged that the claim would be made by another, non-native member of his traveling party.[1] By July of the following year, news had reached the United States, and aspiring prospectors began flooding from San Francisco via ship from Seattle, landing at Skagway or Dyea, Alaska. From there, they took the Chilkoot Trail up to its highest point, known as Chilkoot Pass, which was the passageway for thousands of gold-diggers through the coastal mountains which separate Alaska from British Columbia.[2] The trek through the steep and hazardous pass was 26 miles long. Having been used by the Tlingit indigenous people for trade, it consisted of 1500 steps carved in ice, and it rose 1000 feet over its last half mile. Prospectors scrambled up by foot, and many foundered along the way. At the top Canadian Mounties were posted, ensuring that each fortune-hunter had brought a year's worth of supplies. From there, the prospectors built rafts and boats at Lake Bennett and sailed 500 miles down the Yukon River to Dawson City, Yukon.

Twenty-seven years later, Charlie Chaplin would happen to view a photograph of the seemingly endless line of prospectors journeying up the Chilkoot Pass. In the aftermath of *A Woman of Paris*, the comedian was under pressure to deliver a big hit for United Artists, the production company he'd started with Douglas Fairbanks and Mary Pickford. His partners were understandably concerned about continuing to bear the debt of the company themselves, and his latest film had not helped much in that regard. Chaplin was stimulated by the image of Chilkoot Pass. In addition, he would read about the infamous Donner Party, a group of travelers who had become lost in the Sierra Nevada on their way to California in 1848. Stranded without food, they resorted to cannibalism, eating the flesh of their fallen comrades, and according to some reports, boiling and eating their own moccasins.[3]

The Gold Rush opens with perhaps Chaplin's most elaborate, extravagant image, and certainly one of his most memorable. We see before us the Chilkoot

Pass, the vast mountains of merciless whiteness obscuring the sky, up which a thin, seemingly endless line of men travels, insect-like against the icy infinity. The spectacle was recreated using Mount Lincoln in Truckee, Nevada, with 600 real hobos transported up from Sacramento.[4] The authenticity and scope of the image announce Chaplin's aim: this is the epic, the masterwork.

We see shots of the men trekking, stumbling and falling; we are told the hardships, struggle and peril of the prospectors. Then we see our old friend the Tramp, blithely waddling along a snow-encrusted mountain ledge, replete in derby and swinging his trusty bamboo cane. He has had a two-year vacation from the screen, yet he is more instantly recognizable, and enthusiastically welcomed for that reason, than ever before; he is more himself, somehow, than ever before. In *The Gold Rush*, and in the three remaining films he appears in, the Tramp is defined for all time, is "frozen" and becomes the quintessential icon that will float around in the collective subconscious of humanity forever after. If, in a film as late as *The Kid*, he could erupt in a sudden flurry of frenetic violence, if in *The Pilgrim* he could furtively size up the take from a church or kick a child to the floor, from *The Gold Rush* on he is more the industrious fellow, the romantic ever working in the service of a dream. He isn't above cadging a drink or two, or stealing food when necessary, but he's not in the business of making trouble — he isn't doing prima ballerina routines in front of stunned onlookers. His grace, his ingenuity, will now be put to use for practical ends. He'll certainly give as good as he gets, but his fights are now fought for the furtherance of ideals — and dedicated to the romantic, poetic vision which he ever dreams of. In each of his final four films he will rescue a female from economic hardship and oppression.

Plucking his way through the Arctic wilderness, his tiny figure sliding down the icy wastes, his essential predicament is made manifest, his basic situation is portrayed here and throughout the film with stark geometrical precision. Survival, the main theme of Chaplin's work, at the heart of the Tramp's drama, is brought to the fore, concentrated on here with a frightening intensity. The bitter cruelty and mercilessness of nature and the struggle to exist in the face of it have never been far from the surface of these films — and now this becomes the undeniable theme.

It's certainly evidence of Chaplin's genius that he was able to seize on the stories of the suffering of prospectors during a gold rush, on the horrible tragedy of the Donner Party, and use them to build a comedy. The snowy frigidity gives a theme and a look to the movie as a whole, but the solemn whiteness, which so diminishes the tiny humans who travel through it, also has symbolic truth — it conveys the Tramp's utter insignificance to the vast indifference of the universe around him. It conveys the manner by which that indifference is malevolent to his very survival, and outlines the endless struggle for mere subsistence that his existence ever more will be.

If hunger has been a motivating concern for Charlie in the past, here it becomes massive, grotesque, primitive, tragic. A blizzard begins and he is blown about like a rag. We have already met another prospector, Big Jim McKay — played by Mack Swain, the old cohort from Keystone, here playing his defining role. The Tramp is blown into a cabin of another prospector — the criminal, Black Larson. Charlie gnaws ravenously at a bone he finds in the cabin, but Black Larson enters and orders him out. The Tramp does his best to leave, but the wind keeps blowing him back in. In short order, Big Jim, too, finds his way to the cabin. Black Larson points his rifle at Big Jim and Charlie and orders them both to leave. When Big Jim attacks Larson and defeats him, appropriating the rifle, the Tramp quite passionately affirms his loyalty to the larger man.

The three men huddle, without food, in the cabin as the blizzard rages outside. At one point Jim leaves the room and returns sucking his teeth and belching, causing Charlie to nervously whistle for the dog. It is decided that they will split the cards to decide who will leave to get some provisions; Black Larson leaves. We see him come upon two policemen, ensconced in a tent in the vast whiteness — he kills them in cold blood.

Meanwhile, the Thanksgiving holiday has come upon Charlie and Big Jim in the cabin. In order to do the occasion justice, the Tramp has gone to the trouble of boiling one of his rather large boots — he places it, steaming and sumptuous, on a plate with all the care of a practiced gourmet chef. He brings it to the table under the appalled gaze of Big Jim; Charlie starts carving up the carcass of the boot — you can almost hear him ask "White or dark meat?" — placing a portion of the boot before Jim, who stares at it in outraged disbelief. Jim observes with awed disgust as Charlie chews the boot, twirling the laces around his fork and swallowing them like spaghetti — "Try it! It's good!" the Tramp's eyes and gestures say to his friend. Big Jim, scornful, doubtful, yet desperate in the pain and delirium of his hunger, bites into the leather, and manages to swallow a piece.

The transformational gift of the Tramp is once more on display, yet here it exists not as an irrepressible outburst of exuberant whimsy but as an absurd triumph of delusional adaptability. He sucks the nails of his boot like bones, even inviting Big Jim to get into the spirit of things and break the "wishbone" with him — the latter demurs. The Tramp's ability to derive pleasure and satisfaction from eating footwear is ridiculous, of course — but at another level, and one which is never far from the comedy, it is an act of ultimate desperation, an evocation of the pain of gut-grinding hunger and deprivation, the sharp, painful edges of need exposed bare.

As if this were not enough, it is followed in the next scene by Big Jim breaking down completely, crying, "Food! I must have food!" His agony causes him to take leave of his senses: he begins seeing Charlie as a large chicken. The Tramp is perplexed by his friend's behavior at first, but when Big Jim begins chasing him around the table with a rifle, the panic of self-preservation takes over. He is chased out into the snow before he is finally able to make his friend come to his senses—Big Jim, chastened, goes back inside as Charlie prudently buries the rifle in a drift. It isn't too long before the chilling intertitle informs us: "Chicken or no chicken, his friend looks appetizing." Big Jim leaps from his chair to pursue the Tramp with an axe—Charlie runs outside, digs up the rifle, and the two men face off.

It's all been an entirely logical progression. This basic horror has been at the heart of Chaplin's comedy all along. While it is fun to see Chaplin in the large chicken outfit, scratching and pecking, and to see Mack Swain smacking his lips, trying to entice him as he stalks him with the rifle, we are not let off so easily. The essential implication of the fun—that Big Jim wants to kill the Tramp and then eat his body—is thrown full force into our faces in the next scene. The "Chicken or no chicken..." signifies Big Jim's clear-eyed intention to cannibalize his friend—only Charlie's dexterity and ingenuity will prevent his being slaughtered by Big Jim's axe.

But hasn't this always been the case? Charlie's mission always been simply to subsist, which would be hard enough in and of itself, without being hunted down by authority, by hunger and need, by the brutes which rule his world and are only waiting for him to suffer a momentary lapse of attention so that they may slay and consume him whole. Always there has been the larger man in pursuit of the Tramp, some burly manifestation of angry power ready to smash Charlie to the earth. Here, the cruelty of nature and the stark whiteness of his images allow and inspire Chaplin to express the truth of the situation—his artistic vision—in the barest and most primal, primitive manner. The basic dynamic between Charlie and his nemeses is painted in broad slashes. It is now a matter of the smaller animal being hunted and pursued by the larger animal—the prey and the predator. He takes it right to its farthest extreme, and in hindsight we realize that we should have expected no less. Charlie must stay up all night in order to keep an eye on his would-be slayer—his rifle keeps Big Jim at bay, though the latter is seen to be ever at the ready to put his axe to use. In the morning, Big Jim attacks the Tramp again, throwing a blanket over his head and trying to strangle him. It is only the arrival of a bear in the cabin which saves Charlie from becoming Big Jim's meal—when the Tramp is able the shoot the animal, the two men excitedly prepare for a feast, and Charlie's skin is saved.

It was in this same manner that the Tramp was saved from the wrath of Black Larson when he'd first entered the cabin—a larger organism arrived and took the heat off him for awhile. The slapstick chases and fights of the past—the battles with furious clouts to the skull and energetic kicks to the ass—have now been refined and reduced into the most essential fight of all, the one which compels one to destroy or be destroyed. This has been the fierce inspiration for all the ass-kicks and bludgeonings up to this time. Chaplin is able to show us, in all its gruesome glory, what's been on his mind all along.

The two friends part, with Big Jim leaving to inspect his claim. When he arrives, he finds that Black Larson has usurped it. The two behemoths battle, and Black Larson slams Big Jim over the head with a shovel. Larson makes his escape, scampering off with his sled, but an intertitle informs us: "The North: A law unto itself." In a rather spectacular shot, the snow Black Larson's standing upon crumbles and falls from the side of the mountain, and he is pitched, by capricious and cruel nature, into the abyss. Big Jim pulls himself to his feet and stumbles, in a concussive daze, into the wilderness.

Certainly the plotline of *The Gold Rush* is one of Chaplin's most ambitious and original. These desperate and dark characters are brought in, in their feverish search for fortune, in this pitiless environment, in a mission which is a battle with destiny itself. There is something which is harsh and ruthless at the heart of the film, which gives it depth and majesty.

We now see the Tramp enter a small mining town. He trudges through the streets, and comes to the door of a dance hall. He stands, his back to us, watching the revelers within; he sees the people dancing, drinking, laughing and talking with each other. The Tramp stands alone, watching them as though they are residents of another world, of another way of being, that he will never know — and this shot is held for a considerable length of time. We admire Chaplin's acting skill in evoking such emotions simply by showing us his back, without using his facial features. We see also that his composition of the shot, as director, speaks as eloquently of the Tramp's essential solitude, his aloneness, his estrangement from humanity. It is this aloneness which is among his most salient characteristics, and in this iconic image of isolation, Chaplin lays out another defining moment for the Tramp.

It is the beginning of a sequence which is one of Chaplin's most accomplished sustained pieces since the café scene in *The Immigrant*. He moves into the dance hall — at every side there is laughter, gaiety, merrymaking. Charlie moves through it all like a ghost. Nobody looks at him, nobody really even sees him. The people are as indifferent to him as the howling blizzard outside. He looks about expectantly for a moment of communication, of human connection, but he is like an image projected on the surface of their world — to them he simply does not exist.

Unexpectedly, a pretty female smiles at him. He returns the smile with surprise, then with delight as she greets him. He does not see she is speaking to the man standing behind him. She steps towards him, her hand extended, and Charlie moves to meet her, his smile disappearing from his face, replaced with hurt puzzlement — a real pain seemingly as deep as any pain which has been experienced on earth — as she slides swiftly past him and takes the other man's hand.

The female is Georgia, the dance hall girl. We have been introduced to her as well as to Jack, Georgia's burly, aggressive would-be suitor and a described "ladies' man." We have seen Georgia in her domain, in an earlier quarrel with Jack. She had been examining some photos of herself with some friends, and he had crudely grabbed at the pictures, confiscating one tauntingly. She had angrily and spiritedly grabbed the picture back, then threw it at his feet, telling him off all the while.

Georgia is played by Georgia Hale, an actress of 19, and the perfect performer for the part. She is young, petite, lithe, and sexual: it is evident that Edna Purviance could not have played the role, for she had never had the sultry, defiant hint of vulgarity which the part requires. Like Edna's character in *A Dog's Life*, Georgia is a dance hall performer who seems actively encouraged by the management to subsidize her onstage performances with offstage ones. Where Edna was naïve and innocent, however, Georgia is a good deal worldlier. She looks apathetically around the hall, complaining to her friend, as Marie did in *A Woman of Paris*, of being bored, of wanting to find someone who would make a difference. As she had bypassed Charlie without a glance when she had taken the other man's hand, so now she laments her fate as she looks about, her head one inch away from the Tramp's face. She gazes off, actually looking through the Tramp, not seeing him there at all — as he stares at her with meek yet grave adoration.

This new insignificance of Charlie in the presence of "normal" people — much like tramps in real life are thoughtlessly discounted, not looked upon as worthy of attention or consideration — is quickly enlarged upon. The brutish Jack approaches and demands that Georgia dance with him. He tries to manhandle her and she refuses, defiantly looking about and choosing the Tramp as her dancing partner: "I'm choosy about who I dance with," she tells Jack spitefully as she leads Charlie to the dance floor, and here we have a new development in the evolution of the Tramp character. Certainly he has been a misfit in the past, an outcast and a pariah, but never before has he been an object of ridicule and disdain. In the eyes of Georgia he is a sad and sorry specimen, and his abject unworthiness of her charms is a decisive rebuke to Jack. Chaplin would later speak of his difficulty in contriving scenarios in which young and attractive women could become interested in a rag-attired hobo whose movements and gestures suggest a permanent infestation of fleas.[5] The romantic element is necessary especially in the feature films, to push along the plot and to add tenderness and sentiment. So Charlie becomes the hopeful suitor, here and in the next two films, whose dreams of romance must grow from misapprehension, and must always shatter because of his absolute aloneness and irrevocable estrangement from humanity, must always be edged in pathos and tragedy.

She pulls him out to the dance floor, and he dances with earnest, reverent grace, a grace somewhat impaired by the ill-fitting trousers he's wearing, which seem determined to slip from his waist. He tries to keep them hitched up with his cane for awhile, and when there's a pause in the dancing he grabs a piece of rope from a table uses it as a belt to secure his pants. When the music starts up again, we see that the rope is attached to a large dog, who sleepily lumbers about the dance floor following him. Inevitably, a cat appears and the dog bolts, pulling Charlie onto his backside.

It is after this that Jack approaches Georgia again, roughly demanding her attention. She presents a flower to the Tramp, that recurring symbol of the Tramp's romantic nature, his higher yearnings, his poeticism. She exits, presumably to her room, and Jack angrily tries to follow her. The Tramp sternly bars the way, his miniscule frame in contrast to his hulking opponent giving him the same absurd heroic stature as was seen in *Easy Street*. Jack pulls Charlie's hat down over his eyes so that he flails about blindly, and the crowd laughs at him, along with Jack. In casting about, the Tramp punches a post, and a large clock falls, felling his opponent. He walks from the dance hall triumphantly, as the crowd stares with awe.

In the laughter of before, though, we've seen that Charlie can now be a figure of ridicule for the larger world as well. In his earlier, more dynamic and transformational incarnation, the people didn't laugh at the Tramp; he laughed at them. Now there is an uneasy new vulnerability to his character; if he had triumphed over the denizens of his world with almost superhuman agility in *Easy Street*, *The Rink*, and *The Adventurer*, he is now more at the mercy of them. This is all a part of having the drama of his destiny form the narrative arc of the longer films—if we in the past had stood with the rest of the characters in the films, awed and outraged by the whirling dervish of violent creativity that was the Tramp, we now stand with the Tramp in his more human disappointment and determination against the crowd which surrounds him.

At the same time, this also requires that we believe the Tramp believes that Georgia is actually showing interest in him, rather than just using him to punish Jack. This would at first seem to be a stretch, since we know Charlie is anything but stupid. Yet here and in his next two films he is overcome by his romantic and poetic nature to believe and to hope that the hand he outstretches to beauty and love will be accepted, all prior indications notwithstanding. In his final incarnation he is defined by this earnest poeticism, and by all the underlying sadness inherent in it. If the films contain less of the violence and savagery of the earlier works, there could be said to be a greater cruelty in them, in the disparity between the Tramp's expectations and his bitter reality.

He finds residence at a cabin a "stone's throw away from the dance hall." One afternoon, Georgia and her friends are out cavorting in the snow; they happen upon the cabin. Georgia and Charlie meet again, and she puts on a show for the benefit of the other girls, encouraging the Tramp's romantic hopes. When he leaves for a moment to get some wood, Georgia lifts a pillow from his bed to serve as her backrest — and sees the flower she'd given him at the dance hall, with a crumpled picture of her. For an instant an expression of self-reproach, of taken-aback emotionality, flickers over her features. But as he returns, she continues the charade for her friends, even asking him if he'll have them over for dinner. They make a date for 8:00 on New Year's Eve, to the great ecstatic delight of Charlie — in their absence he swings from the roofbeam, and punches a pillow so that a blizzard of feathers erupts— and to the great amusement of Georgia and her friends.

The pathos is in the contrast between his deadly serious, gentlemanly, gallant pursuit of love, and the frivolous, derisive, coarse attitude of Georgia and her friends. He is seen shoveling snow for money to finance the big night, then carefully preparing the table, laying out party favors and gifts, basting a roast in his makeshift oven. The night arrives and he sits at the table, expectantly waiting. He falls asleep, and in perhaps the most effective use of Chaplin's old standby, the dream sequence, we see Charlie's vision of perfect happiness— he sits at the table with Georgia and her friends, all of their faces shining with excitement and glamor. They are all having the time of their lives, and are delighted by the little presents the Tramp has given them. They ask him to stand and make a speech — but tellingly, he is so happy and excited that he can't express himself in words. His emotions can only find voice through action, movement: he'll dance for them, he says. He picks two rolls from the table, inserts forks into them, and does a little dance with them, the rolls and forks becoming his feet and legs, his head oversized and floating strangely above them, his features outrageously insouciant.

It is the quintessential Chaplin moment. The happiness of the Tramp bursts from him in this performance uniting two of his most recognizable traits: his gift for transformation and his gift for dance. Just as the depths of pathos have been plumbed, Charlie's incorrigible exuberance of imagination bursts through. With easy grace and elegance, he is once again the artist, living creatively, tossing off this bit of poignant whimsy and poetry with the nonchalance of an ostrich spreading its wings. As always, he wins our respect and admiration for the sheer ingenuity in conjuring magic from the most banal of realities. In the dance is the beauty, charm and inventiveness which define Chaplin as a clown and as an artist — he is magical, an otherworldly being, an alien.

The dance wins the love of Georgia and her friends as well — she kisses him, which causes him to faint dead away. But the dream in which Charlie is loved for his wonderful artistry must end, as it always has in the past, and leave him to face a desolate and depthless loneliness.

They have not come; it's now midnight. In the dance hall, the revelers are celebrating, singing "Auld Lang Syne." Georgia and Jack are there, a couple — she has chosen the brute primitiveness of Jack, while the lonely romanticism of the Tramp has never even registered on her radar. Charlie stands in the doorway, listening to the far-off music, his face unreadable. He makes his way out into the night, to the dance hall, and once again he stands with his back to us, watching through the window at the people celebrating, peering at a world he can never be a part of.

Georgia has a sudden inspiration—"Let's go up and have some fun with the little fellow," she suggests to Jack. They go up to the cabin when Charlie isn't there and Georgia sees the carefully laid-out table, the decorations and the presents. "The joke has gone too far," she says, overcome with remorse. Jack reacts to her sudden sobriety by demanding a kiss; he paws at her, and in her anger she slaps him across the face.

She is Chaplin's most complex, most realized heroine. Like Marie in *A Woman of Paris*, she is in a relationship which she is fundamentally ambivalent about: she is mistreated by her oaf of a boyfriend yet she can't wholly sever herself from him either. Her mistreatment of the Tramp would seem to make her quite unsympathetic, yet her own plight with Jack, and her spirited reactions to his coarseness, as well as the proddings of conscience she has experienced regarding the Tramp, allow us to view her in a manner not entirely negative. We are ambivalent about her, as maybe Chaplin was.

The basic complexity of her character is seen again in the next segment as she begins a letter: "I'm sorry for what happened last night...." We might think it is directed to the Tramp, but she is writing to Jack, and she rounds the letter off with "I love you." She directs a waiter to take it to Jack, and she watches from the upper floor of the dance hall as he opens it. She sees him as he snickers, and passes the note around to the women seated at the table. She is let down, her belief in love destroyed, as was Marie's, by the cavalier insensitivity of her lover.

It is here that Charlie makes his entrance again, ambling into the dance hall; Jack has the good idea of passing the note on to him, and the Tramp is instantly transported into overjoyed excitement. He races about, trying to find Georgia as Jack chortles, enjoying the spectacle. What the Tramp believes to be his new romantic adventure is forestalled, however, by the sudden appearance of Big Jim. The prospector has stumbled into the dance hall in search of Charlie, for he knows that only his old companion (and former potential stomach fodder) can lead him to the cabin, in proximity to which his gold stake is located. He seizes the Tramp, and after Charlie runs to Georgia and bids heroic farewell, the two men make off to the wilderness to claim their fortune.

They arrive at the cabin and bed down for the night. A blizzard comes and the cabin is blown about the arctic wastes. In the morning it balances preposterously on the very edge of an icy cliff. When the men awake and move about, the cabin tilts—at first, Charlie is quick to persuade Big Jim, and perhaps himself, that the gravitational disorientation they are experiencing is merely a result of stomach trouble. The tilting continues, however, in strict accordance to the laws of physics, and the expected hair-raising brushes with annihilation ensue. Straying further into the realm of the fantastic than he has before, and reviving the shifting floor seen in several of his films to date, it is a final bravura routine which Chaplin throws into the film as its climax, a last blast of comic invention, flawlessly executed as always. When the cabin finally drops into the infinite abyss, the two men make their escape at the last moment—and find they have fortuitously landed at the site of Big Jim's gold claim.

In the final scene Big Jim and Charlie are millionaires, attired in the requisite suits and top hats, returning home from Alaska on a steamer. Some journalists ask Charlie to dress in his prospector's clothes for a photograph. Meanwhile, Georgia is also seen to be on board, solemnly heading home from the gold rush. With Charlie now in his Tramp clothes, they collide; she assumes he's the stowaway the boat's authorities have been looking for, and she tries to hide him. He is uncovered and about to be arrested when the journalists come and tell the authorities—and Georgia—who he really is. The photographer asks him to pose with Georgia for a picture. The photographer asks them to move closer, closer, until Charlie's and Georgia's lips meet, and on their kiss the film ends.

Leaving aside the striking autobiographical connotations of the scene—Charlie is a millionaire obliged to dress in the costume of a tramp (and certainly the making of Chaplin's fortune had been no less fantastical and fraught with hardship and adventures than the Tramp's)—we see the necessity of Charlie meeting Georgia again dressed as the Tramp. She must be seen to be a caring person, in offering to pay his fare, so that she can be accepted as the Tramp's romantic partner. In doing so, it is just as easy to observe that what Georgia feels for Charlie has been mainly pity and remorse—in describing the relationship later, Chaplin would write that she pitied him and the Tramp mistook her pity for love.[6] And certainly her act of charity now does little to balance the cruelty she had shown to him before. There is evidence in her new solemn demeanor that she has changed, perhaps because of her disillusionment with Jack, which has caused her to leave the North and travel home.

Even so, her sudden acceptance of the Tramp as a romantic partner might strain credulity except for that it comes after she is told that the Tramp is no longer a tramp, but a millionaire. If all that she had felt before for him was pity, certainly the reason for pity now would be gone—replaced by a new interest in Charlie, inspired by new and heretofore nonexistent possibilities. Survival and love, those twin obsessions of Chaplin, come into play again, with Georgia, his archetypal heroine, making her decision of necessity. Again, Chaplin's perspective is compassionate, and mindful of the material actualities which influence the pursuit of love and happiness for all of humanity. If her kiss is offered with motives not entirely romantic in nature, Charlie's moment of triumphant happiness need not be dimmed: he remembers only the "I love you" of the note, and is only too ready to trust Georgia's kiss. We leave him in utter ecstasy in the fulfillment of his dream—if only for that moment.

When Chaplin rereleased *The Gold Rush* seventeen years later in 1942, he added a musical score and replaced the intertitles with his own spoken narration, in an attempt to appeal to a new generation. Leaving aside the question of the artistic success of such additions—in this writer's opinion, the original version of the film is far superior to its later incarnation—they amount to a reimagining of the film as a whole. Chaplin also took the opportunity to make the character of Georgia less cruel in the early part of the film — her statement "Let's go up and have some fun with the little fellow" in the New Year's Eve sequence is changed to reflect more genuine concern for the Tramp. As well, instead of having her write a letter asking forgiveness of Jack and professing love for him in her penultimate scene, she writes the letter to Charlie to begin with, and has it delivered to him; the text of the letter is changed to: "I'm sorry for what happened last night. Let me explain." As she is softened into a more compassionate, responsible person in the later version, so is the ending of the film less extreme in its depiction of the new union. The tender, surprisingly sexual, kiss is gone; now the couple simply walk off together, as Chaplin's voice intones: "And so it was a happy ending." But even if it is more sedate, and less contradictory than the earlier conclusion, it is only happy in the ambiguous sense that all Chaplin's "happy" endings are. There are still many questions left unanswered, and Chaplin's realism about human nature will not allow any of them to be wrapped up tidily.

It is this realism which gives depth and gravity to Chaplin's "epic," even as it includes such bizarre sights as men eating a boot, a human-sized chicken, dancing dinner rolls and teetering cabins. Chaplin has forged another comedy from the gravest of situations, and the ambition, audacity and scope of *The Gold Rush* made it a peak in his career. The plot, accumulated, as he remembered, from a series of routines improvised around the central theme, rises and falls in the capricious rhythms of fortune with which the film is so concerned. More than any of his other works, the film benefits from a uniformly strong cast: Georgia Hale, Mack Swain as Big Jim McKay, Malcolm Waite as Jack, Tom Murray as Black Larson, and the reliable Henry Bergman as the kindly Hank Curtis, all are strong and memorable in their roles. As well, the unforgettable images and photographic effects achieved by Rollie Totheroh — the opening scene of Chilkoot Pass, the sight of Black Larson meeting his ignominious fate, the cabin tilting off the cliff — mark the film as a technical accomplishment in a way that none of Chaplin's other works qualify.

On more than one occasion, Chaplin stated that *The Gold Rush* was the film he wanted to be remembered by. He would equal it in elegance of expression and in profundity in other films, but he would never quite reach the heights of invention, originality and audacity attained here.

10

The Circus

The Gold Rush grossed over six million dollars, easily taking care of Chaplin's debt to United Artists. The film had also taken nearly a year and a half to make. As has been noted, *A Woman of Paris* had been seven months in the making, and the lengthy time Chaplin had taken in the creation of the two films meant that the Tramp had been absent from the screen for two and a half years before returning in *The Gold Rush*. There was now another two and a half year gap before the next appearance of the Tramp in *The Circus*—though 13 months of that can be attributed to the production of the new picture being suspended because of one of Chaplin's protracted and painful divorce battles.

In his new freedom, Chaplin was taking unheard-of lengths of times to make his films—the obsessive taking and retaking which began to be seen in the Essanays and Mutuals, and which, as outtake material discovered in the 1980s show us, were his manner of composing and refining the action of his films, now were allowed free rein in Chaplin's quest for perfection, to his brother Sydney's frequent trepidation. As well, Chaplin's freedom meant that if he wasn't feeling inspired, he simply didn't work, and his cast and crew would be sent home from the studio. It also meant that if he hit a snag in his ongoing improvisation of plot, he could retreat and think it through until he had it untangled — as his cast and crew waited nearby.

Certainly such unique working conditions aided the creation of the singularly impressive, timeless classics Chaplin was now producing. At the same time, it was undeniable that he was now no longer a mere slapstick clown who occasionally showed flashes of great art; to his audience and to himself, he was now an artist who chose slapstick clowning as his method of expressing his artistry. For in addition to the constant and conscious artistic development in his films, the lengthier wait times between his works took him out of the common run of comedians—the occasion of their release took on more the appearance of rarefied events, so that he was no longer the reliable lifter of spirits he was ten years earlier as the Keystones were flooding into the theaters at a rate of three per month. "The funniest man in the world," as he was largely known, had moved into a class of his own — his great success at making all of humanity laugh had afforded him the freedom and time to take that gift to its highest possible refinement.

The Circus is a film about making people laugh in which Chaplin returns to making people laugh as his first priority. *The Kid* and *The Gold Rush* both had many classic comedy sequences—but they also both broke new ground dramatically. *The Circus* has no such ambitions; unlike most of Chaplin's other features it attempts nothing new or audacious. It consolidates the gains of the past, and quite consciously states its aim: to be a film about laughter which creates laughter. It is a film in which the Tramp becomes a clown who can only make people laugh when he doesn't try to; when he tries, he's unfunny. Notably, the film's credits designate it as "A Comedy"—in contrast to *The Gold Rush*'s "A Dramatic Comedy," or even *The Kid*'s "A picture with a smile and perhaps a tear."

Comedy though it is, there are certain formed conventions which need to be observed, and *The Circus* begins with the standard establishment of an oppressed female character. In each of these masterworks, the final four films in which the Tramp appears, he rescues a woman compromised by material need. Here, the equestrian girl, played by Merna Kennedy, is abused by her nasty ringleader father: she missed the hoop in her routine, so he throws her violently through a paper-covered hoop backstage. Emblazoned across the front of its surface is a star. The clowns don't fare too much better — they are doleful, unimaginative and unfunny, and the virtually nonexistent audience causes the ringleader to bark poisonously at them.

Into this miserable, loveless excuse for a circus comes the Tramp, and immediately as he enters a triumphant comedy sequence speeds into motion. He hangs around the sideshow, hungry — we first see him again from the back as he moves through the crowds. A pickpocket steals a wallet and watch from a man, and when the man's suspicions are aroused, the pickpocket hurriedly shoves the wallet into Charlie's pocket, unknown to Charlie. The man grabs the pickpocket, then releases him, unable to find the stolen articles on him. The pickpocket then returns to collect his ill-gotten gains from the Tramp's trousers. He is intercepted in this by another cop, who returns the wallet and watch to the bewildered Charlie. Quite pleased to now be in possession of a billfold full of money, Charlie now goes to a stand and orders a large number of hot dogs. As the Tramp prepares to pay, the original owner of the wallet passes by and recognizes it. He cries out to a cop, who comes and chases Charlie. In the meantime, the pickpocket has escaped the custody of his cop, who now is chasing him. The pickpocket and Charlie come abreast of each other as they run from their respective cops. Charlie elegantly tips his hat to the other man as he runs.

The chase continues into a hall of mirrors, then into the Big Top. The Tramp gets mixed up with a magician's act as the cop chases him, the audience roaring with delight. The Tramp runs off, escaping, and in his wake the clowns of the circus begin their act. The crowd is unimpressed: "Bring back the funny man!" they shout, "We want the funny man!" We see a title simply reading "The Funny Man," and see Charlie sleeping obliviously in a gladiator's cart behind the tent.

The preceding minutes have passed at lightning speed, the quick pilferings and confusions of wallets and watches recalling the similar sleight of hand which accounted for the plots of innumerable Keystones, most notably one of Chaplin's first self-directed films, *Twenty Minutes of Love*. As well, there have been other such profusions of business as the hungry Tramp coming upon a baby carried over a man's shoulder, the baby holding a tempting hot dog inches from his face. The Tramp grins and coos at the baby, all the while taking bites from the wiener — even taking care, as he must, to season it to his liking. There has also been the eerie chase through the hall of mirrors providing us with striking myriad images of the Tramp and his pursuers, and there has been the moment when the Tramp reincarnates himself as robotic mannequin in front of a fun house, shifting from side to side so mechanically that one could swear one hears the clatter of bolts inside of him. There has been the invention of the magician sequence, with the Tramp disappearing and reappearing in the cabinets.

It has all been exquisitely executed and we, like the audience in the film, have been greatly amused by the actions of the quick-moving little man. But with the sequence's final image we are given a disquieting end to the hijinks which would never have been seen in the Keystones: the vision of the lonesome, slumbering Tramp, and the bitter irony of his desperate, perilous life as a source of amusement for the circus crowds — and for us. It is almost like a rebuke to our laughter. The film will continue this way — like a circus it will unfold in a series of masterfully performed acts, but around the edges there will always be this bitter irony, this icy elegance. It is a new self-consciousness for Chaplin — it had been there, lurking in the First National films. But with *The Circus* it comes to the foreground.

The crowd in *The Gold Rush* had laughed at the Tramp as well — there seems to be the same type of cruelty here as was exhibited there. The crowd might be assuming that the Tramp is a clown, but there is a certain cruelty to the idea of Charlie's merely existing as who he is, with the best intentions, and being more ridiculous and funny to the world at large than clowns are. The Tramp here is more divorced than ever before from society — his appearance and manner seem to be as outlandish to the crowd in the film as they are to us.

The equestrian girl doesn't have any happier a time of it — her ringleader father deprives her of food as punishment for her not accomplishing her feats. When the Tramp prepares himself a small dinner on the circus grounds, she comes begging for sustenance. The ringleader intervenes, striking the girl to the ground, and Charlie is stunned — but must hold his tongue, since the ringleader has promised him a tryout for the following morning.

The tryout is the next gag sequence Chaplin graces us with, showing with exemplary skill and audacity how he can wring laughs from the very attempt to create comedy. The sad clowns are directed to run through their routines for Charlie's edification, after which he is called in to give them a try. The routines are two circus clown standards—a William Tell sketch, in which the famed archery trick is sabotaged by the inability of the archer's assistant to stop eating the apple which is placed on his head; and a barber shop sketch, in which two rival barbers succeed in dousing their prospective customer and each other with prodigious amounts of shaving cream. In each case, Charlie creates havoc through his inability to conform to the stale, mechanical conventions of the comedy. In the William Tell sketch, he is unable to bite into the apple, for as he describes fluently through his gestures, there's a worm in it—he helpfully places a banana on his head instead. During the barber sketch, he can't allow himself to get doused when it's his turn to get splashed with the shaving cream—he reflexively jumps back. When he finally does understand that he must get hit, he becomes blinded with shaving cream and can only flail with his brush in response—before directing it into the face of the ringmaster.

Besides being an inventive comic routine, the sequence can be seen to be continuing the autobiographical note sounded with "The Funny Man" intertitle—for Chaplin was surely aware that the connection would be made with his own off-screen destiny as the world's favorite funny man. The clowns' sketches are not much different from the action Chaplin had participated in the Keystones not so long ago; as Chaplin had done in his film career, Charlie breaks the tired conventions of comedy and asserts instead his own comedy of attitude and personality. He can't conform to the stale manner by which things are done, and instead sounds a new note: he substitutes a banana in place of an apple. Like Chaplin, Charlie cannot be just another clown—there must always be some new miracle of the unexpected which he presents to us. It isn't that he is unwilling to conform to pre-established norms, it's that he simply can't—the essence of his being won't allow it. This follows in the logic already established by the Tramp's first oblivious success in the Big Top—he succeeds only when left to his own devices, only when he can be most uniquely himself.

This is proven in the next gag sequence. For his failure at his tryout, the Tramp is banished, but when the circus's property men quit, he is hired on. He is carrying a stack of plates when a donkey who's taken a perverse dislike to him chases him out into the Big Top—the crowd roars with laughter as he again makes a mess of the poor magician's act. The ringmaster observes: "He's a sensation but doesn't know it." It is in this manner that the Tramp finds his place in the circus, but the element of cruelty persists—the Tramp of old was many things, but he wasn't stupid. Yet Charlie here is oblivious that he is the stimulator of laughter. He goes out each night and the donkey is released to chase him into the ring, the ringmaster observing to his swarthy head property man (Stanley "Tiny" Sanford): "Keep 'im busy and don't let him know he's the star of the show." It is puzzling that one so savvy and knowing as the Tramp should be used in such a manner, yet Chaplin might be pointing to something deep in the heart of the Tramp character: that the crowd, like us, laughs at Charlie's desperate shambling in his quest for survival, but in the desperation of that quest there is something real and tragic, something whose roots spring from a grim reality which is anything but amusing, in Chaplin's life and in all our lives. This recognition accounts for the wry aftertaste which follows the comedy throughout *The Circus*.

In between times, Charlie forms a friendship with the abused equestrian girl, Merna, sneaking food to her, etc. Merna is Chaplin's least interesting heroine — she is less complex than Georgia had been, perhaps because of her youth, and she exists mainly as a pretty-faced ingénue — a plot device — someone the Tramp can become enamored with and, later, rescue from her miserable existence. Though Merna shares with the other Chaplin heroines the plight of being victimized as a result of material circumstances, little time is devoted to the implications of these circumstances, as disturbing as the images of her being shoved and struck by her father are. Whereas in *The Gold Rush*, Charlie's crush on Georgia came to define the film, the romantic element here seems to function as a structure on which the comic routines of "the clown" can be placed.

The next routine up is Charlie in the lion's den: in the course of his duties as a property man, the Tramp swallows a horse's pill — in the panic that this causes, his nemesis, the donkey, chases Charlie straight into the lion's cage, the door of which locks shut directly after. It is the old thrill-comedy routine, yet it is remarkable here for what Chaplin does with it — the lion lies slumbering at the far end of the cage, and Charlie treads softly to avoid waking the beast. He knocks a pan of water from the shelf and dexterously catches it before it hits the floor. He tries to escape through another door, but finds that it leads into the domicile of a ferocious tiger. Only Chaplin would also add the complication of a loudly barking dog who happens upon the scene, leaping up at the cage and yelping — Charlie puts his foot through the bars to shoo him away, but the cur leaps up and grabs the Tramp's pantleg. Merna comes by, but she faints dead away when she realizes the fearsome reality of the situation — Charlie must frenziedly splash water on her face from the cage in an attempt to wake her up.

When it is the lion who wakes up and slinks desultorily over to inspect the petrified Tramp, then pads uninterestedly back to his corner and returns to his slumber, Charlie becomes emboldened. Merna comes to, and opens the door of the cage for him; he assumes a nonchalant air, striding over to the lion to display his newfound relaxation with the animal's proximity — until the lion lunges with a roar, and the Tramp streaks from the cage across the grounds and up to the top of a very high pole. His descent from the top, sliding down with his arms fluttering bird-like for Merna's amusement, is one of those pieces of mime which alone would make the entire film worthwhile.

In the ensuing scene, Merna tells the Tramp that it is he who is the real star of the show—so that when the ringmaster arrives and begins to throw Merna to the ground in customary fashion, Charlie is able to insist: "If you strike that girl I'll quit!" Thus the Tramp's success as a clown assures Merna of safety. This balance is maintained until the arrival of Rex, a new tightrope artist. For awhile, Charlie is given reason to hope, as he has heard the Fortune Lady say that love lies ahead for Merna, in the form of a dark, handsome person close to her. The Tramp looks into the mirror and does a little ass-kicking dance of joy through the circus. Later, though, he hears Merna confess her love for Rex to the same Fortune Lady. Charlie becomes dejected—his broken heart infects his performances, so that the audience stops laughing at him.

The ringmaster tells him in no uncertain terms that he'd better get funny or else, but Charlie hasn't entirely given up on Merna. He's been practicing tightwire walking in the hopes of winning her from Rex. When Rex doesn't show up one night, Charlie leaps at the chance to fill in, and we have the climactic, piece de resistance comic routine: Charlie on the highwire. He bribes a property man to affix a harness to him, which is useful for awhile until it flies off. The Tramp quivers and falters on the wire—and a bunch of escaped monkeys are added into the mix: they scamper out to Charlie and climb over his face, bite his nose, pull his pants down, stick their tails in his mouth. He endures all of this, then falls onto the seat of a bicycle on a lower wire and speeds out of the tent.

The tightwire scene was said to have been the situation around which the entire rest of the film was built: Chaplin had a vision of himself in "a high place troubled by something else ... monkeys or things that come to me and I can't get away from them."[1] From this central image of anxiety and peril came the film as a whole. After the routine is done, there is little left but to tie up the ends of the perfunctory plot. The ringmaster beats Merna backstage, and Charlie promptly attacks him—for which the Tramp is thrown out of the circus. That night, Merna comes to Charlie where he has camped in the countryside. She wants to go with him, but the Tramp realizes he has nothing to offer her— he hits upon the idea of sneaking back to the circus and persuading Rex to marry her. Rex and Merna are married, Charlie happily throwing rice on them as they leave the church. They return to the circus and the ringmaster is forestalled from laying his customary beating on Merna by the fact that she is now married. The circus is pulling up its stakes and leaving town: the Tramp is rehired by the ringmaster and the newlyweds offer him a ride in their caravan. He refuses, gesturing "two's company, three's a crowd." The circus caravans depart, leaving the Tramp standing alone in the dust.

In serving to unite the two lovers at the end of the film, Charlie takes on the standard role of clown or comic relief in the film—he is the happy, self-sacrificing eunuch, quite far from the striking sensuality of the final moments of *The Gold Rush*; he helps to fashion a happy ending in the manner by which jesters and clowns have done so from time immemorial. In this sense, *The Circus* has more in common with the films which served as the "vehicles" for funny men before and after him, than it does any of his other films. Merna, the ringleader, and Rex don't have the complexity of depth of any of the characters in *The Gold Rush*—even a minor character like Black Larson in the earlier film has more grit and personality. But the characters of *The Circus* don't need to possess these qualities; the film's focus is more abstract, more utilitarian. The Tramp is heroic in attacking the ringleader when he beats Merna, and he is admirably self-sacrificing, almost saint-like, in his arranging for Merna and Rex to marry. The ending, like the ending of *The Vagabond*—a film which shares much with *The Circus*—would seem imperfect in that Charlie's sacrifice and wisdom seem too ennobling and martyrlike for the Tramp — though Chaplin will enlarge upon these qualities in his next film. Yet these are not the point of *The Circus*—and the haphazard manner of the plot, in glaring contrast to the methodical care taken elsewhere (Chaplin doesn't even bother to tender an explanation for Rex's absence on the night Charlie takes the highwire), attests that Chaplin did not consider the story of Merna to be the central point of *The Circus* either — as much as it addresses the recurring Chaplin concern about female servitude.

The central point of *The Circus* is in the comic routines, in the flair and grace with which they are performed. With exemplary skill, all the expected comic opportunities of the circus are mined and their vignettes are performed impeccably: the fun house, the magician's act, the lion cage, the tightrope. Chaplin is plying his trade, displaying why he is the master of it, and an intelligence is watching us calmly, keenly from within the routines as we laugh. For the film is about laughter as well, and crowds—the audience here being perhaps Charlie's true screen partner. But the laughter never sounds without an ironic, bitter echo, and Chaplin is saying that it never can again.

It is about the star on the front of the paper hoop which begins the film and which Merna smashes through in her routine. It is about the star through which she is thrown by her ringmaster father backstage. It is about the same star on a piece of tattered paper which the Tramp finds on the ground after the circus caravans leave; he picks it up and stares at it wryly. The elegiac poetry of Chaplin's images glimmers not with the sad sentimentalism of pathos, but an even deeper sadness, the futility of all things, as seen when Charlie takes the star, representing "stardom" and the world of people in which he seemed to have found a place for awhile, crumples it into a ball, kicks it into the air behind him, and makes his way into an unimaginably vast emptiness.

It is part of the icy, deceptive nature of *The Circus*—like the myriad mirrors in the fun house — that despite such an ominous ending, it is one of the most uncomplicatedly funny of all of Chaplin's features: the clowning routines are that potent, and this focus on the purely comedic makes it unique among his longer works. *The Circus* is Chaplin's circus, and he displays his wares for all to see. At the same time he shows us, in the image of his slumbering figure adorned with the title "The Funny Man," as well as in his frenzied, monkey-bedeviled tightrope walk and in his final abandonment by the circus and its crowds, the inherent pain of his vocation, the cost of his comedy. With cold, precise skill he presents his mastery against a background of pain and exploitation, in a glittery world of stars and mirrors and deception, which, when all is said and done, can be crumpled into a ball, tossed over the shoulder, and kicked into the vast ether of oblivion.

11

City Lights

A crowd has gathered in a city square. Dignitaries line the stage. The occasion is the unveiling of a new statue for the square, one titled *Peace and Prosperity*. An official steps to the microphone to deliver himself of a few remarks. A buzzing, honking cacophony rings from his lips, albeit in the familiar cadences of officious, pompous speech. He graciously introduces a female dignitary, who titters and preens, then clucks and cackles in a high-pitched version of the same grating drone, the rhythm of her repellent quacking mirroring the same familiar tone of gracious self-importance. The crowd cheers and a ribbon is pulled: the large white marble structure is unveiled, and in the lap of one of the sculpture's noble, gleaming figures lies a dirty, slumbering old tramp. The crowd shouts in angry horror. The dignitaries shout with dismay, shaking their fists. The little man looks about in sleepy incomprehension at the angry crowd, as he wakes in the lap of Peace and Prosperity.

The people shout for him to get out of there, to go away. He clambers down from his perch apologetically. But the sword of one of the figures pierces the seat of his sizable trousers. He tries to extricate himself from the sword — this enrages the crowd further. The band starts playing the national anthem, and he tries to pull himself erect, hanging there from the sword, but he keeps faltering, his patriotism at the mercy of gravity. The band stops playing, and he seats himself on the face of one of the sculptures. The crowd roars its disgust. He leans over to remonstrate with his critics but the hand of another of the sculptures makes him look like he's thumbing his nose at them. Finally, he skips over a fence and makes his way out of there.

Befitting its name, *City Lights* takes Chaplin back to the city, to the urban landscape which had been the Tramp's world, a Darwinian universe of angry cops and irascible employers, of misplaced wallets and sidestreet chases. Chaplin's city has never been a contemporary city but rather a timeless, nameless place encapsulating aspects of both 20th century North American cities and 19th century London — as seen in *Easy Street* and especially *The Kid*, which has such British touches as the gas meter in Charlie's hovel; in *City Lights*, an automobile figuring in the action has its steering wheel on the right side, European style. The Tramp is a character of the street, of the anonymous shufflers making their way through the pathways of the grimy labyrinth — power and wealth on display all around, poverty and punishment always at one's heels. This is his essential world, and the adventures he has in exotic settings are but diversions from it. He is a creature of pavement, cement, slamming doors, billy clubs, gutters, alleyways, thieves, pickpockets, tantalizing window displays and empty stomachs.

It had been ten years since Chaplin had thrown his Tramp into the merciless, winding streets — he had not been seen in his indigenous homeless milieu since *The Kid* in 1921. As well, it had been three years since the Tramp had last graced the screen in *The Circus*. In the latter interim, a change had come over his medium which was cataclysmic to Chaplin as an artist: the technology for sound films had been introduced, perfected, and become commonplace.

Since the inception of motion pictures there had been constant attempts to wed them with sound: in 1888, Eadweard Muybridge had met with Thomas Edison to combine Edison's sound technology with Muybridge's zoopraxiscope. The chief obstacles to making films talk had been the difficulty of synchronizing sound with image and the problem of amplifying the sound so that it could be heard in large theaters. In the 1920s, these obstacles were surmounted — a man named Lee DeForest had invented a process in 1923 by which the soundtrack was photographically recorded and printed on the side of the film, so that it couldn't go out of synch with the images.[1] As well, fidelity electronic recording had been perfected, with electronic amplification allowing the sound to be heard in venues of any size. In 1927, the voice synchronization in *The Jazz Singer* made it a sensation; in 1928, the first all-talking picture, *Lights of New York*, premiered, and by 1929 sound had conquered Hollywood.[2]

These last had occurred during the conception and creation of *City Lights*; Chaplin observed it all, and turned back to his work on what was essentially a silent film. Chaplin was the master of gesture and facial expression; his uncanny ability to communicate non-verbally was the most essential aspect of his screen character. The Tramp expressed himself so evocatively and gracefully that he was already beyond words, beyond sound. It could only limit him, make him less than he was. Silence was his oxygen, his world. "I knew that he could never talk," Chaplin said, speaking of the Tramp.

As well, Chaplin must have known that the unique manner in which his films were created was threatened by sound. His development of the plot, scene by scene, the improvisatory nature of his filming, his ability to control the performances of his actors by miming precisely what he expected them to do — these would be lost, owing to the need for dialogue and the greater preparation sound shooting required.

It was not that Chaplin shrank from the challenges of sound — it was simply that he had no need of it. As he well knew, sound had nothing to offer his art — in fact, its introduction would only inevitably decrease it power. And so Chaplin's main concern was to stave off its approach for as long a time as possible. Both *City Lights* and the film after it — his last as the Tramp — would be, aesthetically, silent films. He would be Hollywood's last holdout against sound. This, along with the extensive length of time between his releases — owing to his unheard-of painstaking method of filming — conferred on him further the status of being a singular cinematic talent, the "King." It is undeniable that Chaplin was concerned about financial success, but he recognized no need to conform to the dictates of mainstream Hollywood. He was no mere funnyman, trying to win the favor of his audience. He regarded himself, and was regarded by his audience, as an artist, making art.

It is important to note that *City Lights* and the film which follows are silent films only in the aesthetic sense for literally they are not silent films at all — they are sound films with a silent sensibility. The first gag of *City Lights,* the quacking dignitaries (whose sonorous honks were made by Chaplin himself with an instrument in his mouth), as well as one of its follow-ups — Charlie trying to remain erect as the anthem plays — are dependent on sound. There are sound effects throughout both of the films which are integral to their comedy. They also boast Chaplin-composed musical scores, as all his films from this point on will. Chaplin, a musician and songwriter, had long been interested in the music which accompanied his films, even selecting the pieces for screenings of *A Woman of Paris*.[3] Now he added another dimension to the complete mastery of vision he wielded in his films. His music was like all other aspects of his art: elegant and sentimental, simple and soulful, with its roots in the English music hall. Chaplin remembered that his old boss Fred Karno had used music to underscore his slapstick sketches, and that it was never funny or quirky, but always graceful and melancholy.[4] In his films, Chaplin took the same tack, never indulging in cartoonish effects: his accompaniment is always consummately tasteful throughout, evocative, often haunting — an extension of the sensibility within the images.

Adding to Chaplin's determination to stay with the silent film aesthetic was the fact that his new project was, as he would remember later, "an ideal silent picture."[5] In bringing his Tramp character back to his authentic habitat, Chaplin was also exploring definitively all the implications of the Tramp's poverty, alongside of his pretensions to dignity; he was exploring all the aspects of the fundamental cruelty of his timeless city, how the whims of the wealthy may answer the prayers of the poor, or dash them to pieces, and how all of us are made less by the presumptive labels placed on us by the degree of our material ownership, or lack thereof. The Tramp, ever at the mercy of material reality, had always achieved at least a spiritual triumph over it, simply by retaining his basic decency and dignity. In the last few films he had attained heroism by rescuing a woman who was even more oppressed by economic realities than he. Now this aspect of the Tramp would be taken to its ultimate, definitive end, and his self-sacrifice in the rescue of his romantic ideal — always tied, for him, to higher, spiritual virtues — comes to its apotheosis.

Throughout Chaplin's work, flowers have signified these higher, romantic-poetic yearnings. And so the scene which announces Chaplin's new heroine opens with a close-up of flowers. They are being sold by a blind flower girl, who sits at a corner of the teeming, diabolic city proffering her wares, calling out to the rushing crowd. We have seen the Tramp awaking on the statue before the outraged crowd and we have seen him being taunted by a pair of urchin newspaper boys — as he has been in his last few films, he is notably apart from the rest of society, a figure of spectacle and of ridicule for the common mass of people in a way in which he was not in the earlier films. If there is one who is more vulnerable, more to be pitied than he, it is the beatific-looking flower girl, calling out sightlessly to the passersby. The oppressed female has been a constant in his last several films, and now we have one who seems almost martyr-like.

The situation Chaplin is setting up is rich in implications and subtleties, but it must be handled delicately — it is emotional intricacy he is aiming for, and so he must focus with laser-beam precision here as he does in no other film. Nowhere is this delicacy and precision found more than in the scene establishing the Tramp's relationship with the flower girl.

Making his way through a traffic jam, and avoiding a cop along the way, Charlie passes through an idling limousine. The slamming of the door as he emerges on the other side alerts the flower girl and she calls out: "Flower, sir?" The Tramp stops in momentary surprise that he has been solicited — then ambles over and agreeably selects a flower. He becomes a bit annoyed when she extends a flower to him with one hand when he has already pointed to the one in her other hand. As well, he shows some impatience when his flower is dropped to the ground, and after he has bent and picked it up, she still searches on her knees for it, asking "Did you pick it up, sir?" He exasperatedly shows her the flower in his hand — but when she merely continues smiling obliviously into the distance, understanding dawns on the Tramp, and a new solemn gravity overtakes him as he watches her. She places the flower in his lapel and he stares at her in a sort of dazed wonder.

The same car door slams again — the girl calls out, assuming he has left: "Wait for your change, sir." This allows the Tramp to tiptoe around the corner so that he can continue to observe the girl. She gets up and refills her flower bucket at a fountain near where he sits. He stares at her in mute adoration — with rapt interest, as well as with curiosity. She rinses her bucket out, and throws the water into his face. He hoists himself dripping from the scene.

The slapstick conclusion comes at the end of three minutes of exquisite poetry in motion — it's one of Chaplin's most remarkable sequences, and the fulcrum on which the entire film rests. The Tramp has discovered one who is even more naked to the twists of cruel fate than he: this accounts for his quick absorption in her, once he realizes her blindness. As well, she is one who accepts the Tramp precisely because she cannot see him; in fact, she imagines him to be at least reasonably well-off, owing to the slamming of the car door. The Tramp's adoration of the girl is founded in his fascination with her helplessness, which awakens the gallant, heroic aspect of his character. But it also is fueled by her handicap, in that it promises him the acceptance he can find nowhere else — an acceptance of himself for himself in a world where he seems largely a figure of ridicule or scorn.

This world, the mythical city of Chaplin's dreams and nightmares, is further defined in the next sequence, when Charlie, cradling the flower given to him by the girl as though it were a religious artifact, makes his way that night down to the waterfront. Down the stairs to the water comes another of Chaplin's archetypes, the Drunk — albeit a wealthy one, attired in a tuxedo. He is carrying a large stone and a rope and makes preparations to hurl himself into the water with said rope and stone tied around his neck. The Tramp intervenes, forestalling the Drunk from his suicide with flowery bromides about life's beauty and all the rest. The expected dunkings in the water ensue, until the Drunk, in gratitude, takes the Tramp home with him to his mansion and plies him with drinks. Charlie is quite happy, if a little perplexed, to avail himself of his inebriated friend's largesse, though the Drunk's clear-eyed butler is less than thrilled to have a ragged, dirty vagabond so welcomed into his master's home. He tries to ensure that at least Charlie is stopped from sitting on the couch and ruining the upholstery.

The Drunk, like the similarly well-heeled drunk in *The Idle Class*, is in the process of a painful divorce — and so is periodically given to brandishing a revolver and pressing it to his temple, announcing his wish to die. When Charlie, now rather inebriated himself, delivers a few of his sunny platitudes and brings the Drunk back from the edge of self-annihilation, the Drunk passionately, frenziedly declares, "I'll live!" and takes the Tramp out on a harried night on the town. They arrive at a nightclub, but their drunken antics there do not have the anarchic hostility that was displayed by Charlie and his drinking partners in *The Rounders* and *A Night Out*. The day of the ass-kick has long passed, and most of the Tramp's crises arise from misapprehension. He becomes quite confused at his difficulties in keeping his cigar lit, owing to the fact that his sodden friend keeps obliviously holding his cigar up to Charlie's mouth each time he tries to light it — in an inventive and impeccably timed routine. He eats a seemingly endless streamer dangling from the ceiling in the belief that it is a strand of spaghetti; he leaps to the defense of a woman in an Apache dance, breaking up what he thinks is a domestic quarrel. In the main, it is this type of genteel, low-key humor we see throughout *City Lights*. Restraint and refinement are the concerns here, for as the opening titles have told us, this is a "comedy romance."

We see what Chaplin is setting us up for. The Drunk, masterfully played by Harry Myers, is an extreme version of all the drunks and rakes Chaplin has depicted in many of his films to date. He is capable of only two temperaments—either functionally comatose, completely numbed to his feelings of despair, or maniacally suicidal. He is the world which has always presided over Charlie, the power which rules only through the simple fact of its wealth, which, in its utter, amoral indifference, determines in its momentary moods or fanciful whims the destinies of a thousand Charlies. He is the representation of a capricious universe, and on a smaller scale, a capricious society, wielding its power with destructive thoughtlessness. With an arbitrariness which can only be cruel, the forces of commerce at one moment embrace, at the next cast one into the abyss of non-existence — and this is simply accepted as the way things are. It is another example of Chaplin concerning himself with the unavoidable injustice at the heart of society.

The Drunk is balanced by his opposite, the blind flower girl — perfectly embodied by Virginia Cherrill, a young woman with no acting experience whom Chaplin found, amazingly, at the beach.[6] As the Drunk symbolizes all that rules over Charlie, the flower girl in her wounded beauty is that wounded world Charlie tries to redeem, the "infinitely gentle, infinitely suffering thing," which never fails to draw his adoration and wholehearted dedication, which it always becomes his mission to save.

City Lights consists of the Tramp running back and forth between these two poles, these unchanging fixtures in Chaplin's landscape. The film goes to the heart of the Tramp's dilemma, his search for beauty and tenderness in a world which denies him these. The injustice the Tramp suffers here is not so much the result of a corrupt or evil society, but of a deeper, more frightening senselessness, which is cruel and unjust precisely because of its senselessness, its utter lack of meaning. The Tramp's search is a search for dignity, for meaning in the face of meaninglessness—in the face of the Drunk's mercurial, anguished insanity, of the girl's tragic destiny, and of the Tramp's own outlandishly precarious existence. Ever since the formation of his character the Tramp has been defined as one who has nothing, and also who has no meaningful human connection — who is fundamentally, existentially and forever poverty-ridden and alone. Here, he is taken under the wing — sporadically — by one who has everything; and he also has the promise in the blind girl of one who can, finally, accept him for who he is.

Both hopes are illusions, for we see that the Drunk's embracing of Charlie is frivolous and alcohol-inspired, and we wait only for him to rip the carpet from beneath the Tramp's feet; we know also that his acceptance by the flower girl is predicated on her blindness. The tragic undertones of these illusory hopes give weight and definition to the Tramp's search for meaning — they give a definitive, ultimate dimension to this familiar, heroic aspect of the Tramp.

Nowhere is this seen more than in the Tramp's second meeting with the flower girl. After his night out with the Drunk, they arrive back at the Drunk's mansion in his limousine. The Tramp admires the limousine, so the Drunk tells him to take it as he wanders off to bed. Charlie drives off and comes upon the flower girl, walking to her corner in the early morning air. The Tramp speeds back to the mansion, saying "Let's buy some flowers!" to the Drunk, who gives him money — Charlie returns to the girl and buys her entire supply of flowers, offering her a ride home. The Tramp pulls up to her home in the slums and escorts her to her door. "May I see you home again?" he asks. "Whenever you wish, sir," she replies. He bends low to kiss her hand.

In Charlie's gallant gesture we see the noble posture he has summoned in the past, his romantic solemnity worthy of a knight errant, or an actor playing Romeo. But of course he is playing the part only in fantasy, for he is not the rich man in her mind's eye — he is indulging himself, and misleading her, in playing that part. We have seen in an earlier scene the flower girl's loneliness, being left behind as her peers in her neighborhood set off on their dates. Now she trembles and fidgets, her face beaming as Charlie kisses her hand, her romantic dreams awakened. There is a cruelty in the tableau towards both characters, and the tenderness of the kiss is absurd and heart-rending.

Directly after this the Tramp returns to the mansion of the Drunk — who, now sober, brushes past him without an inkling of recognition, gets into his limousine with briefcase and bowler, and motors off to work. Charlie is left standing in dumb astonishment. In the Drunk's blank gaze is all the mad indifference of the universe to the Tramp's plight.

This is what is illuminated by the lights of the city — the unanswerable, senseless cruelty of power, the unending and voiceless suffering of the powerless. The flower girl retreats to the hovel she shares with her grandmother, recounting, "and then he brought me home in his car." "He must be very wealthy," the grandmother muses. "Yes, but he's more than that," the flower girl asserts, and in that vague observation we have a thread of hope that in her blindness she is able to appreciate Charlie's inner qualities in a way that all others, with sight, have been made blind to by his trampishness.

That afternoon, the Tramp happens upon the Drunk coming out of a restaurant — he is now in full drunken manic mode and enthusiastically embraces Charlie, shouting, "My friend!" So passionate is he in his newfound commitment to their relationship that he vows to throw a party for his pal: that night, a host of revelers descend upon the mansion, and again the Tramp becomes tipsy — his difficulties here include swallowing a party whistle, which causes him to disrupt a singer as well as summon an array of dogs to the party — this rather overlong sequence is entirely dependent upon the soundtrack. The next morning, he awakes from a drunken slumber beside the Drunk in his bed; his bedmate awakes, naturally, devoid of any memory of the Tramp, and the butler is only too pleased to be told to remove him from the premises.

Charlie makes his way back to the flower girl's hovel — he peeks through the window to see that a doctor is visiting, telling the girl's grandmother: "She has a fever and needs careful attention." The Tramp is so moved by this that he actually seeks gainful employment, with the goal of helping the girl. He becomes a street cleaner, and Chaplin is able to work in the clever gag of Charlie, chagrined at having to clean horse waste from the pavement, assiduously avoiding a team of horses going down the avenue, only to find that the street he's chosen is a thoroughfare for a team of elephants. There is also clowning in the old style with the Tramp's fellow street cleaner, old Karno confederate Albert Austin (who is also given the title "Assistant Director" on the film, along with Henry Bergman and Harry Crocker — the latter played Rex in *The Circus*). The perpetually aggrieved Austin's gastronomic particularities haven't changed any since *Behind the Screen*, as he prepares himself a sandwich of onions and cheese. Unfortunately, Charlie's substituted a cake of soap for Austin's cheese while washing up, with the result that the latter gets an unpleasant surprise when biting into his sandwich. He bawls Charlie out, spewing a prodigious flurry of bubbles.

On his lunch break, the Tramp visits with the flower girl at her rooms. He brings along a newspaper clipping, which tells of a cure for blindness having been perfected by a Viennese doctor. "Wonderful! Then I'll be able to see you!" the girl enthuses, and the Tramp shares in her happiness — for a moment, before he realizes what her sight will mean for him. In his momentary happiness-uneasiness is the paradox of his situation: his love for her seeks the greatest good for her, her sight — but her sight also means the end of the false pretense he's maintained before her. It means that he will have to trust in her acceptance of him as he is, something which, the quick despair in his eyes tells us, he has little hope of experiencing, having been denied such acceptance so often in the past. As if to enlarge on this, we are then given a gag on the same theme: she commences to gather some yarn for her knitting, asking Charlie to hold it while she winds the strand up. Instead, she starts obliviously winding a dangling thread from Charlie's wardrobe — he is about to tell her of her mistake, but then realizes he dares not: no affluent gentleman as he pretends to be would have threads dangling from his suits. So he sits, painfully shifting from side to side, as she unravels what we presume to be his undergarments, gathering the thread into a sizable ball.

The Tramp comes upon a letter of eviction in the girl's room: he vows that he will take care of it for her in the morning. We have been shown that the Drunk has left on a voyage to Europe, and so the Tramp comes upon boxing establishment willing to pay him $100.00 to step in the ring. Charlie is able to cut a deal with a boxer in which they'll fight and split the take fifty-fifty, the boxer promising not to hurt him. Unfortunately, that boxer receives a telegram from a pal telling him that certain authorities are closing in, so he takes a powder. Charlie is left to face a different opponent, the hulking Hank Mann — an old Keystone stalwart — who remains quite impervious to the Tramp's attempts to be ingratiating. In fact he becomes convinced, quite understandably, that they are more in the nature of sexual invitations.

They step into the ring and a boxing routine ensues, a situation Chaplin has mined before in *The Knockout* and in *The Champion*. Here there is little rough knockabout — Chaplin's style had changed in the intervening years, and he was now 40 years old, as well. But more so, *City Lights* is a more abstract, stylized comedy, so that it isn't long before the boxing match evolves into a dance. Charlie positions himself dexterously behind the referee; Charlie's opponent steps to the side to throw a punch, the referee steps to the side, and in unison Charlie steps to the side. They step, shuffling from side to side, all about the ring. Rarely is a punch thrown — the three figures become locked in a lockstep ballet: every so often they change position, Charlie shuffling from side to side in front of his opponent while the referee shuffles along behind him. It is a dance, as so many of Charlie's most triumphant moments have been — here the dance is the Tramp's magic dance of survival, supernaturally positioning himself with otherworldly grace out of harm's way, and taking his opponent along with him. He creates a dance, a trance of stately elegance by way of avoiding annihilation.

The dance can only last so long, however, before deadly physics and gravity assert themselves once again. The boxer lays Charlie low, so once again he is cast into the streets to look for money. In a crowd spilling out of a theater is the Drunk, returned from Europe and in the manic phase of his cycle — he embraces Charlie and takes him back to his mansion. "I'll take care of the girl, don't worry about that," he assures the Tramp, and pulls out some bills. "Will a thousand dollars be enough?" he asks, counting the money into the ecstatic Charlie's hand.

But there are thieves in the house — they emerge to knock the Drunk unconscious, and they move to surround Charlie, but he is able to make to a phone to call the police. The police come, the thieves escape, and in the confusion the Tramp is apprehended. The butler comes in, telling the police that his master has been robbed; Charlie is searched, and they find the thousand dollars on him. The Tramp insists that the Drunk has given him the money, and as the Drunk comes to, Charlie desperately pleads for him to tell them what has transpired. As expected, the Drunk's face assumes its blank, uncomprehending expression: "Who is this man?" he asks.

The Tramp is able to make his escape with the money. He streaks out of the mansion, back to the flower girl's hovel. "This is for your rent — and this is for your eyes," he says, placing the bills in her hand. She thanks him profusely — it's nothing, his gestures say, as he snaps his fingers. When she kisses him gratefully on the hand, he is moved to give her an extra bill he'd secreted away for himself. It has always been part of the Tramp's character to assume the attitude and bearing of one considerably more affluent than himself — it has always been in the contrast between the fastidiousness and delicacy of his gestures and the woefulness of his threadbare reality that much of his comedy has existed. He has been able to indulge farther than ever before in this grandiose vision of himself while with the girl — her blindness has made it possible. But now it is at an end.

"You're not going away?" she asks. Yes, he says sadly, nodding his head. He departs, and out on the street, near the two paperboys we have seen earlier in the movie, he is apprehended by the police. He is placed in jail, and we see the calendar pages fly — from January to autumn.

The flower girl now has a smart flower shop with her grandmother. We see the flower girl pause to fix her hair in a mirror. Her beauty and grace are now unimpeded by her former handicap — she is joyful and confident. A limousine stops before her store and a top-hatted gentleman comes in; she looks up hopefully as she takes his order, thinking it must be her benefactor. But no — she is disappointed again.

Out on the street, a small ragged man drags himself along, his slouched posture giving every indication of his broken spirit within. Jail has been hard on the Tramp — he is lower than he has ever been before. He ambles directionlessly. He comes by the corner where the flower girl used to sit and looks woefully around. What he has become is a real tramp — the spunkiness and invention and grace which had defined him are gone, showing that they have always been impossibilities, that they were but artful distractions from his appalling true situation. Like all real tramps, he has become broken, hopeless, with a sadness so vast it has made him numb. His clothes now really are soiled, tattered rags, his hat is broken, and his faith has been so crushed that he really is more like some sort of beaten animal or abused child than a man.

He shuffles along, his empty eyes scanning the pavement at his feet. The two newsboys of before begin taunting him, blowing peas at him which hit him in the back of the head. He turns to them not with the haughty disdain of before, but with a sulking petulance — he waves his finger at them, his eyes pain-filled and tragic. He is utterly without the defining characteristic of before — his dignity, his resilient élan. He has been reduced to something less than human.

Then he comes to it — outside of the flower girl's store, the waste has been swept out into the street, and there, in the gutter, lies a flower. Even in his misery he manages to bend down and pick it up — that symbol of truth and beauty so important to him. The newsboys laugh at him; one reaches forth to grab a rag from where it is protruding from the seat of his pants and pulls it out, screaming with laughter. Charlie reaches and grabs the pitiful rag back, using it to wipe his nose. The newsboys laugh at him, as do the flower girl and her co-worker, watching through the window of their shop.

The flower girl is further amused by the antics of the little man as he turns and stares at her through the window, first in shock, then with a growing, dazed happiness. This really sets her off; she turns to her co-worker: "I've made a conquest!" she says of the pitiable figure staring slack-jawed at her though the glass. The little tramp does not even notice when his flower begins falling apart between his fingers. She points to it, presenting a new flower in her other hand — but he merely continues staring at her in dumbfounded adoration. She makes a move to get up and come to him, but he scampers away, afraid, almost in horror.

She comes out to the street with a flower and a coin for the little beggar. She calls to him — he stops and turns. She holds out the all-important flower to him, and as she touches his hand, and looks into his eyes a new understanding comes into her eyes—a painful, disbelieving understanding, a shocking understanding. He gazes into her eyes, morosely, adoringly, hopefully, with a hope beyond hope, entirely prepared to be disappointed. She looks at him, half unbelieving, choked with emotion, beyond disappointment. "You?" she asks. He nods, his hand at his mouth holding the flower, his gaze heavy with ardor and fear.

"You can see now?" he asks. She nods, smiling: "I can see now." One of Chaplin's great skill as a silent film maker has been his sparing, tasteful and effective use of intertitles. These would seem at first to verge on the superfluous. Yet the Tramp's observation is not merely comment on the obvious. In a deeper sense, the flower girl sees the real truth of the situation, sees the Tramp for who he really is. The flower girl's reply is equally telling — she smiles as she says it, and we can see her mouth the word "Thanks." We then see a close-up of Charlie's face smiling beatifically, joyously, ecstatically as the film ends.

The scene is a bookend to the earlier scene of their first meeting, in which a flower was exchanged. In going down to his lowest depths, in descending into the lowest implications of his tramphood, the Tramp has ascended to his highest heights as a hero, in his romantic, self-sacrificing saintliness. For in his final gaze is not the expectation of the hopeful lover, or the thrill of acceptance which has meant so much to him in the past, but the joyfulness of the believer whose faith is vindicated. In this way he attains dignity, and triumphs over the humiliation and shame of his situation, over the perverse and nonsensical gear-shiftings of the Drunk, over all the material forces which bring him low and oppress him, over the cruel taunting of the newsboys. In his pure adoration and delight at her sight he is beyond the subterfuges of before — through his sacrifice he has given sight to the blind, has given meaning to a meaningless world. The Tramp is Christ.

It is the highest moment of Chaplin's art. His rescue of the child in *The Kid* had been the most outright emotional moment in his work, and is a great sequence of filmmaking; but this is more open-ended and nuanced, more consciously controlled. The great revolution he had brought to film comedy from the time of his earliest Keystones— the emphasis on character and attitude and subtlety —comes to full flower in these final moments. They contain some of his greatest acting, and perhaps some of the greatest acting anyone ever did in any film. If Virginia Cherrill was so inexperienced as an actress that Chaplin had to school her and drill her extensively for every scene, it was worth every minute, for she is excellent throughout, giving the best performance of all of Chaplin's heroines; her performance in this final scene is note-perfect and extremely moving.

The implications of all the various facets of the plot of *City Lights* make it one of Chaplin's greatest instinctual creations, a shining display of his great genius at devising evocative situations which touch on great truths: the Tramp is accepted by the Drunk only because of the latter's alcoholism, the Tramp is accepted by the flower girl only because of her blindness. The Drunk is suicidal, the girl is in peril, and the Tramp flits between the two of them like a ghost. The injustice and accepted misery of the city, the stark helplessness of the Tramp's situation and of all the powerless, are redeemed and given meaning by the Tramp's final smile. The tragic and pitiless city is redeemed by his vision of beauty which floats above it like a vapor. It is here also that the Tramp comes to the apotheosis of his gallant, heroic, romantic visions— it is here that he is redeemed.

If *The Kid* was Chaplin's masterpiece of emotion, and *The Gold Rush* is his masterpiece of ambition, *City Lights* is his masterpiece of refinement. It is here that he shows to the highest degree his mastery in focusing so much emotion — and so many kinds of emotion — into one situation, and molding it with great skill to articulate his singular, inimitable vision. The final scene is his highest achievement in cinematic poetry.

12

Modern Times

The Tramp began as a violent, coarse little man. His most salient characteristics were kicking, punching, and thumbing his nose at people. With time, he became a slightly more gentle character, but still unpredictable in his sudden attacks of viciousness. He became a more surreal character as well: his frequent displays of his magical gift of transformation — of himself as well as of objects and other people — and his supernatural grace and skill, his ingenuity, made him more magnetic. He was a metaphysical anarchist breaking all previously known universal laws, and his dispensing of his enemies made him almost a Superman in comparison with them. As Chaplin moved into larger forms, this idea of the Tramp as an exceptional being frenetic with imaginative energy was tamped down a bit, so that Charlie became a more sympathetic, romantic figure. He still stuns us with a spontaneous display of grace, but he is often at the mercy of physical reality as well. He'll certainly deliver a kick in the pants if one is called for, but generally he's just trying to get along. He is the Little Fellow, the Everyman.

It's important to note of this final incarnation of The Tramp, as seen in these last four films, that as genteel as he has become, he is still a tramp. As Buster Keaton, Chaplin's peer, noted, "Charlie's tramp was a bum with a bum philosophy. Lovable as he was he would steal if he got the chance." Charlie hasn't got a problem with eating the baby's hot dog in *The Circus*, and he isn't above loitering around a store window so he can examine a nude statue in *City Lights*. As well, the Tramp remains a radical revolutionary, for his presence invariably stimulates societal upheaval in some form. He is still breaking laws, but on a more sublime level. He may perform his magic tricks which leave us in awe, but he also has romantic yearnings for love, home, acceptance, which we share and empathize with. He is an amalgam of all the characteristics of the Tramp since his inception. But his most primary characteristic is that he is outside of whatever society he is in. He is also the least member of his society. It is in his inability to conform to this lesser role, in his constant transcending of it through his uniqueness, through his inimitable singular embodiment of what seems to be the very spirit of creativity itself, that makes him still an artist, an anarchist, a rebel, who must cause upheaval in any society he passes through. He has nothing, lives nowhere, is loved by no one, yet in the end, if only for a moment, he rules over all creation.

Make no mistake, no matter how low the Tramp may become, no matter how ridiculed he may be by the world around him on occasion, he is always in firm possession, though he may lose all else, of his dignity. The Tramp may cause problems through misapprehension at times, and he may find himself the victim of cruel and perverse fate, but he is no fool. He is simply too alive to be confined by the rules of society. His preposterous situations arise from his helpless inability to conform — as in his botched rehearsal with the clown troupe in *The Circus.* He is both blessed and cursed by his tremendous life energy, which sends him ricocheting through the world like a mad champagne cork and keeps him always alone. Neither stupid or bumbling — as many clowns are — he is simply so completely unique that he is as far from the other characters in the films, and from us, as one of an alien species from another planet might be. He roams the earth in eternal solitude, his boots jutting out to either side as he waddles.

His is the language of facial expression and gesture, of the shoulder shrug, the mustache twitch, the delicate hand gesture. His body is a tool of expression as fluent and fluid as the pen of any poet. He is a dancer, an athlete, a musketeer. At times he is almost like more of a pleasing geometric shape than a human being. His is a world of silence more expressive than the sum total of all language, and his nonverbal communication bypasses our conscious minds entirely — it goes straight into, and finds communion with, the wordless knowing whose understanding is at once intuitive and visceral, existing long before the creation of the Tower of Babel.

The Tramp's arrival as the world's most famous symbol of laughter coincided with a war exploding across Europe, a war of a magnitude that had never been seen before. Following the war had been a time of economic prosperity and indulgence — Chaplin commented upon these, consciously or unconsciously, in *A Woman of Paris* and *The Gold Rush*, two films concerned with riches, their attainment and their effects. The prosperity came to a sudden end with the Great Depression, an event which threw millions out of work as the economic system crashed, and North American society found itself vulnerable, stumbling to regain its balance. There were riots, strikes, shantytowns of the homeless, unrest — and it seemed to some that the answer to the economic dysfunction was communism.

Coinciding with the Depression was the arrival of sound in the motion picture industry. Chaplin had proved his aesthetic decision to ignore sound to be correct with the production of *City Lights*, an undisputed masterpiece. At the time of the film's release, he claimed to believe that sound was a mere novelty or fad, which would eventually disappear: "I give it another three years," he said.[2] At the time he made the statement, sound films had already been customary for three years.

His denial regarding sound was understandable, considering that he knew that this revolution in his medium meant the end of the Tramp. There was no necessity for the Tramp to speak, and so sound would inevitably be a violation of his artistic essence — the ingenious and energetic manner by which he expressed himself so completely and so precisely in a universal, primal language would be lost. The arrival of sound was an artistic and professional crisis for Chaplin: it brought upon him fears of being thought of as old-fashioned, and he would even later ascribe his increasing involvement in political matters to his "irritation" at the coming of sound.[3] His involvement in politics would end with his being effectively barred from America, twenty years in the future.

There was pressure from the industry and from the public for Chaplin to succumb to the talkies. His next film, coming five years after *City Lights*, is Chapin's answer to the pressure. He has faced the inevitable, and in the appropriately titled *Modern Times* he completes the legend of the Tramp — he finishes him off and puts him to rest. *Modern Times* is a sound film with a silent film aesthetic in the same manner as *City Lights* had been, with a Chaplin-composed score and appropriate sound effects. But here, as there had not been in *City Lights*, are words and human voices explaining and propelling the action — and they are not the kazoo-like squawks as heard in the opening moments of the earlier film. As well, in the film's final ten minutes, for the first and final time we hear the Tramp's voice, and the sound of his oversized shoes padding the ground. If the modernity of the times must insist upon the death of the Tramp and the death of the Tramp's world, Chaplin faces the reality bravely, making that very cruel result of "progress" the point of his new film — and affirming again the Tramp's humanity and ingenuity in triumphing even over that which announces his obsolescence.

Along with the unemployment, the strikes and riots of this new age, Chaplin had become aware of the gruesome byproduct of another technological advance: he had heard stories of the Ford plant in Michigan, of how the assembly lines first adopted in 1915 took strapping young farm boys and turned them into nervous wrecks through the repetitive and strenuous work they were subjected to in the factory.[4] This dehumanizing labor made a deep impact on the comedian; to him it represented the dawn of a new, "modern" age, less hospitable to human individuality. For as the assembly line presented a series of identical parts to be fastened in an identical fashion in order to make a series of products in which one was seamlessly identical to the others, it seemed to demand of its workers an identicality, a conformity of movement and mind which paralleled the uniformity of the products of mass production. Looking into the future, Chaplin saw a crass, dehumanized sameness as a result of this supremacy of the machine which might have brought to mind the brutal damage the arrival of sound signaled for his art. He would always say he found the silent medium to be more poetic, the implication being that the new, modern innovation, sound, which had taken over his art was inevitably less poetic, more prosaic and crass.

Modern Times begins with the title: "A story of industry, of individual enterprise — humanity crusading in the pursuit of happiness." We are then shown sheep rushing feverishly through a gate; this dissolves to an image of people rushing furiously out of a subway terminal, on their way to work in the factory. Chaplin has injected social commentary into his films in the past, and in one sense it can be said that it has been at the heart of all his work. We have seen the tableau of the slave pulling the boss on his wagon up the impossibly steep hill in *Work*, and we have seen the crowd of immigrants staring up at the promise of the Statue of Liberty before being roughly pushed back by the authorities in *The Immigrant*. But this, as the opening shot of the film which sets the tone for all that comes after, is far more blunt and explicit in its diagnosis than anything seen previously — "industry," "enterprise," "modernity" in Chaplin's assessment, were turning humanity into a flock of sheep, who were rushing mindlessly, madly, to their own slaughter.

This is soon expanded on, as the workers flood into a futuristic factory — actually described as a steel mill in the film — and take their places on the endless assembly lines, amongst the demonically turning cogs and gears. The mechanical monstrosity is presided over by its laconic president, who, when not amusing himself by putting together jigsaw puzzles or reading the funny papers, checks up on his workers via closed circuit television and barks at them, with real words we can hear: "Increase the speed! Keep it moving!" Among the uniformly harried workers is the Tramp, feverishly tightening the bolts on an infinity of nameless steel devices. He has suffered in his occupations of the past, from his oppression in *Work* through his employment in the service of an array of sociopathic bosses. But his situation here is far more insidious and malevolent. He is made into a helplessly jerking, spastic automaton by the repetitive demands of his duties. However fast he tightens the bolts it is never enough — he's hectored to increase the speed. When he escapes to the washroom for a smoke, an immense screen appears on the wall and the face of the president shouts: "Back to work!" Lunchtime offers no respite — that's when the management has decided to try out its new time-saving device: a machine to feed the employees while they work. The Tramp is strapped into the machine, which goes berserk, shoving food down his throat, mashing it into his face. At one point the machine throws that old Keystone standby into his face — a pie — to show just how far automation has come.

As we anticipate, the Tramp cannot be the Tramp and continue to suffer such abuse so ignominiously. It is perhaps telling, though, that in the earlier films he was able to assert his dignity by a mere thumb of the nose or a kick in the chest — here, his only recourse is to go mad. He breaks from the assembly line to go on a lunatic rampage, sabotaging the factory and its workers, turning all the controls of the machinery the wrong way, spraying oil into his fellow employees' faces. The most notable aspect of his free-for-all is the fact that it is a dance, so important as a form by which the Tramp has transformed banal, dismal reality in the past into awe-awakening transcendence; it is a mad ballet in which the Tramp breaks from the uniformity, conformity, and the crazed inhumanity of modern life. His irrepressible individuality comes bursting out, sending the system which confines him into disarray. He is packed off to a sanitarium.

The factory set is the most elaborate and impressive prop Chaplin has yet gifted himself with, and this first scene is one of his most inspired and iconic. He has done battle with demonic mechanisms in earlier films — most notably the wicked folding bed of *One A.M.* But there can be little doubt as he slides slickly through the innards of the machinery here that this is something new and far more ominous than the affronts of the past.

He's released from the sanitarium. Ambling down the street, he helpfully picks up a flag which has fallen from a truckload of lumber — he walks after the truck, calling to it. A parade of marchers calling for "Liberty" rounds the corner behind him, and follows him as he waves the flag. Police on horseback arrive, break up the march and arrest him as a "communist leader." He's taken to jail.

At his point we are introduced to a "Gamin," a street urchin played by Paulette Goddard — Chaplin's wife at the time. She is seen stealing bananas from a boat, and is introduced as "one who refuses to go hungry," announcing a theme which persists throughout the film — the perception that one is driven by necessity to theft. The Tramp, of course, has always stolen. But never before has theft been so clearly linked to oppression, and affirmed as being the only manner by which one can survive and maintain one's dignity in a brutal world of deprivation and unrest.

The Gamin's father is identified as "one of the unemployed." She also has three younger sisters. When the father is killed in what appears to be a labor dispute, the officials arrive to take the Gamin's siblings off to the orphanage — but she escapes.

Charlie has meanwhile settled into a happy routine in his jail cell, amiably relaxing and chatting with his guards; after reading of the strikes and riots and breadlines in the wicked world outside, he tosses away his newspaper with the philosophic shrug of the upper class gentlemen apprised of trouble with the peasants. At mealtime, however, the Tramp unknowingly spreads some smuggled cocaine on his food, and after eating it, in the manner of his drug injection in *Easy Street*, he becomes a wild-eyed dynamo. His manic exuberance foils a prison break — unfortunately for him, since he is given his release as a result. "Can't I stay a little longer?" he asks. "I'm so happy here."

On the street, the Tramp makes the acquaintance of the Gamin — she is on the run after stealing a loaf of bread, and she collides with him. When the police arrive, he is only too happy to take blame for stealing the bread himself, anticipating his readmission to jail. A woman bystander approaches and identifies the Gamin as the thief, however, much to the Tramp's chagrin. Purposefully, he strides off and orders a sizable meal in a cafeteria; when presented with the bill, he nonchalantly beckons a policeman in from the street. To his delight, he cop seizes him and throws him into a paddy wagon. Inside the wagon, Charlie meets the Gamin once more — he tips his hat and offers his seat to her. She suddenly makes a run for it, pushing past the cop at the back door of the wagon, as it swerves and casts the Tramp, the Gamin and the cop out onto the pavement. The policeman is unconscious — the Gamin runs off, pausing to call to Charlie, inviting him to come with her. After a moment's hesitation, he follows.

The Gamin is unlike any of Chaplin's other heroines. She is more akin to the child in *The Kid*, as she is a younger mirror image of the Tramp. Their relationship is that of comrades, rather than potential lovers: when they move in together, Chaplin takes care to show that their relationship is chaste — the Tramp is seen sleeping in a piano crate outside of the shack while the Gamin sleeps within. She is wild and desperate and free, like the early Tramp, and her presence revivifies Charlie, reconnects him to those anarchic roots. If the Tramp has been so oppressed by the modern world that he has become convinced that jail is the only livable place, the Gamin beckons to him, calls him to the treacherous freedom beyond the machines and the billy clubs.

They scurry off to the suburbs; resting beneath a tree, they observe a happy husband and wife parting for the day, the husband scampering off energetically to work, his spouse ecstatically summoning him back for another good-bye kiss, then skipping cheerfully into the house. In a small flurry of pantomime which in itself would make the whole film worthwhile, Charlie mocks the banal contentment of the suburban couple, but their happiness causes the Tramp and the Gamin to envision their own dream home. It is the last and one of the finest of Charlie's visions of Paradise — a dream sequence which allows him to soar from his barren reality into the essence of the ideals which inspire him. His vision of "home," that much-desired ideal which has so eluded him, is a place where oranges hang from branches accommodatingly leaning into one's window, where if the lion does not exactly lie down with the lamb, the cow comes to spurt its milk into a pitcher without need of assistance in the matter. The dream is accompanied here by eerie, otherworldly music, and when it ends, as it must, hurling the dreamers back into their hungry, pitiless world, Charlie is inspired: "We'll get a home even if I have to work for it!"

He finds employment replacing an injured night watchman at a department store. The first order of his new occupation is to let the Gamin in, so they can feast on the food and avail themselves of the luxuries offered by the store. They gambol up to the toy department, where Charlie straps on a pair of skates and glides with effortless, uncanny grace across the floor — and provides a thrill-chill sequence when, blindfolded and showing off, he skirts along the edge of an unprotected balustrade. Later, thieves break into the store, brandishing a gun at him and yelling "Freeze!" — but the poor Tramp finds himself stuck on an escalator, his roller skates making it impossible to accede to their demands.

Critics have noted the episodic structure of *Modern Times*, claiming that it is nothing more than a series of two-reelers stuck together. This viewpoint has merit, but the structure of the film matches its content in that the story it tells — of downtrodden misfits trying to survive in a world wracked with unemployment and social chaos — necessarily insists upon an episodic structure, as the wanderers drift from place to place in their search for home and sustenance. Along with the humiliation and deprivation poverty bequeaths to its sufferers is just this very sense of instability and unpredictability, this lack of security and no rest from the terrors which pursue them.

This, by coincidence — or perhaps not by coincidence — is the same world the Tramp had last known in his two-reelers, those short immersions in jobs and situations which ended in disaster and escape — the world out of which the Tramp had been born. And this world was not much different than the "episodic" life Chaplin and his mother had known in London, as they ventured from one claustrophobic rented room to another — compared by Chaplin in his autobiography to the movements of "a game of draughts" [checkers].[5] In Charlie's resourceful diligence to get himself recommitted to jail, we can see some of Hannah's determination in getting herself and her sons discharged from the workhouse in order to have a day of freedom in the park, before getting them all readmitted to the workhouse again. Throughout the film, Charlie's constant admissions to and discharges from jail parallel the same peripatetic existence Chaplin knew as a child, when he and his brother were put into, and yanked out of, workhouses on a regular basis.

All of which is to say that *Modern Times* mirrors the world of the unsettled and poverty-stricken, and that Chaplin knew whereof he spoke on the matter. But as importantly, the film also mirrors and recreates the world of his finest two-reelers: we have seen the remembrance of *Easy Street* in Charlie's drug-inspired heroism in the jail; and now we have, for all to see, the opportunity for the Tramp to display his magical roller skating abilities as he had done in *The Rink* twenty years earlier; there is also the use of an escalator as a prop, bringing to mind *The Floorwalker*. In his final look back at the world of the Tramp, Chaplin tellingly evokes some of the high points of his Mutual films, the works which, to this writer's mind, best represent Chaplin's genius for pure, unfettered, inspired clownery. These scenes, and *Modern Times* as whole, are a warm, affectionate last look back at the world of the Tramp, a summing up and acknowledgment of all that Charlie has known and experienced and which has brought him to his present point — and which has brought Chaplin here, too. They are a celebration of all that the Tramp is — and a farewell to it all.

This is made explicit by the scene which occurs after the factory has reopened. The Tramp rushes to get a job there and is employed as an mechanic's assistant — under Chaplin's old Keystone comrade, the fellow he once described as "the funniest man in the world," Chester Conklin. The stoic Conklin performs a gentle routine with Charlie, in which the Tramp inadvertently flattens several of Conklin's possessions in the factory's machinery, then somehow gets Conklin himself swallowed by the hungry cogs and gears, his head sticking out of the metallic guts of the mechanical behemoth. Unable to extricate him, Charlie thoughtfully feeds Chester's lunch to him.

If any more proof were needed that these scenes are Chaplin's tribute to his free, slapstick sketch–oriented past, we need only look at the prevalence of swallowing and digestion which takes place in *Modern Times*—if these have been longtime obsessions for Chaplin, they come to full flower here. Certainly the emphasis on survival would guarantee a certain fixation with food consumption, but here we have Charlie being fed by the out-of-control feeding machine; then we have Charlie himself being fed into a machine; then we have the clever sound gag of the grumbling stomachs when the minister's wife visits in the prison; then Charlie's leisurely lunch in the cafeteria in his attempt to revisit jail; the ongoing stealing of various food products by the Gamin; Charlie's customary haughty disgust at the slovenly bum's odious belches in the paddy wagon; poor Chester Conklin being fed into a machine; then Charlie helpfully feeding Chester in the machine — with the odd gag of using a fried chicken to "funnel" coffee into Conklin's mouth; and the roast duck which Charlie delivers as a hapless waiter in the final reel. The Chaplin obsession with mastication, digestion and excretion has come to its apex at last.

In amongst all the time-honored, vulgar slapstick foolishness is the social commentary of the film, which has also come under criticism through the years. Some reviewers at the time discerned communistic leanings in the film — others took offense that Chaplin make any kind of political statement at all, however vague. The sentiment is understandable, given that Chaplin the man had become by this time a celebrity of such status that his off-screen persona rivaled the character of the Tramp as being the public's prime perception of him. At the time of *Modern Times* he had been an international celebrity for twenty years, and one who had recently become given to making public pronouncements on the state of the world, as well as authoring a comprehensive plan for hoisting Western civilization out of the Depression — an "Economic Solution," as he called it,[6] reflecting his growing interest in the subject. So it is not unreasonable that critics of the time looked to his film for political messages.

At the same time, Chaplin's art has always touched upon subjects of solemnity and import — and tragedy. It was part of his genius to enlarge the scope of slapstick comedy to include such things, and as he had used the Great War as the subject of *Shoulder Arms*, so he utilizes the unrest and deprivation of the Great Depression here. The social satire which has always been strong in his work comes to the fore most noticeably in the opening shot of the sheep, and in the scenes following, with the funny-paper–reading factory president and his furiously working employees. It is certainly possible to see the workers as victims of profit, of capitalism, to see the pitilessly grinding gears of the machinery as the crazed, nihilistic workings of a civilization determined to sacrifice human lives to the god of money, much like Allen Ginsberg's later vision of Moloch. But beyond this is also a message of the unavoidable destruction of the human sprit such a system guarantees, a consideration which is beyond mere politics. Chaplin is depicting a reality in which machines, once created to be the servants of humanity, have become the masters—and destroyers—of human beings. Work, a recurring motif in Chaplin's films, has become bereft of dignity, as it insists upon dehumanization.

The world outside is even worse — a chaos of breadlines and riots, so fearsome that the Tramp elects to stay in jail. He only gains the courage to face reality with the inspiration of the Gamin, who awakens the adventurer in him again. What's notable is that the old concerns of the Tramp are present here, but in the context of the new social bleakness he portrays they are charged with new, more ferocious implications. The Tramp has always shown the inclination to steal if the need should arise, but here theft is seen as a necessity, as the only way to reclaim one's dignity and survive. The Gamin steals because she refuses to go hungry, and among the thieves which break into the department store is Charlie's old co-worker at the factory (Stanley "Tiny" Sanford), who exclaims to the Tramp, "We ain't burglars—we're hungry!" before briefly, and movingly, bursting into tears. In Chaplin's estimation, the world had so changed that the mischievous thievery of the early Tramp was now desperate and mandatory.

As well, the Tramp's old bugaboo, the police, are depicted in a more harsh, bitter manner than has been seen before. They have always naturally represented society's authority, ever bullying, ever pursuing the unfortunate Tramp. But the neighborhood cops in the old "park" comedies, and even the police in *The Kid*, have more humanity than the constables depicted here, who are more like goons whose only responsibility is protecting property and cracking down on dissenters—as seen in their breaking up of the protest march, and in their rough treatment of the strikers later in the film. They are more like soldiers in a war that society has declared on its citizens.

As always, no matter how harsh the world is depicted in Chaplin's films— and the harshness here, though more organized and ominous than in the earlier works, is not vastly more intense than that which has been known before—the real focus is the effect of that harshness on the Tramp, the least personage of his society. Chaplin displays that his concern for the plight of the powerless within the corrupt system is more primary than his desire to create political propaganda against that system when he ends Charlie's and Chester's short term of employment in the latter part of the film with the two men being told to get their coats because they're "on strike." The Tramp and his friend stand scratching their heads quizzically—they are buffeted and manipulated, twisted and displaced by forces far beyond their comprehension; forces which are, in fact, absurd and irrational, which can only be survived with a herculean strength of will—with ingenuity, cunning, and imagination.

This, of course, has always been the message of the Tramp, and in his representation of humanity in an increasingly inhuman world, we see here that his simple retainment of humanity has become heroic. Chaplin seems to be saying that the Tramp must go because there is no longer a place in the world for him to exist even in the meager sense he has existed in the past. Technology, we are told, has made society crueler, has made people into a herd of conformist automatons—only thieves and outlaws such as the Gamin are free.

Technology has also introduced sound to film, invading and destroying Chaplin's artistic world as surely as mechanization and greed were destroying the last vestiges of the human, quasi–Victorian world in which the Tramp could at least find occasional respite and shelter.

It is the final act of *Modern Times* in which the Tramp is put to rest. Knowing how momentous the occasion of Charlie's first spoken words was, and knowing that in that instant he spoke the Tramp would begin his curtain call, Chaplin placed the historical event in the last reel; he throws it to the audience as a parting, obligatory gift. As noted, sound has been used in *Modern Times* in a more intensive manner than had been the case in *City Lights*, with human voices featured for the first time on the soundtrack, so we have been prepared for the fateful moment of Charlie's breaking his silence. During one of the Tramp's stints in jail the Gamin has secured a job as a dancer at a café (she was discovered dancing on the street, in a scene reminiscent of the perhaps apocryphal tale of the young Chaplin being discovered in the same manner as a youth). On Charlie's release, the Gamin secures him a job at the café as a singing waiter. Soon the moment comes for his debut; he is unable to remember the lyrics to his song so she writes them on his cuff. In the opening flourishes of his dance, his cuffs fly off. He is forced to improvise nonsensical sounds to the music.

Upon his entry into the café, Charlie for the first time is in our world, no longer part of that higher order of ghostly grace and dreamlike poise—we see him move in real time, we hear his shoes scrape along the ground, we know that he is now mortal like us, now subject, like us, to the laws of gravity and decay. It is here he begins his decline. He is no longer the angelic sprite but a man performing a music hall turn, executing a comic song in much the same manner as Chaplin's own father did to success on the stage of the British music hall.

But Chaplin fools us again here, for Charlie's song, the words he sings, are not of our world, they do not relate to any readily translatable meaning—rather his vaudeville turn is a performance piece on how utterly meaningless, superfluous language and sound are. Chaplin knows there is no meaning which the Tramp could express in words which he cannot express a thousandfold better in movement. And so he has the final laugh, for the noises the Tramp makes—a bizarre mixture of vaguely French and Italian-sounding syllables which just might be the official language of an alien race existing in the far corner of the next solar system — are merely the accompaniment and the backdrop, as all else in Chaplin's films are, for the main event, as has always been the case: the magic fluency of the Tramp's—of Chaplin's—gestures and expressions. Through these, he gives us a little movie within the movie: a man spies a pretty young thing on the street; he entices her with his ring, offers her a ride in his car; she acquiesces, but when he tries to get fresh, insists upon receipt of the ring; she receives it, they make love, and she dances off ... a tale as old as time itself and given new life as expressed through the Tramp's body.

The Tramp's improvised song and dance meet with success, and he embraces the Gamin happily. But now that he has been contaminated by sound, Charlie must go. The authorities from earlier in the film arrive at the cafe to arrest the Gamin; the Tramp helps her to escape. They run to the outskirts of the city, and rest a moment by the side of the road at dawn; another potential home for them has been lost. The Gamin starts to cry: "What's the use of trying?" she asks bitterly. The Tramp consoles her: "Buck up! Never say die — We'll get along!" he tells her. They get up and she takes his arm, heartened, regaining her determination. They walk resolutely away from us, off a winding road, into the future.

If Chaplin has sounded the death knell for the Tramp in allowing sound to invade his domain, so now he finishes the job by retrieving him from the existential solitude of his most iconic image — the trip down the endless road is now made with a companion, so that there is no need for the little shaking off of care as he disappears from view. This is as it should be: it would have been unfathomably tragic to have Charlie depart from us in the utter loneliness which has always defined him — even for a tragedian like Chaplin, there are limits. He extends a gracious generosity to his creation by allowing him, finally, a companion and helpmeet for the long struggle ahead. For ultimately, Chaplin's message, beyond politics and social issues, is of the importance of the very human need for acceptance and understanding, the need for simple encouragement to bear the burden of existence at the very moment it seems most unbearable. The Tramp has always embodied persistence and determination, and in a world growing ever more cruel and unstable, we see that he continues, and will continue, to make his stand.

Chaplin's generosity in finally ending the Tramp's solitude is also seen in his manner of bidding good-bye to the Tramp's world—for as relevant to the study of assembly line production in the early twentieth century as it is, or to Depression-era labor issues, the structure of *Modern Times* provides the space for Chaplin to enjoy some of the lighthearted freedom that he had known in the shorts which had catapulted him to fame. Unencumbered by the romantic wistfulness, pathos, or self-consciousness seen in his last three features, Chaplin's performance as the Tramp here is one of his most playful and energetic.

With admirable bravery he has faced up to the end of his era, and he has given it a fine finale which not only looks back, but looks ahead: the more blatant social commentary here will form the basis for his next two films, and the sound, while artfully used at some points—the Tramp's song, and the routine in which both the Tramp and the reverend's wife at the jail suffer from loud indigestion—is, as it will be in the future, used less well at others—the gimmick of playing a phonograph record to explain the feeding machine is awkward, and the lengthy explanation itself is, as will be the case with the use of dialogue in the future features, over-elaborate, serving only to slow the film down. Even in a film which is the summation of an era, there is much that is new and experimental, and as per its title, *Modern Times* remains one of Chaplin's freshest films, and the one of which it can be said has the most "modern" sensibility. It is also perhaps his best-looking film, and boasts some of his finest music. As much of a tribute to the past as it is, as much of an indictment of a harsh and maniacal world as it is, it is in the end, like the Tramp's final exhortation before taking to that endless road ahead, an expression of hope and confidence, even as we, along with the Tramp and his pal, advance into an unknown, ominous, calamitous future.

13

The Great Dictator

Adolf Hitler was born in Braunau am Inn, Austria, exactly four days after Charlie Chaplin was born, April 20, 1889. In contrast to the poverty stricken, perilous childhood Chaplin knew, Hitler was the child of middle-class parents. As the young Chaplin became a child actor and dancer, Hitler too dreamed of becoming an artist. Hitler applied to the Vienna Academy of Fine Arts with his artistically mediocre, spiritually barren paintings. He was rejected by the school twice, and after his second rejection in 1908 — the same year that Chaplin signed with Karno and entered the "school" in which he received training in his art — Hitler, bitter, furious, and distraught by his mother's recent death, drifted into the street life of Vienna, becoming a homeless dropout. He was a tramp, living in hostels and hanging around soup kitchens and cafes, for five years. For a transient, he was quite garrulous, haranguing anyone near him about politics; he was embittered at bourgeois society, and later he would identify this period as the beginning of his fanatical anti–Semitism. He began to seek release from his own feeling of failure and mediocrity by focusing blame and hatred on the Jews.

The world war came: Hitler fled from Vienna to Munich, and joined up with the Bavarian army. He found a place where he finally fit in, and later remembered the war as the greatest time of his life.[1] In the same year that Chaplin rocketed to fame via the rapid release of his Keystone films, Hitler won the first of two Iron Crosses for bravery. Four years later as the war was ending, Chaplin sent his Tramp into battle in *Shoulder Arms*; rather than being struck by the piece of limburger cheese Charlie threw from his trench, Hitler was felled by a poison gas attack, and during his three-month recuperation, the unthinkable (for him) happened — Germany capitulated and Armistice was declared.

Overwhelmed by the shame of Germany's humiliating defeat, Hitler returned to Munich, and shortly thereafter joined the German Workers' Party. Predictably, Hitler blamed Germany's loss on the Jews, whom he saw as the financiers of the war. He began addressing the party, which soon changed its name to the National Socialist German Workers' Party, and which adopted many of Hitler's ideas into its program; Hitler discovered he had a powerful talent for oration, and after several years was able to take over leadership of the party. From his first written political statement, he specified the "removal of Jews altogether"[2] as being the aim of a future nationalist government of Germany. Not only did he see the Jews as the orchestrators of worldwide capitalism; he also saw them as the exponents of Bolshevism in Russia[3]— this rather glaring contradiction seems not to have bothered Hitler or his growing legion of followers. His concept of Marxism as the political manifestation of Judaism figured heavily in his contention that Germany, in search of "lebensraum"[4]— living space — and economic expansion, was destined to invade and take over communist Russia. He began to see history as a racial struggle between what he termed "Jewish Bolshevism" and Western culture, which could only result in the destruction of one of these forces.[5] Conjoined with this was his conception of a superior German race, the Aryans, whose enemy was Judaism, as well as Hitler's adherence to a crude social Darwinism which saw war as the natural state of society.

Inspired by the fascist dictatorship of Benito Mussolini in Italy, Hitler conceived of himself as a leader, or Fuhrer figure. As Mussolini had marched on Rome to seize power, so Hitler marched on Munich with 3000 of his followers in a Putsch to take over the government. His action failed — he was arrested and put in jail for five months.[6] During this time he wrote *Mein Kampf* (My Struggle), articulating his worldview. By the time of his release, he had become a national figure. Aided by his future Minister of Propaganda, Joseph Goebbels, who strengthened the image of Hitler as a messianic leader, Hitler gained notoriety, and if in the elections of 1928 the Nazis were able to take only 2.6% of the vote, by 1933 they were able to take control of the government, chiefly due to the onset of the Depression and the resultant instability.[7]

Hitler's ideas, aside from being illogical and irrational, were not even very original. Anti-Semitism had been rife throughout Austria and Germany, and the concept of a German "master race" had been written about years ago. It was Hitler's obsessive joining together of these ideas in order to form his all-encompassing sterile and crude vision, and his fanatical dedication to that vision, along with his ability to convey his absolute emotional commitment to others, which drew his followers to him. For it was not merely ideas he articulated — in his frenzied, vituperative speaking style, he had the ability, as Chaplin had, to convey emotional truths emphatically, beyond the power of mere words. "False ideas and ignorance may be set aside by means of instruction," Hitler would note, "but emotional resistance never can. Nothing but an appeal to hidden forces will be effective here."[8] In this, Hitler can be said to have found his true "art" and to have excelled at it.

As it can be said that Chaplin's great success, beyond his supreme talent as a clown, was due to his being able to divine, intuitively, the zeitgeist of his time, and to express it, the same can be said for Hitler's popularity in Germany. But where Chaplin had gained favor through his brilliance in depicting the spirited adventures of the "least" one of society, and his ultimate triumph, Hitler presented the Darwinistic Nazi philosophy "which promotes the better and the stronger and demand(s) the subordination of the inferior and the weaker in accordance with the eternal will that dominates the universe."[9]

In his histrionics Hitler expressed the fury of a country humiliated by war and by the punitive debts leveled on it by the rest of the world as a result of that war; his fervent cries for national pride and unity spoke to an unstable country reeling from the Depression. It was the phlegmatic rage and unashamed, unhinged emotionalism of Hitler's speeches which caught the attention of Chaplin and caused him to remark that Hitler was "one of the greatest actors I've ever seen."[10]

Along with his incendiary speaking style and Goebbels' stage management of his image, Hitler was aided by his iconic appearance. It would seem that it was in the immediate years after the war that Hitler trimmed the handlebar mustache he had worn up till then, adopting the more truncated facial hair which he could not have failed to realize was identical to that worn by the most famous comedian in the world at the time. This alteration in personal grooming was certainly beneficial for it coincided with Hitler's "finding himself" by joining the German Workers' Party. The minute mustache gave Hitler, as it had given the Tramp, a central focal point on his face, to which the eye was unavoidably drawn. With demonic brilliance, Hitler seized upon the world's premier symbol of mirth and healing laughter and harnessed its power in the service of his vision of rage and destruction.

True to his word, Hitler was not long in acting upon much of what he had laid out in *Mein Kampf*. From the boycotting of Jewish shops in 1933 to the nationwide attack on Jewish persons and property that was the "Kristall-nacht"—the night of the breaking glass—in 1938, and subsequent incarceration of Jews in concentration camps, Hitler carried out his barbaric, brutal mission. The world watched in a sort of stunned, paralytic horror as his troops marched into Austria, then Czechoslovakia, then Poland...

Like many, Chaplin watched from afar with a rising dread, and appalled fascination—he saw that Hitler was a deranged grotesque, even "obscenely comic,"[11] until one realized the consequences of his jabbering oratories—Chaplin remembered that his first impression of Hitler was that he was "a bad imitation of me."[12] It was the director Alexander Korda who had first suggested that Chaplin do a parody of Hitler, based on mistaken identity resulting from the similarity of appearance between the world's greatest bringer of laughter and the world's greatest bringer of misery.[13] Chaplin seized on the idea as being a perfect way to introduce himself into sound films—as "Hitler" he could speak as much as he wanted to, and as the Tramp—or the "Jewish Barber" he made the Tramp into for the sake of contrast—he could remain silent. Along with this was undoubtedly a bit of show business ego, for it was likely not lost on Chaplin that the mediocre Hitler had stolen his image just as the coming of sound films had rendered the Tramp artistically obsolete: Hitler had appropriated the "look" which Chaplin had used to communicate so many truths about humanity in the early part of the century, and was now using it to communicate newer, darker truths about humanity as the mid-century approached. It made perfect sense that Chaplin would want to reclaim his image from the new, repellent meaning Hitler had invested it with; in what is perhaps an apocryphal story, the screenwriter Garson Kanin, after the premiere of *The Great Dictator*, asked Chaplin why, in his burlesque of Hitler, he had not flattened and combed his hair to match the Fuhrer's. "Well, God damn it!... why should I?" Chaplin replied, "I was using that makeup before *he* was!"[14]

As well, Chaplin was disturbed by Hitler's invective against the Jews at a time when many were effecting a disinterested neutrality. Chaplin's wife at the time was Jewish, and Sydney, his brother, was half–Jewish; from his earliest successes Chaplin himself was often thought to be Jewish, a misapprehension he made a point of never correcting, for he felt that this would have played into the hands of anti–Semites—he'd actually been identified in Nazi propaganda as a "little Jewish acrobat, as disgusting as he is tedious."[15] He would later state that he made *The Great Dictator* "for the Jews of the world." Beyond this is the fact that whether Hitler had singled out Jews or any other race for persecution, "One doesn't have to be a Jew to be anti–Nazi," as Chaplin noted: "All one has to be is a normal decent human being."[16] Hitler was the face of the new, brutal inhumanity Chaplin saw taking over the world.

As always with Chaplin, perhaps his most compelling reason for making the film was simply that he was inspired as a clown by the prospect of lampooning Hitler. For from his unique perspective he could see that Hitler was not simply grotesque but absurd—and he saw the necessity of laughing at such a ludicrous, pathetic figure, of ridiculing his ideas which were certainly vile and immoral, but also preposterous. "I was determined to ridicule their mystic bilge about a pure-blooded race," he recounted.[17]

In making *The Great Dictator*, Chaplin was not simply creating a film, but, as his biographer David Robinson would note, bringing about "an epic incident in the history of mankind. The greatest clown and best-loved personality of his age directly challenged the man who had instigated more evil and human misery than any other in modern history."[18] It was felicitous that behind the interest and attention this incident demanded, the event of *The Great Dictator* being Chaplin's first all-sound-and-dialogue film was largely ignored—he was able to make his entry into the field with little scrutiny or fanfare.

The opening scenes of *The Great Dictator* display the pitfalls of sound for Chaplin's art, and give plenty of justification to Chaplin's avoidance of it until this time. The film opens during the First World War, with the ersatz "Tramp" character shambling about in uniform. If Chaplin had intended the Jewish Barber character as some sort of incarnation of the Tramp, he must have envisioned him as a watered-down, emasculated version so as to contrast with the far extreme of the other side of his character as represented by his "Hitler." The Barber is far too genial, gentle and subservient ever to be mistaken for the Tramp — his first spoken words are "Yes, sir." The sound of his voice, too, Winnie the Pooh–esque with clipped British enunciation, identifies him as a milquetoast, a meek little fellow, whereas the Tramp had never been identified as anything, or anyone, at any time. As the Barber shuffles about, pulling the chain on the Big Bertha super-cannon which is supposed to destroy Rheims Cathedral but succeeds only in pulverizing an outhouse, or ambling up to defuse a missile which turns and pursues him no matter which way he dashes, Chaplin proves his fears about sound were justified, for he had worried that once he spoke he'd be "just like any other comedian."[19] Truly, as he runs through the war gags at the beginning of the film, Chaplin could be Danny Kaye, Don Knotts, Martin Short, or any other clown — he's not the balletic magician anymore, but a fumbler and a stumbler, mumbling his apologies, surrendering to a gravity and a banality which possesses him absolutely. In order to spice things up in these sequences — and in later pantomime sequences involving the Barber — Chaplin makes use of undercranking, speeding up the action slightly so that it approximates the feel of the silent films. But the process which had given "oomph" to the action in the silent days only succeeds in being disorienting, and seeming dishonest, in the context of the sound world. Sound insists that the Tramp lives under the physical laws that all the rest of us live under — so he can't be the Tramp anymore. He doesn't transcend his situation but merely stumbles around like everyone else.

The Barber rescues a pilot (Reginald Gardiner) lying half-conscious beside his plane — he carries the pilot to his aircraft and they fly away. Chaplin here makes use of a clever gag by which the plane comes to fly upside-down, unbeknownst to the two soldiers; the Barber opens a canteen whose contents magically flow straight up, his pocket watch hovers at the end of its erect chain. In short order they crash, and the Barber is taken to the hospital, going into a coma for the next twenty years. In the interim, the war ends, the Depression comes, and a dictator named Adenoid Hynkel seizes power of Tomania, the Barber's homeland.

The first fifteen minutes of the film have been a display of the effect of sound on Chaplin's art — we see the uneasy relationship between his clowning and the dialogue, which often sounds obligatory, stilted, uncharacteristic. Chaplin's performance as a fifty year old man also emphasizes the more sedentary, passive nature of the Barber as compared to the heroic, dynamic Tramp. The Barber is lukewarm, an obliging little English peon, a far cry from the magical, mischievous sprite who autopsied the alarm clock in *The Pawnshop*.

With the introduction of Adenoid Hynkel, however, mid-flight in one of his furious, frenzied speeches, we are given something else entirely. Hynkel is an overflowing volcano of rage and hysteria — he howls a guttural spiel of German-sounding phrases and noises as he thrashes the air with his hands. His spasmic, feral outbursts are retched up from a place in his being which bypasses the mental process entirely — they are primal, biological, scatological, sexual — he must pause at one point and pour part of his glass of water down the front of his pants to cool himself off. Chaplin's performance as Hynkel here and throughout the film is a tour de force, one of his greatest performances of all, and certainly his greatest performance in a sound film. He is able to get around the arbitrary and limited "meaning" which dialogue implies by screeching his vaudevillian German doubletalk of utter gibberish — the result is sound without defined meaning, as was his gibberish song in *Modern Times*, Chaplin's most artistically appropriate use of sound and also the finest weapon by which to satirize the disturbing and disturbed speeches of Hitler as seen in the newsreels. The Hynkel speeches throughout the film are displays of Chaplin's greatest triumphs as a "sound" comedian — he pulls out every low comedy trick in order to ridicule this unhinged would-be usurper of his beloved mustache. What is most evident in his rabid gesticulations is the utter spiritual contempt Chaplin holds for Hitler, the disdain with which he mocks the coarse and vulgar blasphemy of existence at the heart of Hitler's philosophy.

Hynkel assaults his crowd with his thundering barrages of vociferation, alternating between teeth-gnashing expressions of hatred and shameless displays of maudlin schmaltz. As Hitler would frequently do in his speeches, Hynkel details and dramatizes his early years of struggle; as Hitler had his trusted Minster of Propaganda, Goebbels, and his fieldmaster Goering, so Hynkel has Garbitsch and Herring — the latter played beautifully by the great Billy Gilbert. "Garbitsch shouldn't smelten fine from Herring," Hynkel helpfully informs us, "and Herring shouldn't smelten fine from Garbitsch."

But it is when Hynkel speaks of "the Juden" that he becomes particularly animated: his nostrils flare, his eyes bulge, and he snorts like a pig. It is then when his hatred overcomes him completely, and he becomes rigid, almost paralytic with his vehement, deranged fury.

How banal, lackluster, and colorless is Chaplin's performance as the Barber, and how focused, brilliant and impassioned is his portrayal of Hynkel by contrast! The ease and power with which Chaplin embodies viciousness is, of course, no surprise to anyone who has witnessed the performances of his early career — now, after the last several films in which he has concentrated on the more romantic, poetic aspects of the Tramp, he has an opportunity to let the demonic savagery of which he is capable flow unimpeded once again. As well, it is simple fact that at this point in his career Chaplin had more in common with Hitler than with the Tramp. Chaplin and Hitler had both been "outsiders" who had lived on the street — "tramps" — and had attained positions of high prominence — certainly it could be said that Chaplin had "conquered the world" in his own chosen field. Chaplin reigned over his studio with the absolute power of a dictator, and his directing style was, to put it mildly, dictatorial — he acted out all the other performers' parts and insisted they perform them as he did, and he was known for flying into powerful rages when he worked. At this stage, he had spent as much a part of his life being a powerful, internationally famous man as he had spent as one of London's downtrodden unfortunates. After the last several films in which he had glorified, almost deified the penniless Tramp, he was able to guide his energy into this cathartic explosion of power-crazed insanity, which was closer to the truth of his own present life, and through which, by way of satirizing Hitler, he was able to reconnect with the more primal, rawer, sadistic roots of his art.

Hynkel completes his speech, and departs with Garbitsch; the latter feels that the presentation could have been a bit harsher on the Jews, to keep the populace's minds off their empty stomachs. We are taken to a Jewish ghetto, where a Mr. Jaeckel is commiserating with his associate about life under Hynkel; we are introduced to Jaeckel's boarder, Hannah, the female lead of the film, played by Paulette Goddard. The Nazi storm troopers conduct periodic raids on the ghetto, and they bully Hannah, throwing tomatoes at her. It is to this ghetto that the amnesiac Barber returns after emerging from his coma; he enters his barber shop, staring uncomprehendingly at the cobwebs and dust on his chair and mirrors. He becomes rather peeved with the storm troopers who come to paint "JEW" across the front of his window, and is roused to engage in a tussle which brings to mind the struggles with police of old — but here the Keystone Kops are Nazi storm troopers (some of them are even played by old Keystone Kops, such as Hank Mann, the boxer from *City Lights*). The Barber is aided in his scuffle by Hannah, who wields a frying pan from a window; she accidentally smashes it against the Barber's skull in her efforts, and he does a nimble, dazed dance down the street and back in semi-conscious reverie — before drifting into a lightheaded dance with a storm trooper who's been similarly afflicted, and sinking to the ground with him.

As brave and admirable as Chaplin was in drawing attention to the plight of the Jews under Hitler at the time, or even in depicting it at all, it is scenes like these that make *The Great Dictator* as much an oddity, or a historical document, as a comic film. There cannot help but be something eerie and strange about seeing slapstick intermingled with the barbaric horror that was life for the Jewish people in Hitler's Germany — particularly knowing, as we do now, how far Hitler would go in his hideous fanaticism. Chaplin would later note that he could never have made the film if he had known the full extent of the Nazi horrors.[20] The scenes in the ghetto are unsettling in all sorts of unintended ways — but they are unsettling for reasons which are entirely intentional as well, and the depictions of violent oppression are inevitably heavy with a darkness that the knockabout hijinks can't really balance out.

The Barber refuses to deface his own shop at the storm troopers' request — so they make ready to hang him. At this point the pilot the Barber had rescued during the war, now a corporal, comes by and saves the Barber from his fate. And from here, following the rhythm which defines the film, alternating with pendulum-like regularity between the ghetto and Hynkel's palace, a typical day of the "Phooey" is portrayed. Hynkel is a peevish, petulant, short-fused jack-ass who flies into rages as the slightest provocation as he goes about his business—recalcitrant pen holders infuriate him as much as the complaints from the concentration camps that the sawdust in their bread isn't of a higher quality. He speeds from room to room, from painters and sculptors who wait for two-minute snatches of time in which they can attempt to capture his heroic likeness, to demonstrations of new military gear by the intrepid Herring. A man is displayed wearing a collapsible parachute-hat. He leaps from the window, shouting "Heil Hynkel!," and Hynkel and Herring gaze down, following his silent descent. Turning from the window, Hynkel remarks witheringly: "Why do you waste my time like this, Herring?"

More pressing are the concerns articulated by the sleekly sinister Garbitsch, who warns that a new distraction is needed for the people. The much-anticipated invasion of neighboring Osterlich is picked as a likely candidate, but money must be borrowed to finance the enterprise. They seek to borrow the funds from a man named Epstein, a Jew, and so Hynkel resolves that all oppression of the Jews shall cease — at least until the loan is procured. Back in the ghetto, the Jews wonder at the sudden peace: when Hannah trips on the sidewalk, spilling her groceries, storm troopers help her up, assist her with her burden, and she wonders aloud if this is the way it will always be.

Paulette Goddard as Hannah is less effective here than in *Modern Times*, chiefly because her role is less a character than a symbol of the Jewish people under Hitler's persecution. Her too-earnest, too-contrived dialogue strikes a false note the like of which hasn't been heard before in Chaplin's films, since it deals in the breathless generalities which are the enemy of art. Chaplin, whose art at its height has been in the complexities and nuances of human behavior as portrayed through the fine instrument of his body, is becoming seduced by words into making grand, sweeping statements, which, in attempting to mean everything, mean nothing. The Barber, too, is no more than a symbol, an amiable, nostalgic ghost of the departed Tramp, merely another of the powerless under Hynkel.

Like the ghetto world they live in, the characters are necessarily bleak, ill-defined and shadowy, for though one of Chaplin's main themes has been the struggle of the powerless against the powerful, here there can be no triumphant kick in the ass, cunning escape, or crushing defeat such as Charlie was always pleased to dispense upon Eric Campbell. They are frozen in their oppression, trapped in a manner that the Tramp never was. The greatness of the film, as contemporary critic Basil Wright noted, is in the contrast between the scenes of these people in the ghetto and in Hynkel's palace.[21] The alternations between the two give the film a driving force and make it something in the nature of a sweeping epic.

It is back in Hynkel's office that the reptilian Garbitsch slithers up to the

Dictator again — he speaks of Jews, and of the majority of union disrupters at the factory being brunettes. "They're even worse than the Jews," Garbitsch notes, so Hynkel orders: "Get rid of 'em!" Garbitsch posits a vision of the future in which Osterlich is conquered and then the world, a world of blonde, blue-eyed Aryans, ruled by the emperor of the world, the black-haired Hynkel. "Stop!" cries Hynkel, suddenly flustered and coquettish, embarrassed and excited: "You make me afraid of myself!" he cries, prancing across the room and climbing the curtain.

The triumph of Chaplin's satire of Hitler is that he allows him no vestige of seriousness or dignity; to Chaplin, Hitler is simply a barbarian, bestial in his drives and his rages, and fearsome for that reason. But as far as Hitler's ideas and philosophy are concerned, he is nothing more than a buffoon, his mission serves no purpose but to be ridiculed and laughed at. Chaplin displays the innate absurdity of Hitler's singular hatred of the Jews, an absurdity as egregious as hating brunettes, or any person based on arbitrary, superficial reasons. As well, Chaplin points out the glaring (but mostly ignored) absurdity of Hitler's desire to breed and rule over a race of Aryans when the Fuhrer himself was less than a prime specimen of Aryan purity.

Above all, it is Hitler's lust for power which is portrayed, a lust which is sexual, aesthetic, romantic, tragic, demonic, where all begins and from which all else proceeds — and which comes to the fore in its own little vignette which is the centerpiece of the film. Dismissing Garbitsch, Hynkel climbs down from the curtain and stealthily approaches the large globe which has place of prominence in his office. He seizes it and lifts it from its stand — he touches it tenderly like a lover, then releases it: it floats, balloon-like, into the air. He allows it to waft above him, then he seizes it again. He tosses it aloft, letting it drift away, but never letting it get too far, always making sure it comes back to his hands. He twirls it around, his eyes flashing at it, laughing a nasty, guttural laugh. He throws it up, and for old time's sake, gives it a back-kick into the air. Leaping onto his desk, he crouches down and lets the world bounce off his posterior a couple of times. He dances with the world as though it is his lover, his sexual partner, his quarry — until he squeezes it so hard that it bursts with a jarring bang. He collapses with bitter tears — he weeps not with remorse but with self-pity that the victim of his domination, his power-lust, is no more.

Directly after this, one of Chaplin's greatest set pieces, comes another of his classic scenes, another dance. We are back in the ghetto, and the Barber is administering a shave to a customer — played by that old Keystone confederate, Chester Conklin. The radio is tuned to Liszt's Hungarian Waltz No. 5, so the Barber shaves Chester in perfect time to the music, in a neat routine that might have been performed in the British music hall. Since Chaplin felt that sound film had doomed the art of pantomime, an art of which he said he was "without false modesty, a master,"[22] he must have been pleased to no end to place two pantomime pieces back to back, totaling 5 minutes, in the middle of a motion picture released in 1940.

The peace, of course, cannot last. Word is forthcoming from Epstein that he will not deal with a medieval maniac, so Hynkel furiously resumes his attacks on the Jews. His commander Schultz — the same pilot the Barber had rescued in the war, and who had saved the Barber from being hanged in the ghetto— objects to the measures. "Your cause is doomed to failure because it's based on the stupid, ruthless persecution of innocent people!" he cries: "It's more than a crime, it's a tragic blunder!" That Hitler's cause was considerably more than a tragic blunder is borne out by history. For his troubles, Hynkel condemns Schutlz to a concentration camp. He also unleashes hell on the Jewish ghetto, and here the world of the ghetto and the world of the palace are brought into stark contrast — we see the Barber and Hannah embarking on a night out just as the crazed voice of Hynkel bellows from the loudspeakers— the people in the street scurry into their homes. We see the face of Hynkel fill the screen as he delivers his tirade of hate, and the savage aspect of Chaplin has never been more evident, for he looks truly frightening, and truly evil. The storm troopers stream through the ghetto and set the Barber's shop on fire. As the Barber sits on a roof with Hannah, watching his shop burn, we are given a quick cutaway shot to Hynkel in his palace, playing the piano. The recurring Chaplin theme of the whims of the powerful destroying the worlds of the little people is expressed forcefully.

Schultz has escaped from custody and seeks refuge with the Barber and Hannah in the ghetto. The storm troopers track him down and a chase ensues, with Schultz and the Barber being captured and sent off to a concentration camp. Hannah and her employer Mr. Jaeckel, however, are able to escape Hynkel's rule, migrating to the seemingly idyllic country of Osterlich.

It is the same country of Osterlich which Hynkel has been intent on invading. Just as he's about to get it under way, however, he receives news that his fellow dictator, Benzino Napaloni of Bacteria, has stationed his troops on the Osterlich border. He resolves to meet Napaloni at his Palace to discuss the situation.

If the dance of the globe is the centerpiece of *The Great Dictator*, then the meeting with Napaloni is its climax. Chaplin admirably brought in Jack Oakie to play the role, a notably sound-oriented comedian, and his bombastic presence brings a real kick to this last third of the movie. With his chin and lower lip jutted out to mirror Mussolini, his real-life counterpart, Napaloni is a crude, imbecilic vulgarian, easily the equal of Hynkel in his desperate lust for power which is infantile and sexual all at once. From the moment he barges into the movie he is engaged in an asinine game of one-upmanship with Hynkel in which Napaloni's obnoxious boisterousness assures him of victory. Interestingly, there also seems to be a similar, yet subtle, parallel game going on between the two comedians in these scenes which gives them an edgy energy — for Oakie is the more brash, self-assured, raucous clown of the modern sound age, while Chaplin is the pantomime master, nervously holding his own as the king of the bygone silent cinema. It's also worth noting that Chaplin invariably gives all the best business in these scenes to Oakie.

They go to a military display, and Napaloni takes note of a massive clock tower at the top of which is a huge sculpture of Adenoid Hynkel giving his "Heil." "It's about a five-a minutes off," Napaloni says in his Italian-English, checking the timepiece against his own pocket watch. Garbitsch prepares Hynkel for a meeting with Napaloni — he plans to enable Hynkel to impose his will on Napaloni by making the Bacterian dictator feel inferior: he arranges that Napaloni will enter through a door at the far end of the room so that he'll have to walk a distance towards Hynkel at his desk; he places a tiny, ridiculously low chair for Napaloni so that he'll be seated considerably beneath Hynkel; he arranges that a large bust of Hynkel be placed to look down on Napaloni, to intimidate him further. Napaloni enters through a door directly behind Hynkel, however, taking him by surprise, slapping him on the back so that he falls against his desk; he notes that the chair is low and so sits on Hynkel's desk, towering over him; he strikes a match against Hynkel's bust to light a cigarette. All of this flusters Hynkel so much that, far from appearing imposing, he is unable to speak, and must gesture for Garbitsch to fill in for him (notably, in an earlier scene, the Barber found himself suddenly unable to speak due to fear, and had to gesture silently to Schultz that the storm troopers were on the way). The two dictators decide to go to the palace barber shop for shaves, and there they surreptitiously pump themselves higher in their respective barber chairs, each one determined to rise above the other. They pump themselves impossibly high into the air, until the chairs collapse and they skid to the earth.

All of this leads up to their decisive conference on the Osterlich question. It occurs in a banquet room to which the two men retire during a gala ball: Napaloni proposes the signing of a non-aggression treaty, after which he'll pull his troops from the border; Hynkel wants the troops removed before he signs. The discussion grows more heated until they are accompanying their words with the throwing of food from the banquet table; typically for Chaplin, expression is found through digestibles, and the splattering continues until Hynkel mistakenly puts hot English mustard on his strawberries — he leaps weeping onto a couch with the pain, which is much enjoyed by Napaloni until he finds that he too has dolloped his sandwich with a surplus of the mustard. He collapses, writhing on the couch beside Hynkel, the two men overwhelmed with the pain. Recovering, they resume their screeching at each other, each one slashing the air with his native salute, each one yelping his cultural credo.

It is in this tableau, every bit as expressive as the dance with the globe of before, that Chaplin achieves a grim irony in his satire that would seem years ahead of its time — its bitter vision of political realities anticipates *Dr. Strangelove or: How I Learned to Stop Worrying and Love the Bomb*. Riding upon the jabbering of these two ludicrous baboons are the destinies of millions of people, and the utter foolishness of the dictators is as tragic as it is comic — within it are all the reasons one needs to pity all of humanity.

The two leaders are at an impasse until Garbitsch summons Hynkel and informs him that it doesn't matter whether he signs the treaty or not — it's merely a piece of paper and they can invade Osterlich in any case. Hynkel signals his new willingness to sign and is embraced by Napaloni. This whole sequence is a direct comment on Hitler and Mussolini's non-aggression pact regarding Austria, and its subsequent abrogation by Hitler. From here, the film wends its way to its conclusion and final piece de resistance: the Barber and Schultz escape from the concentration camp, dressed in a couple of their captors' uniforms; Hynkel invades Osterlich; we see headlines, "Ghettos raided," "Jewish Property Confiscated"; the storm troopers appear in the newfound paradise of Hannah and Mr. Jaeckel, beating them and vandalizing their cabin. Hynkel, in a Tyrolean outfit, is duck hunting in the country near the Osterlich border as part of the invasion plan — he's arrested and knocked unconscious by some soldiers who mistake him for the Barber. And the Barber, naturally, is discovered in the country and mistaken for Hynkel. He is ushered to a massive podium to address the world as the new conqueror of Osterlich.

As co-star Jack Oakie would note, "Chaplin only made that movie so he could deliver that long speech at the end."[23] It's true that one can view the entire film, and certainly the complex machinations of its final third, as a prelude and a rationale for Chaplin to address his public directly, to give his true views on the matter of world peace and individual responsibility completely and didactically. For if the meek Barber steps up to the podium, mumbling apologetically, "I'm sorry, but I don't want to be an emperor. That's not my business...," he soon gains remarkable confidence and passion, exhorting the troops gathered before him: "Soldiers! Don't give in to these brutes! ... In the name of democracy, let us all unite!" In the course of his six-minute speech, we become aware that the face intensely, solemnly speaking these words directly to us through the camera is not the face of the Barber, of Hynkel, or of the Tramp. It is not even the face of Charlie Chaplin — it is rather the face of Charles Chaplin, internationally famous celebrity and the confidant of Albert Einstein, Mahatma Ghandi, George Bernard Shaw, Aldous Huxley, and Winston Churchill.

The speech is an artistic aberration — and it is intended to be. As the entire film has been an act of Chaplin committing his most precious gift — his art — to the cause of lampooning what he believed to be humanity's most dire threat of the time, so now Chaplin goes further, breaking every dramatic law which has governed his art till now, breaking through the "fourth wall" in order to communicate his message desperately in a frenzied, hectoring, inartistic manner. So perilous were the times for humanity, so crucial was Chaplin's message, that the aesthetic violation is entirely justified — this seems to be the spirit behind the speech. As well, one can say that the crude political pamphlet-language of the address fits in with the rest of the film in the sense that the whole production can be seen as extended political cartoon or editorial.

But what is it, exactly, that Chaplin states to us so directly, so stridently? "The way of life can be free and beautiful," he states, "but we have lost the way." The greed of humanity, he tells us, "has goose-stepped us into misery and bloodshed." "More than machinery, we need humanity. More than cleverness, we need kindness and gentleness." He pleads with the soldiers not to give themselves to dictators, to "machine men with machine minds and machine hearts! You are not machines!" The specter of soul-destroying technology and regimentation as seen in *Modern Times* announces itself again, in the face of the new wave of inhumanity swarming the earth. "In the seventeenth chapter of St. Luke it is written that the kingdom of God is within man — not one man nor a group of men, but in all men! In you!" "Let us fight for a new world!" Chaplin cries to the huddled masses of the planet.

These grandiose sentiments are akin to the earlier statements of Hannah, and while they are admirable, they call to mind Buster Keaton's anecdote about Chaplin's political philosophy: one night as they drank beer in Keaton's kitchen, Chaplin extemporized, "What I want ... is that every child should have enough to eat, shoes on his feet, and a roof over his head!" Keaton noted: "But Charlie, do you know anyone who doesn't want that?"[24] If Chaplin's gospel of kindness and gentleness is unoriginal and trite, it is no less profound or necessary, and there can be no doubting his passion and deep concern as he makes his statement to humanity. But at the same time there is an unbecoming pomposity displayed, an indulgent sense of self-regard. "Let us fight to free the world," he shouts, "to do away with national barriers, to do away with greed, with hate and intolerance!" He who had been so expressive, unique, subtle, artful and subversive in his silent communications now becomes lead-footed, cliché-ridden, obvious and puerile in his use of speech.

The speech is the birth of the new Chaplin, who will stop the action of his films to philosophically pontificate for minutes at a time, who will cast out his ponderous epigrams like pearls, and generally succumb to the temptation sound presents by using it to indulge himself in lengthy monologues. Since the coming of sound had robbed Chaplin of his art, this is his new "art," with the endless articulation of his thoughts replacing the poetry of his gestures and movements of before. Like the speech which portends them, Chaplin's remaining films will be odd, overlong, difficult, erratic and more "interesting" as events, as creations by the great Chaplin and as windows into his mind, than artistically successful.

Again, it's entirely arguable — and was argued by Chaplin — that the speech is suitable, and even necessary, given the times. As it comes to its close, Chaplin's voice reaches Hannah, where she lies on the ground after being beaten by the storm troopers. He beckons her messianically to "Look up! The soul of man has been given wings and at last he is beginning to fly! He is flying into the rainbow...." The film closes with her standing and looking into the distance, heartened by his words, and along with this unmasking of himself which he has effected in this closing speech, Chaplin makes a personal statement in giving his heroine the name of his own mother — who had never regained her sanity, whom Chaplin and his brother had brought to America in 1921, and who had died during the production of *City Lights*. As the Hannah of the film was chased and persecuted by the storm troopers, so Hannah and her sons had been chased and persecuted by the horrors of poverty, and the forces which blighted them and drove Chaplin's mother into madness before his eyes were no less malevolent and destructive in their results than much of the oppression which was unleashed by Hitler. Chaplin knew the face of evil when he saw it, and he called out and named the prime demonic practitioner of his day — yet he also saw the impulse behind it was not unlike that which rushes to crush the weak in every society, and he calls out to the spirit of his mother, as one crushed by that force, with a message of hope just as the clouds are about to gather and usher in an even more brutal stage of history. As the Hannah of the film stands, she is moved by the words, but she, and we, are left with no guarantee, only the sentiment that "a new world is at hand," which was certainly the case. But not in the manner Chaplin — or the Jewish Barber — hoped.

"The hate of men will pass, and dictators die," we have been told, and the real-life counterparts of those two titans, Hynkel and Napaloni, whose worst problems consisted of eating too much hot mustard and bouncing around in pain on a couch, came to particularly nasty ends: Mussolini was hanged, then his body was dragged behind a car through an Italian village, so that his former citizens were able to beat and abuse his corpse; Hitler shot himself through the head in his bunker as the Russian troops were about to close in on him — after which, as he had instructed, his aides poured gasoline on his corpse and incinerated it. Before this, he had managed to carry out a fair portion of his mission — he had conquered Denmark, Norway, the Netherlands, Belgium, Luxembourg, and France, and had invaded the all-important Russia, but that didn't go quite as planned. He also had begun the extermination of the Jewish population from Europe, first by interning them in concentration camps and working them to death, then by conscientiously gassing them to death, and incinerating their remains in large ovens designed for the purpose. In this manner six million Jews were killed, along with five million handicapped people, Gypsies, homosexuals, and others deemed unworthy of life by the Nazis. As well, it is estimated that a total of 62 million people were killed in the war Hitler began, 25 million of these being soldiers, 37 million being civilians.

Hitler could not have accomplished any of what he set out to do without the willing and unwilling assistance of literally millions of people. It is not in the exhortations of the final speech of *The Great Dictator* which give the film its relevance and greatness, but in Chaplin's portrayal of Hitler as a leader unworthy of respect or veneration — as a small, crass, ridiculous, mediocre loser whose ideas were crackbrained and absurd, and certainly undeserving of serious consideration, much less the horrible actions carried out in their name. By making the film, Chaplin made his own stand as a person, at a time when many were afraid to, or were simply unaware of the gathering crisis. But more than this, Chaplin fulfilled his duty and destiny as humanity's premier clown, and the duty of all clowns and jesters throughout history, as he brought the spirit of truth and love, of "gentleness and kindness" and healing laughter to bear, however vainly, against a small, clenched figure of hatred, prejudice and violence.

13

Monsieur Verdoux

Monsieur Verdoux follows *The Great Dictator* by seven years, and it exemplifies the difficulties which sound presented for Chaplin. Without the high concept and the broad political caricatures of the earlier film, *Monsieur Verdoux*, as a slightly more realistic work, displays more plainly how Chaplin's art was handicapped by the new technological development. Sound had necessitated not merely the addition of dialogue to his artistic template; it required a reconstruction of his entire approach to film. The added technical concerns, with the required hiring of an array of experts in their fields, along with the increased cost, meant that Chaplin could not create his films in the improvisatory, organic manner by which he had brought his silent films into being. Now, all had to be planned out well in advance of stepping before the camera. Whereas he had created his greatest films without a formal script, he now devoted years to writing his films. There could be no more of the long, agonized contemplations which led to the subtle manner by which the audience finds out that Marie is being kept by Pierre Revel in *A Woman of Paris*, nor could there be the endless series of takes by which the exquisite ease of the Blind Girl mistaking Charlie for a rich man is arrived at in *City Lights*. Instead of these nuances, so painstakingly fashioned by Chaplin in his silent films, and representing the peaks of his art, the sound films are often clumsily constructed, and make their points in a sometimes surprisingly crude and ham-fisted manner.

The fact is that Chaplin was a genius at expressing himself through movement, gesture and facial expression. The command of verbal language is so out of his sphere that the fact that he is as good at it as he is entirely due to his driven perspicacity as an artist. His artistic template had been formed without sound so he never quite knew what to do with it, or what space he should allow it to inhabit — here, as at the end of *The Great Dictator*, his tendency is often to philosophize, or to over-employ the dialogue, making it do more than it needs to do. What's surprising about these later films is how "talky" they are, how much the plot is advanced through words, and how little is communicated through physical business or images. It is as though Chaplin wants to show how very capable he is in embracing and mastering sound, to show how little he needed to fall back on what might be seen as silent film methods. Far from saving time, as one might think dialogue would do in telling the story, these later films are all overlong, lumbering works. As a creator of silent films, Chaplin had few, if any peers. But as a creator of sound films there are times when he is barely adequate.

This is not surprising, considering that at the time of *Monsieur Verdoux*'s release he was fifty-seven years old, and past the point of being able to radically reformulate his technique. As well, it is undeniable that as the sound films progress, there is an increasingly shabby look to them, with an increased reliance on indoor shooting and the unconvincing use of process shots. These were undoubtedly resultant of the new economic and technical realities of sound, but they are reflective as well of Chaplin's new focus in the films: the technical niceties were not so important to him as was the "message" he was communicating. In this, the shabby look of the films parallels the leaden, crudely motivated plot twists of the scripts—the technical proficiency of the films, and the elegance and fluency of their plots which he had so labored over before, were not as essential now to Chaplin as the statements he wished to make through his films, now articulated straight out in dialogue. It is these "messages" which replace the poetry of image and gesture which have constituted Chaplin's art to this time. From *The Great Dictator* on, all of his work will be imperfect, flawed—more intensely personal, cheap-looking, idiosyncratic, messy, brilliant, erratic statements from a man less concerned with advancing his art technically than with making a stand. They are still works of genius, but they are, inevitably, the lesser works of genius. As such, they remain completely unique creations and worthy of attention.

The inspiration for *Monsieur Verdoux* was Henri Landru, a French "Bluebeard" killer who had been guillotined in 1922 for 11 murders. He was a secondhand furniture dealer in Paris, who in 1914—the same year of Chaplin's rise to fame in the Keystones—had begun putting personal ads in newspapers, luring unsuspecting females, romancing them, then killing them shortly after gaining access to their assets. Over the course of five years, Landru used many aliases, keeping track of them and the relationships they pertained to in ledgers; he generally cut the bodies up with a hacksaw and incinerated them in his stove, spreading the ashes in his garden. Orson Welles had suggested Landru as a role for Chaplin, proposing that Welles direct him in it; Chaplin was interested, until Welles signaled that he expected Chaplin to help with the writing as well. The comedian drew back, but later found himself intrigued by the mass killer story, and so bought the basic idea outright from Welles, fashioning it into a vehicle for himself.[1]

"Good evening!" a disembodied voice calls out: "My name is Henri Verdoux!" We see the Verdoux headstone in a cemetery and we hear the chatty voice go on to explain his occupation as a "liquidator" of women, noting that such a profession requires a surplus of optimism. He welcomes us into the movie, into the story of his life. Suddenly we are with the Couvais family as they wonder about the whereabouts of their sister Thelma. The Couvaises are an assemblage of oafs, crones, dullards, and nags who are among the most unpleasant individuals Chaplin has ever featured in a film — and the manner in which this sequence has been shot typifies all the weaknesses of the Chaplin films in the sound era. It is in fact one of Chaplin's worst scenes ever, with the awkward staging and the incompetent acting — the film features one of Chaplin's least accomplished casts — enabling it to resemble a community theater production on an off-night. The purpose of the scene is exposition — to clumsily set up the premise that the Couvaises are concerned about their sister, who married some queer duck then vanished, and now they've just received a wire telling them that her life savings have been withdrawn from her bank.

In a flash we go from the cretinous, loudmouthed Couvais family to the refined Monsieur Verdoux in his garden — he has just cut himself a lovely bouquet of roses, as behind him a thick black cloud of smoke uncoils from the chimney of his incinerator. A neighbor lady complains to another that he's kept that incinerator burning for three days; the other observes that she hasn't been able to put out her wash because of it. Verdoux strolls along with his roses — pausing to solicitously pick up a caterpillar and place it on a branch out of harm's way.

Monsieur Verdoux is Chaplin's bitterest and most bizarre film. After reconnecting with the darker side of his character in his previous film, it's no surprise that he felt himself drawn to the role of the French gigolo who goes around seducing and marrying women, then murdering them. There is much in the character that is reminiscent of his role in *Tillie's Punctured Romance*, in which he had devilishly swept the gargantuan Marie Dressler off her feet for purely monetary reasons. As Dressler was in that film, most of Verdoux's prey is hulking, slovenly and awkward, in contrast to his compact, trim figure. The role also calls to mind that cheerfully amoral French bon vivant, Pierre Revel from *A Woman of Paris*. Verdoux is charming, cultured, graceful — the world around him is ignorant and coarse, and none are more coarse and ignorant than the women he knocks off with efficient grace.

Hynkel had been a murderer too. But where Hynkel was furious, unhinged with rage, writhing and screeching, Verdoux is self-possessed, calm, poised — his manners are impeccable, his temperament, at least on the face of it, seems ever-agreeable, accommodating — up to a point, anyway. Yet Verdoux is in his way more frightening than Hynkel, for he seems more cheerfully sane. Chaplin had said that he never could have poked fun at Hitler had he known the full extent of his atrocities, yet here with Verdoux we have a Chaplin fully aware of what transpired in Hitler's death camps. He had heard the trials in Nuremberg and heard the testimony of the Nazis who blandly claimed they were "only following orders" displaying the point of view which later inspired the phrase of

Hannah Arendt — "the banality of evil." Verdoux is obviously, for Chaplin, a man of the times — a fellow who can clip some choice roses as he incinerates a corpse in the manner so many had been incinerated in Auschwitz — and then repair to the nearest phone to buy some stocks.

There is much as well of the Tramp, and of Chaplin himself, in Verdoux, who is one who seduces and charms — like the Tramp, like Chaplin — at the same time as he cannily guarantees his survival. He is, like the mid-period Tramp, a superior being, who, for the most part, triumphs over his doltish, dull-witted fellow humans — here he follows the strain of the old films to its logical conclusion and puts his adversaries out of their misery altogether. With wicked perversity, Chaplin associates Verdoux throughout the film with those longtime symbols of the Tramp's romantic and poetic ideals — flowers. But Verdoux makes mockery of the old chivalrous dreams, for they are only a pose he assumes so that he may slaughter and make off with his lucre. Yet he does it all in an extraordinarily efficient manner. He is not "businesslike," for to him it *literally* is his business, as he makes clear several times throughout the film. In a world where killing has become big business, business is finally, literally, murder. If the Tramp's mission had been to find an honorable way to live, it is now flatly stated that there is no honorable way to live. There is only Verdoux's way, and he is not to be blamed if he happens to excel at it more than most.

Behind Verdoux there is a palpable rage and hostility emitting from Chaplin towards his audience, as if to say, "Look what you've made me into." Verdoux, it is explained, fell into his present way of life after losing his job as a bank teller during the Depression — the same period in which sound asserted itself. As Verdoux moves through the movie, with his chilly, efficient precision, his modus operandi begins to exclaim, with increasing persuasion: "Look what we have made ourselves into." As survival has always been one of Chaplin's main themes, *Monsieur Verdoux* brings it to its apotheosis. And for Chaplin, finally, survival is murder — reality had driven this fact home to such a degree that the Tramp was no longer suitable to reflect it. So we have the affable, charming, insouciant Verdoux.

When a woman comes for a viewing of the house of his now deceased wife, Verdoux is only too quick to jump in and start romancing her, scoping her out as a new source of revenue, even as he is cremating his last conquest. When his stockbroker informs him that he needs some quick cash to cover his investments, Verdoux speeds off via rail — the recurring image of train wheels symbolizes his industrious expeditions throughout the film — to "liquidate" another of his wives. She is a monstrously unpleasant individual, a po-faced, bellyaching hag whose sour petulance contrasts with Verdoux's refined poise. He convinces her that a worldwide financial crisis is imminent and that she should therefore bring her deposit box home from the bank posthaste. With considerable grousing she does so, and that night we see them disappear together into the bedroom. Morning comes, and only Verdoux emerges, humming a cheerful tune as he carries the deposit box, heading to the phone to call his broker. He counts the money, his fingers rippling through the currency impossibly fast, with crisp, magical efficiency—one of the few notable bits of physical business in the film, and one which recurs throughout.

The train wheels blaze again and we see Verdoux arrive at a small chalet in the country. The music swells to the romantic heights we now recognize as hallmarks of Chaplin's composing style. A little boy rushes to greet Verdoux— he has a son. Then Verdoux walks to greet his wife, who is seated in a wheelchair. As he embraces her, the camera pans down and, in the most jarring and confounding close-up to be found in a Chaplin film, remains focused on the woman's useless feet in their braces in the wheelchair for a prolonged length of time.

What are we to make of this? The music and the idyllic setting would seem to suggest that the woman's handicap makes the death of Verdoux's other, more unpleasant wife, acceptable—even necessary. For certainly the other wife is depicted as being so hideous that we were relieved to be rid of her ourselves, while this wife is cultured, like Verdoux, and an invalid besides. She and the son know nothing of Verdoux's other life—only that his business keeps him away for extended lengths of time. As Verdoux says, his wife and son are Verdoux's "world" for which he works—they are his Paradise. But it is a Paradise attainable only through Verdoux's "business." At home he is a most cordial paterfamilias—it's pointed out that he and his family are vegetarians, and he rebukes his son for playing too roughly with the cat: "Violence begets violence!" he admonishes.

There is a wickedness to *Monsieur Verdoux* which is beyond all else in Chaplin's films—a wickedness he obviously delights in—sometimes too much so. In the use of his familiar soaring music in the scene at Verdoux's home, we see him devilishly subverting the usual expectations we might have of the familiar Chaplin touch of the heartstrings—all the while Verdoux evinces tender love for his family we know him to be a monster, and the manipulative ambiguity of the sequence makes us, in way, complicit in Verdoux's villainy. "You must be making a killing!" remarks an old friend Verdoux runs into, seeing his large bankroll. "Yes!" Verdoux replies with a pert nod. In the surreal pastoral vision of Verdoux's home life we see articulated the basic truth that one must be inherently amoral in business in order to succeed—an amorality which can be laid outside the door of one's serene abode each night after work. When Verdoux, later in the film, asks a character to describe her husband, she says that he's "kind and generous—but in business quite ruthless." "Business is a ruthless business, my dear," Verdoux notes. In this, Chaplin echoes the sentiment voiced by Berthold Brecht—a recent friend of his—in his play *The Good Woman of Setzuan*: that one cannot be decent and succeed, one must necessarily divide oneself into two identities, one of them possessing the amoral ruthlessness needed in order to survive.

Business calls once again, and Verdoux dispatches himself to Annabella, another one of his wives primed for liquidation. She's different from the others in that she is younger—though no less vulgar and obnoxious—and has recently won the lottery, which makes for Verdoux's interest. She is also played by Martha Raye, the one memorable member of the cast, and a performer who serves the same purpose here as did Jack Oakie in *The Great Dictator*—she's a spirited, raucous, boisterous, and very sound-oriented comedian in her own right, who plays off Chaplin, and to whom, in most of their scenes together, Chaplin gives most of the best business. Raye was a comedian who'd been a sensation on radio and films, and was famous for the size of her mouth—her prime attribute gets a good workout here. She is very funny as the lanky, loud broad improbably smitten with Verdoux, her healthy vulgarity confounding Verdoux's sinister primness at every turn. For here Annabella is different in another way—among the several archetypal woman characters in the film, she represents an unstoppable, unkillable vitality, as Verdoux finds to his chagrin. As Napolini did to Hynkel in the previous film, Annabella flummoxes Verdoux's usual grace and ease, triumphing in her imbecilic oblivion over his diabolical machinations. Here he is just about to smother her as she sleeps, advancing towards her figure with the grim stealth of a spider, when the maid comes unexpectedly into the house—he retreats to try again another day.

We have seen the standard Chaplin heroines in the films to date—we know that they are generally young women in peril who, until this time, the Tramp has attempted to rescue. Here we have seen Verdoux court and kill older, larger women. Knowing that Chaplin—on film and in real life—preferred younger women, and had little use for women beyond a certain age, we see the rather unflattering autobiographical parallel. The age of the women—and Chaplin was 57 himself at this time—is commented on when Verdoux attempts to seduce the matronly Madame Grosnay: "What difference does age make?" he asks. "A great deal to a woman," she replies. It is possible to see Verdoux's innocent "real" wife as the standard woman in need of rescue here. But a more likely candidate is the young, attractive prostitute Verdoux callously picks up in order to try a new painless, untraceable poison on.

He brings her in from the rain, and gives her a meal of scrambled eggs. He also pours her a glass of wine laced with the poison and watches her furtively as she eats, waiting for her to drink from the glass. As we know, however, Chaplin has always had a weakness for compromised women, and so Verdoux can't help but begin to speak with her. The prostitute is undoubtedly one of the few ladies of the evening ever to carry a copy of Schopenhauer's *Treatise on Suicide*. Noting it, Verdoux asks whether she might not desire death over this "drab existence ... if the end could be simple—say you went to sleep without any thought of death...."

Granted, it's a pretty big leap to Schopenhauer's *Treatise on Suicide* for a guy who not so long ago was kicking people in the ass for a living. But beyond this is the bizarre and strangely evocative situation Chaplin has created—an older man, a killer, restively waiting for a young woman to drink the poison he has provided, all the while engaging her in philosophical debate. In contrast to the Tramp's rescuing of such a woman in the past, Verdoux suggests that she might just be better off dead. As he speaks, we come to know there's no need to infer misogyny from the succession of hellish females slaughtered in the name of Verdoux's business—no need, because Chaplin has Verdoux speak it straight out. "You don't like women, do you?" asks the prostitute. "On the contrary, I love women—but I don't admire them," Verdoux replies. "Women are of the earth ... realistic, dominated by physical facts.... Once a man betrays a woman she despises him," he says with a sudden fierce ferocity. "How little you know about women!" the prostitute replies. She speaks of love, and of her love for her deceased husband, who was an invalid, who she lived for and who, for her, was her "religion." At these words, at this description of self-sacrifice, Verdoux is abashed—he spares her at the last minute, replacing her glass of wine with a fresh, untainted one. As he gives her some money and sends her on her way, she weeps with gratitude: just as she was about to give up, she says, he gave her reason to believe. "Don't believe too much," Verdoux warns: "This is a ruthless world and one must be ruthless to cope with it." "That isn't true," she replies, "it's a blundering world and a very sad one, but a little kindness can make it beautiful."

The scene is the centerpiece of the film and the closing dialogue articulates the dichotomy which has always been present in the Chaplin worldview: the canny, cruel obsession with survival co-existing with the empathetic, sentimental conception of a fallen world. But here there is no room for the type of sentimental platitudes spoken by the prostitute. What's being depicted is precisely the ruthless existence of which Verdoux speaks, and each time the old romantic tenderness seems about to be offered, the rug is unfailingly pulled out from beneath our feet: always, as we are being lulled by glimpses of the old Chaplin, a moral queasiness overtakes us. Chaplin continues to subvert all his old artistic standbys—romanticism, sentimentality; here they are little more than bitter, hollow jokes. The perverse Verdoux decides not to slaughter the prostitute because she has lived in service to a helpless person, as he has—presumably, in his view, all who do not do this are deserving of death. The sequence is as mysterious, disturbing, and revealing as a dream.

The busy Verdoux is next visited at his furniture warehouse—for he's a dealer in used furnishings as was his real-life counterpart Landru—by a detective alerted by the Couvaises who signals his intention to arrest the killer. The official certainly seems to have the goods on him—but Verdoux is little concerned as he refreshes the constable with a glass of poison-laced wine. He agrees to go along with the officer and confess if they can first visit his family and tell them what has transpired. They travel by train—the officer handcuffs Verdoux to himself, then admits to feeling rather groggy and drifts off to sleep. After a time, Verdoux checks the officer's pulse, procures the key from the man's waist-coat, unlocks the cuffs, replacing them helpfully in the officer's jacket, and dis-embarks the train.

After this, it's back to trying to trying to knock off the frustratingly hardy Annabella — he plans to try the poisoned wine on her but, in a rather drawn-out sequence, the poison becomes mixed up with the peroxide the maid's using to dye her hair. This results in the maid's hair falling out in clumps and in Ver-doux — who's ingested the wine by mistake, owing to Annabella's supernatu-ral imperviousness to his designs — having his stomach pumped. Better is the sequence when the two of them embark on a fishing expedition, Verdoux row-ing Annabella out to the deep water. He attempts to dispatch her with a hand-kerchief soaked in chloroform, then with a rope he endeavors to fasten around her neck — but he's foiled when a group of yodelers are found to be nearby. A defining moment of the film is when Verdoux advances on the oblivious Annbella with rope in hand, his features drawn into a mask of determined malevolence — then when she turns, he instantly goes into what many have identified as the old cute, coy, embarrassed pose of the Tramp: he draws his shoulders up and cocks his head to one side, smiling winningly. The whole of the film is in the juxtaposition of those two faces. Chaplin displays the charm which has been so much at the heart of his success to be a facile, deceptive thing — that it has really been nothing more than a carefully plied tool. We see that Verdoux is an artist, like Chaplin, whose art is the enticement of his quarry — and as refined, graceful and inventive as he is in his art, so are his victims crass, clumsy and dimwitted. So dimwitted, in fact, that Verdoux would seem to be doing the world a favor by terminating their existences. In this sense, *Monsieur Verdoux* is a contemptuous and angry film from Chaplin to his audience, to the world. But this is as nothing compared to what is to come.

Hardly perturbed to fail at bagging Annabella for the second time, Ver-doux returns to the courting of Madame Grosnay, a widow he's been pursuing from the beginning of the film via twice-weekly deliveries of roses. Along with Verdoux's wife and the prostitute, Grosnay is perhaps one of the three sympa-thetically portrayed women in the film, and is little-seen or explored for that reason; she is matronly yet cultured, and has had the dignity to repel Verdoux's advances for most of the film. Now, however, she succumbs to his wooing and a wedding is planned. This is the occasion for farcical proceedings when Anna-bella arrives at the reception, and Verdoux must dash about to escape being seen by her. Finally he deserts the proceedings altogether and we then see a mon-tage of headlines: time passes, there's a stock market crash, a crisis in Europe. It's notable that a deficiency in structure forces the film to posit two separate crashes of the stock market — the one in 1929, when Verdoux is supposed to have lost his job as a bank teller, and another in 1932, when Verdoux loses all the money he's "worked" for.

We see him sitting alone at an outdoor café, looking older — his hair is not the salt-and-pepper mixture it has been throughout the film, but is now completely white, as Chaplin's was in real life. He returns the smile of a young female nearby — in a repeat of the gag from *The Gold Rush*, however, she isn't really smiling at him but at a young fellow beyond him. This signals that Verdoux is now retired from seduction. He ambles out to the street and is hailed by an elegantly attired woman riding in a limousine. She's the prostitute, now having struck it rich as he has fallen on hard times: it's a perverse, bitter version of the reunion of the Tramp and the flower girl at the end of *City Lights*. He climbs into the limousine, and when he wonders at her wealth, she explains, "I married a munitions manufacturer." "That's the business I should have been in," he notes wryly. "Yes, it should be growing soon," she observes. So much for the blundering and sad world which kindness can make beautiful.

They adjourn to a restaurant and it is soon apparent to the ex-prostitute that her old benefactor has lost some of his spark. He relates that soon after the crash, he lost his wife and child. She expresses her condolences, but he notes: "They're much happier where they are — than living in this world of fear and uncertainty." Like the lingering camera shot of Verdoux's wife's legs earlier, we are once again pulled up short — did Verdoux, who'd stonily proclaimed to his wife earlier he'd never allow her to return to the poverty they had known in the past, exterminate his wife and son rather than have them meet this fate? It is a question Chaplin puts to us but does not definitively answer. In any case, Verdoux has lost his mission, his purpose — he's a gaunt old ghost, and in the words of his friend, he's given up the fight. So much so, that as they leave the restaurant, he doesn't ride with her; he tells her he's going off to "face my destiny." He's seen the police which have been called by the Couvais family — who've been tracking him down, inexorably, since the beginning of the film. He walks back to the restaurant and turns himself in.

He is tried and is sentenced to death by guillotine. When he is asked whether he has any last words, he delivers an incredible speech. Suddenly Verdoux is an ironic moralist — he admits his crimes, but insists: "As for mass killings, does not the world encourage it? Is it not building weapons of destruction for the sole purpose of mass killing? Has it not blown unsuspecting women and little children to bits — and done it very scientifically? Ha! As a mass killer, I'm an amateur by comparison!" Verdoux rationalizes his crimes by indicting the militarization of society, and to be sure, he's simply evading responsibility for his actions — yet, also, like only a moral pariah can, he speaks the truth. In concluding, he stares balefully around the courtroom, and with a sinister chuckle proclaims: "I shall see you all very soon! Very soon!"

Has the whole film, then, been simply another platform on which Chaplin stands to make another speech? Has this film, like *The Great Dictator*, been made so "Chaplin could make that long speech at the end"? This is, in fact, the opposite of the speech in the earlier film: where he had still hoped for "kindness and gentleness" to triumph in a crisis besieged world, he now has no such illusions. His oration here is a work of reproach, of a sensitive being determined to be more cynical and ruthless than the times he inhabited; it's a spit in the face to the vile brutality which he felt had overtaken the world. And though the film is set in some nether region between the two world wars, it is difficult, knowing the time of the film's release, not to equate Verdoux's citing of "blowing innocent women and children to bits" with the newly created atomic bomb, and with America's use of it in Hiroshima and Nagasaki, resulting in an estimated 124,000 overwhelmingly civilian casualties. Far from taking part in the American triumphalism of having defeated the Nazis and their Axis allies, and by doing so, setting itself up as an empire, Chaplin takes issue with the Americans' "liquidation" of innocents in the name of "business," specifically the explosions which took place and ushered in the new atomic age. And for that, he informs us, they are all going to hell.

It is limiting, however, to interpret the speech and what comes after it on an entirely topical, political level. For as Verdoux explicitly states in his parting to the courtroom — and to us all — we are all as guilty as he. We are all Verdoux. This is the ultimate conclusion of Chaplin's struggle with the question of survival — not only is business a form of murder, but we all take part in a system which makes murderers of us all. "That's the history of many a big business," Verdoux explains to a reporter as he awaits execution with admirable nonchalance: "Wars, conflict, it's all business. One murder makes a villain, millions make a hero. Numbers sanctify, my friend."

If we are then all murderers, all sinners, then what is the meaning of sin, of good and evil? "Arbitrary forces, my friend," Verdoux pipes up. "Who knows what sin is?" Verdoux asks when the priest visits him: "Born as it is from God's fallen angel, who knows what mysterious destiny it serves?" "May the Lord have mercy on your soul," the priest intones. "Why not? It belongs to him," Verdoux observes affably. He is offered a drink of rum before he is led out, and he takes it, remarking: "I've never tasted rum before." He holds it in his mouth for a moment, savoring it, ever the aesthete, ever the bon vivant, the artist. Then he is led away from us, to his death.

The film is designated "A comedy of murders" in its credits—but could anything be called a comedy, even a "comedy of murders," which concludes with this bleak image, which wraps up its story in such a dismally nihilistic manner? Verdoux walks away from us as the Tramp had always walked away from us at the conclusion of his adventures— but Verdoux walks away to be beheaded. He has, in the last several minutes of the film, become a sort of Christ figure in that he is killed for our sins, in our place. Throughout the greater part of the film the social commentary has consisted of ironically comparing the actions of a killer to a small businessman, and by extension the whole idea of "business." In the final 15 minutes the indictment is widened to include the entire new brutal atomic age, and by allusion, the new American hegemony of that age.

Monsieur Verdoux was a failure on its release, in large part because audiences were not ready for the black and vicious comedy it contained — the postwar mood was not suited to savage philosophical iconoclasm or trenchant moral satire. The film's reception was also affected by the groups of men picketing many of the theaters where it was shown. A group called the Catholic War Veterans began to discourage theaters from showing the film across America. Their discontent was not due to the fact that the film compared their country's foreign policy to an amoral French gigolo who runs around knocking off rich widows for money, but to their antipathy for the man who created it. In the seven years since his last release, Chaplin had changed from being one of America's best-loved figures to one of its most reviled.

In 1942 he had answered a call to fill in for the American ambassador to Russia and speak at a rally for Russian war relief — he made an impassioned plea for a second front to help the Russians to beat back Hitler. Energized by the spirited reaction to his boisterous speech, he gave several more — inspired nearly as much by his own hamminess and his "irritations and reactions to sound films" as his hatred of the Nazis, as he acknowledged later.[2] His imploring of America to send troops to fight and die beside the Russians took on new significance once the war had ended, and communist Russia was no ally, but a foe. This significance was joined in the minds of many with the longstanding and steadily growing concern among segments of the populace about Chaplin's personal politics — a concern which had been existent almost from the beginning of Chaplin's fame.

Chaplin had never become an American citizen, nor did he show any inclination towards becoming one. As a matter of fact, he was on record as saying that he considered himself a "citizen of the world," an "internationalist" who believed that "patriotism is the greatest insanity the world has ever suffered."[3] Chaplin's personal life was also a subject of controversy: he had unwisely married and divorced two very young women in succession, the second divorce attracting much attention; he had never officially confirmed the fact that he was married to Paulette Goddard; he had been charged in a paternity suit which resulted in a drawn-out trial at the end of which he was exonerated, but his image was forever sullied — the last occurred during the preparation of *Monsieur Verdoux*, and one can only imagine its effect on the finished film. These personal scandals melded with his dubious politics to create a more unsavory, less amusing image of Chaplin in the public mind, so that some were inspired to stand outside the theaters where his latest film was showing, carrying pickets which read: "Kick the alien out of the country."

In short, *Monsieur Verdoux* was exactly the wrong film to create and release at the time — which is likely why Chaplin did it. Verdoux is the ultimate man of his era, and when he is condemned it is a sweeping, bitter condemnation of all of Western civilization. Philosophically, Chaplin has more in common with writers like Brecht and Albert Camus here than anything else which was being released in Hollywood at the time — Verdoux is a spiritual brother of Camus' antihero in *The Outsider*, who was executed in a like manner, and seemed, like Verdoux, to embody the curious moral myopia of the time, the new, absurd, nuclearized numbness which had fallen across the earth. Beyond all else, Chaplin grapples in his starkest, most extreme manner with the struggle which has propelled his art from the beginning — that of survival — and his anguish and triumph are that the years have brought no solution or solace to the awful problem of the organism's need to sustain its existence. It is the final and most extreme depiction of the polarities of the Chaplin character, which is both criminal and saint, life-giver and life-destroyer, and as Federico Fellini would point out, comprises "the vagabond, but also the solitary aristocrat."[4] Like Chaplin, Verdoux had been displaced by the world, and chose infamy over obsolescence; Verdoux's final testament to a society about to punish him has something in common with the recent pronouncements which had caused Chaplin so much vilification. As messy, overlong and bizarre as *Monsieur Verdoux* is, it's a surprisingly revealing creation of a mind still alive to the unrelenting harshness of existence: Chaplin would later denote it as the "cleverest and most brilliant film I have yet made."[5] It's a brave, ingenious, strange work, the greatest praise of which — and the praise which would likely be the greatest cause of joy to Chaplin — is that sixty years after its creation it still has much in it that is shocking. It is Chaplin as the antisocial, savage radical taken to his furthest extreme — he could go no farther than this.

15

Limelight

The heroine of *Limelight*, the film the sixty-two-year-old Chaplin intended to be his swan song, notes, "What a sad business, being funny." The hero of the film is a music hall clown named Calvero, who is honored for the greatness of his past, yet is regarded as box-office poison in the present. He's a drunk, a figure important throughout Chaplin's career, even forming its genesis—his first great success was as the Drunk in the Karno show, the very role in which he had entranced Mack Sennett. But now the drunk is no comic or heroic figure—he's a sad ghost, a clown who is no longer funny, fading into oblivion with the bitter taste of failure in his mouth. Calvero has been, like Chaplin's own father, taken over by drink and lost his career. Like Chaplin himself, who realized by this time that he, as he would later state it, had "lost the affection of the American public," Calvero has "lost contact" with his audience. He's a wry lost soul, hovering on the edges of existence, not in demand by anyone— least of all himself.

The autobiographical note sounded in *The Circus*—when the Tramp had unwittingly amused the circus crowds, then had fallen asleep in an abandoned chariot, the intertitle commenting: "The Funny Man"—is sounded again here, as Chaplin examines his life and his art. The film was intended to be a retreat from the cynicism of *Monsieur Verdoux*, and a return to the poetic romanticism of his past work: he was closing the circle, returning to Victorian London in the film, revisiting the British music halls of his youth in which his parents had prospered and then foundered, and where he had begun his artistic journey. But as much of an exercise in nostalgia as it is, *Limelight* is a stark self-portrait of the artist as a sexagenarian, his triumphs in the past, isolated and ill-at-ease in an uncaring world which verges on the hostile, each moment of pleasure and beauty overshadowed by death. "As a man gets on in years, he wants to live deeply," Calvero notes. "A feeling of sad dignity comes upon him and that's fatal for a comic. It affected my work...." It is this sense of "sad dignity" which permeates *Limelight*. In a way, the film is a companion piece to *Monsieur Verdoux*, for Calvero, like Verdoux, has been rendered obsolete— Verdoux is executed, but Calvero must find another way to depart the stage.

The film is set in 1914, just before the war which would lay waste to the Victorian era: "The glamour of limelight," the opening title reads, "from which age must pass as youth enters." The drunken Calvero stumbles home to his seedy apartment house: upon entering he smells an unfamiliar odor — repeating a gag he used in a film made in the year in which the scene is supposed to be happening, *Mabel's Married Life*, Chaplin has Calvero check the bottom of his shoe for the source of the odor. It transpires that a young ballerina who's lost the will to live has turned on the gas in her apartment and laid down to die; the old clown breaks in and takes her unconscious body up to his apartment. He nurses her back to health, both physically and spiritually. In the course of doing so, he becomes reawakened to life, and is returned to his art as she is returned to hers.

The ballerina, Terry (played by Claire Bloom), is reminiscent of Chaplin's heroines of the past, of Merna of *The Circus*, of Georgia of *The Gold Rush*, in that she is a performer compromised by material reality who the Chaplin character rescues. She is similar to the flower girl in *City Lights* in that she is cured of her physical affliction. But Terry is more obviously an artist than any of these other characters, and her problems are as much philosophical and spiritual as anything else. As she recovers from her suicide attempt, she finds that the instruments of her art, her legs, are paralyzed — but this is only a psychosomatic condition. Through his help and wisdom, Calvero is able to put her on her feet again, figuratively and literally.

It's worth noting that though Chaplin himself has aged, the age of his heroines has remained the same: here the disparity in their ages allows Calvero to act as a sort of mentor or guru to Terry. And since the autobiographical note has been sounded so strongly — throughout the film it is signaled that Calvero is no one but old Charlot himself — it is relevant to note that Chaplin had recently found happiness which would last the rest of his life with a woman thirty years his junior, Oona O'Neill. The film is an exploration of that type of relationship too.

As with many of Chaplin's earlier heroines, Terry is faintly tinged with the aura of the "fallen woman." Both Calvero and the landlady of the apartment building assume at the beginning she's a prostitute; later Calvero strangely intimates that the illness she suffers from is syphilis. When it is established that Terry is actually a practitioner of that most aesthetically venerated of the arts — ballet — and has fallen on hard times because of an attack of rheumatic fever, Calvero performs a bit of Freudian analysis and ascertains the cause of her breakdown. Her sister had paid for her training in her art — one evening when out with friends, Terry spotted the sister in the course of earning the money she supplied, as a prostitute on the streets of London. Terry ran off and wept — years later when she was established at the Royal Ballet, one of the girls present the night she found out how her sister had supported her was hired. At the sight of the girl, Terry collapsed. Obviously, Calvero concludes eruditely, she broke down because she was overcome by the shame which had attended the birth of her art.

One can only imagine what significance the inclusion of such a strange story had for Chaplin, a man who would write with striking candor in his memoirs that "to gauge the morals of our family by commonplace standards would be as erroneous as putting a thermometer in boiling water."[1] As one from such a family, as one coming from a background of such extreme poverty as well, it isn't difficult to imagine that much of Chaplin's life was a mad dash to escape the shame society and conventional morals attempted to foist upon him — and that his art was an expression and a reflection of that. Terry has allowed herself to be overcome by the shame society would have her suffer under — and so she has lost her art.

Calvero is here to bring her back to life, back to art, with impassioned expressions of his bracing philosophy. He trades in rather bland platitudes which are along the lines of: "Life is a beautiful, wonderful thing!" and other trite truisms which resemble the unfortunate generalities and lazy pomposity of *The Great Dictator* speech. When Calvero proclaims, "Here is the greatest toy ever created! Here lies the secret of all happiness!" while pointing to his forehead, we are not experiencing artistic transcendence but are being subjected to a tongue-lashing from the tiresome, Polonius-like 62 year old uncle we might avoid at a family function. Yet in his fervent, somewhat angry intensity — that of an older person enraged at the youth who would throw life away — Calvero stirs Terry into action, brings her into life.

Strangely, at the same time as he speaks so rapturously of life, he himself is dead to the world, unable to practice his art. As much time as is given to his exhortations for her to live is given to him to diagnose the particular death he lives in. "To hear you talk, no one would ever think you were a comedian," Terry notes. "I'm beginning to realize that," Calvero notes, concluding, "I'm all washed up." In these moments Chaplin indulges in some of the most naked self-portraiture of his career: Calvero "lost contact with my audience — couldn't warm up to them." Alcohol had helped him to perform, but now a heart attack has made drinking dangerous; and so, unfunny, unable to perform, he lives in the netherworld between uselessness and death. The estrangement he feels from his audience would seem to be derived, in some part, from his hostility towards them. "Maybe I love them, but I don't admire them," Calvero observes of his audience, tellingly using the exact same phrase Verdoux had used to describe his feelings towards women. "Individually they're fine ... as a crowd they're like a monster without a head — never know which way they're going to turn. They can be prodded in any direction." Certainly from Chaplin's perspective, after the trials and the picketings and the failure of *Monsieur Verdoux*, he had good reason to be distrustful and angry at his audience. As with Calvero, his sense of alienation had divorced him from the easy familiarity of his best art, had robbed him of the uncomplicated affections of his audience and left him only with his "sad dignity" in the twilight moments of his existence.

"I'm through clowning," Calvero declares disgustedly later in the film. "Life isn't a gag anymore — I can't see the joke ... I hate the theater." His conflicted attitude towards his public is matched by the same attitude towards his art.

Again, the film encourages this type of autobiographical interpretation, for it seems a sort of poem which sums up Chaplin's career as it tries to define the final meaning of that career — it grapples earnestly with Chaplin's dilemma as an aging clown. For like Calvero, Chaplin's problem now is that he is simply old: for an actor who for so long embodied exuberance and agility, whose rapidity and grace of movement defined him, Chaplin could no longer rely on many of his dependable stocks in trade. Now it is talk which defines him as a performer, and the many lengthy philosophical speeches of Calvero make *Limelight* his most dialogue-laden film. Chaplin's genius in the art of pantomime had made the motives and emotions of his characters in the silent films instantaneously apprehendable; now forced to convey the same information in words, he tends to over-articulate, while paradoxically, the motives of his characters become less clear the more he speaks.

The speechifying is interrupted by vignettes of the younger Calvero in music hall sketches — the dreams of the old man which come to haunt him each night. Here, Calvero is seen to have been an entertainer somewhat along the lines of Chaplin's father, Charles Chaplin, Senior — his specialty is novelty songs, the likes of which had made Chaplin, Senior, a star — his image was featured on the sheet music for the songs he introduced. These recreations of British music hall are made ghostly by the fact that there is no laughter meeting Calvero's antics on stage — Chaplin assumed that the audiences viewing the film would supply the laughter, and so there are points throughout the songs and sketches when they are more eerie and poignant than amusing. In puttees and top hat, Calvero sings of being an "Animal Trainer," then moves to a table where he prepares Phyllis and Henry, the two stars of his flea circus, for their show. In this pantomime piece, Chaplin is able to work in the "flea circus sketch" which he had reportedly tried to work into nearly every film he made since *The Kid*. Much of the humor in these sketches is notably biological and earthy, with more than a hint of the vulgarity Chaplin had become known for from the time of his Keystone days.

At the end of his routine, Calvero looks out to acknowledge his applause, but in the sudden silence an expression of panic comes over his features as he scans the pitilessly empty theater. His face dissolves to Calvero's face in the present, staring fearfully into the camera, jolted to uneasy wakefulness by his vision.

Here and in a later instance, the rejection of a performer by an audience is portrayed, and there is conveyed a real terror of the public and the merciless judgment it renders, for all the disdain which Calvero, and Chaplin, effect towards that public. Certainly it is relevant that Chaplin's own introduction to the stage as a boy came in the wake of his mother's rejection by the crowd— her fading voice missed a note, and so the audience had jeered her offstage, the young Chaplin stepping forth to amaze them with a song and dance. Chaplin's father, too, had fallen out of favor with his audience before his death by alcoholism at the age of thirty-seven. By the time of *Limelight*'s release, it had been made all too clear to Chaplin himself that his own time of adoration had passed, and now he was on that downward winding road which both his parents had known so well.

Calvero, however, is able to draw sustenance from the pep talks he gives to Terry, and it is seen as a good omen when his agent gets in touch with him about a prospective job. The aged comedian sets off to the office full of determination that he'll "show them all" now. He finds, however, that he's been booked into a third-rate hall as an act of pity, and is requested to perform under a different name, since his real one has come to be regarded as box-office poison. He gamely agrees to all this, and on the big night he strides out onto the stage and bombs—the audience catcalls, sleeps, makes for the exits. Calvero numbly makes his way to his dressing room, staring at us again with stunned, failure-haunted eyes as he removes his makeup. Back at the apartment, he weeps: "I'm finished—through!" It is time now for Terry to rally him, and in her exhortations she suddenly pulls herself to her feet—in her realization of this she cries: "Calvero! I'm walking!" From this point on, her star is in the ascension—she gets a job with a ballet company and prospers, as Calvero continues to flounder. She is able to get him a bit part as a clown in the ballet she's starring in.

Chaplin would note that in casting the part of Terry he was looking for "the impossible: beauty, talent, and a great emotional range."[2] In actuality, the role of Terry would seem virtually impossible to play, for it consists of long stretches of suicidal depression alternating with near-hysterical expressions of devotion. She is given, via flashback, a romance with a young composer (played by Chaplin's son, Sydney), which is clumsily and tritely established, and which serves to contrast the sense of duty, mistaken for love, which she has for Calvero. For in the aftermath of her recovery she envisions, to Calvero's apparent surprise, a future for herself and the old man as a couple. He gently dissuades her, but we do not know the actual feelings Calvero has for Terry. He has informed her early on that "I have reached the age where platonic relationships can be conducted on the highest moral plane," but there is a sense that Calvero himself does not know the true status of his emotions in this regard—if he is capable of experiencing such emotions to begin with. It is important to note that in Calvero's nightly dreams of past stardom, Terry materializes as a flirting co-star in one of his ribald sketches—perhaps an emanation from the dying embers of the old man's libido. As we did not know, ultimately, why Verdoux killed women, so we do not know what sincere feelings Calvero possesses, beyond his philosophizing, beyond his bitter ruminations on fame and destiny. When the pianist for the ballet turns out to be, as it must, the young composer Terry had fallen for in the past, Calvero will sacrifice himself for her happiness as the Tramp had done for his heroines many times before—though here we do not know the exact nature of that sacrifice. The situation in fact echoes *The Circus*, where the Tramp had withdrawn and arranged for the marriage of the girl and Rex the tightrope walker.

The ballet scene, which runs a good ten minutes, was Chaplin's chance to have dancers perform a ballet to his music, a rather indulgent gift to himself, the occasion of which he called "one of the most thrilling moments of my career."[3] It is notable in that the subject of the ballet—the death and resurrection of Columbine, attended by the clown Harlequinade, played by Terry and Calvero respectively—replicates the events of the film. As well, in utilizing these two stock characters of commedia dell'arte, Chaplin is emphasizing his own pedigree as a clown in a long and venerable tradition—in much the same way as he did in performing the ancient, classic clown sketches in *The Circus*.

At the same time, the staging of an actual ballet in a film by the one clown who was known from the beginning of his career for his balletic grace is significant: Chaplin, a genius of lowbrow humor, had been embraced and elevated by the critics who related his "balletic" style to the ultimate "highbrow" art. He had performed balletic pastiche in *Sunnyside*, but now he presents, somberly, an actual ballet—as though to certify he is worthy of the more refined accolades heaped on his earlier comedy. It is also a statement of his intention to be considered a serious artist. If much of Chaplin's art here is defined by his talk, we note that the subject of that talk—himself, his relationship of himself to his art, his philosophy—means that the phenomenon of Chaplin's genius itself has become the centerpiece of his art: his object, more in *Limelight* than in any other film, is to define himself, as he is and as he wishes to be perceived. It is his last testament. When Calvero enthuses after seeing Terry dance for the first time: "You're an artist, my dear—a true artist!," it is Chaplin's own artistry—his own highbrow artistry—which is being insisted upon and attested to; just as it is Chaplin's own philosophy and "wisdom" which are being affirmed when Calvero is preaching to Terry.

The ballet is a great success. After the show, Calvero slips away to get drunk; later that night he hears Terry's old heartthrob declaring his love to her, urging her not to marry Calvero. Calvero decides to leave—she tours the world with the ballet, and Calvero becomes a street performer. As the Tramp had done in *The Vagabond*, he plays outside the doors of pubs, then goes in with hat in hand to collect. He meets Neville, the composer Terry is in love with, and Mr. Postance, the manager of the ballet, during a day's work; they ask if they can help, but Calvero bears his ignominious fate with saintly composure.

"There's something about working the streets I like," he observes. "It's the tramp in me, I suppose."

Terry seeks him out and they have a tearful reunion. She begs him again to let her accompany him: "I would do anything in the world to make you happy," she pleads. "That's what hurts—I know you would," Calvero states. But there is a plan in the offing: Mr. Postance, the theatre impresario, wants to hold a benefit for Calvero. The comedian seizes on the event as a chance to show the world that he can still be funny—he speaks with sudden enthusiasm about a new musical sketch he's worked out with "a friend." The show will be Calvero's, and Chaplin's, last stand, the clown's final shot of artistic glory before surrendering to the doom which has stalked him, without pause, since the very beginning moments of the film.

As he had given himself magnificent comic partners with Jack Oakie in *The Great Dictator* and Martha Raye in *Monsieur Verdoux*, Chaplin now fittingly graces himself with the greatest partner of all: Calvero's "friend" and partner is arguably Chaplin's only peer as silent clown and comedy film creator: Joseph "Buster" Keaton.

Keaton, five years younger than Chaplin, shared much in common with him. He had also been a child performer: he had toured from the age of three in a vaudeville act with his parents in which he was known as "The Human Mop." The act consisted of the child being tossed and thrown recklessly around the stage by his father. Keaton displayed the same stoic invulnerability to injury as would amaze and mystify audiences in the future; he learned to hide the fun he was having by effecting an expressionless mask, as that made for more laughs. In 1917, while rehearsing for a show in New York, he was invited by old Chaplin confrere Roscoe "Fatty" Arbuckle to drop by the studio where he was beginning his first two-reeler for producer Joe Schenck. Keaton dropped by, played a role, and became Arbuckle's second banana throughout the series, evolving into true partner status and taking a hand in directing the comedies—Keaton's airborne childhood as the knocked-about target of his father's wrath had equipped him to be the ideal silent film comedian. As Arbuckle moved on to features, Keaton was given his own series, and as Chaplin had, began fashioning films which were unique personal visions of the world; Keaton's universe was more quizzical, dry, forbearing, ascetic, and his sense of craft as a filmmaker was strikingly sophisticated. His use of space and composition, of the unique properties of the medium, was certainly more developed than Chaplin's. Keaton made his definitive move into features in 1923 with ease, producing a series of nine classic films which reached their high point with *The General* in 1926, a Civil War epic which blended comedy and drama adroitly and which has come to be recognized as one of the greatest films ever made. It was shortly after this that Keaton's producer sold the comedians' contract to MGM, at which point he lost his own unit with which he'd created all his greatest comedies, and lost the freedom to create autonomously. He was forced into assembly-line products which did neither him or the films he was appearing in any good, and the arrival of sound further sealed his fate, as it robbed him of the world of wonder and majesty as it had for Chaplin. It was at this point his marriage collapsed and he was overtaken by alcoholism — he drifted in oblivion for the next twenty years, appearing in cheap, substandard shorts, getting what work he could as a bit player, and serving as a gag consultant on films for Red Skelton, Judy Garland, Clark Gable, and the Marx Brothers. His last film acting job before *Limelight* had been a role as one of the movie star ghosts in Billy Wilder's acerbic look at what was now regarded as "old" Hollywood, *Sunset Blvd.* Norma Desmond, the deranged silent screen star of the film, rhapsodizes about how "we had faces then," and "I'm still big — it's the movies that became small." Keaton, as one of the has-been actors gathered at Desmond's mansion for a poker game, was a monument to his own obsolescence, a breathing anachronism, a grim sepulchral presence meant by Wilder to symbolize the tawdry ignominy which befell the hapless stars of an earlier time. In reality, the imperturbable Keaton had begun performing live on a new medium, television, at the time.

"I never thought we'd come to this!" he laments as Calvero's partner, preparing for the big show at the end of *Limelight*. It is entirely significant that Chaplin has chosen Keaton to accompany him in this climactic, defining scene at the end of what he conceived of as being his last film. The momentousness of the occasion is commented on by Keaton in the marvelous line: "If anybody else says it's like old times I'll jump out the window!" For rather than simply allowing his era to pass him by, Chaplin definitively rings down the curtain himself, brings the era to a close in his own manner, at a time of his own choosing — his closing slapstick music hall routine brings him full circle and finishes off the entire age of the music hall and vaudeville and of all the greats who had progressed from them and created their own worlds on film, all of the sublime and wondrous clowns of whom Chaplin was the acknowledged trailbreaker and exemplar. This is the end, Chaplin is saying, facing up to and embracing that end, laying down the final vestiges of silent slapstick comedy in 1952.

Calvero, too, actively embraces his doom, sneaking a drink of liquor before going onstage. He relies on alcohol to supply him with the success he so deeply needs, to be genuinely funny once again — but he knows that he risks his life by doing so. Even as he prepares for his final triumph, Calvero remains an ambivalent, gloomy sort: "That's all any of us are, amateurs— we don't live long enough to become anything else," he observes. "Everyone is so kind to me," he says, "it makes me feel isolated." When Terry speaks of them running off together, however, Calvero declares, indicating the dressing room: "This is my home." "You said you hated the theater," Terry reminds him. "I hate the sight of blood too, but it's in my veins." This is Calvero's, and Chaplin's, realization and acceptance of his true destiny, the unalterable elementality of his art within his being, however painful it might be. Calvero's allegiance to his art, his willingness to risk his life for it, is the one sincere feeling he seems to be able to inspire in himself, and as he takes the stage for his last blast, he finally seems to have found the dignity and meaning which had so eluded him.

It is in his return to pantomime that Chaplin finds meaning, and in which he expresses more meaning than all the many words of his script put together. After two solo songs, Calvero takes the stage with his partner, and 8 minutes of pure pantomime performed by the two giants of the silent screen occur. It is important to note that Calvero gives the Keaton character equal prominence to himself—he refers to him as "my partner." They come before the audience to play a duet, Calvero on violin, Keaton on piano, but they are sabotaged by the unwieldy voluminousness of Keaton's sheet music, the breaking strings on Calvero's violin, their inability to tune their instruments, and most of all, the unfortunate habit of Calvero's legs to retract themselves up into his torso at the most inopportune moments. It's the last, and one of the finest, occasions of Chaplin's comic self-transformations: he's wearing a hoop-like contraption under his costume which allows him to give the illusion of shortening or length-ening his legs at will—at one point the poor fellow finds that both legs have retracted, leaving him waddling about the stage like a dwarf. The act is a great success, and Calvero is reunited with his audience and his muse; after the heart-breaking rejections and terror-filled flops he has known, he is finally certified as genuinely funny again at last.

For Chaplin, it is a triumphant return to the uncomplicated pantomime which was his métier, laying aside the political statements of *Modern Times*, *The Great Dictator*, and *Monsieur Verdoux*, and the corollary speech-making of his personal life—and laying aside the ponderous philosophizing which has increasingly weighed his work down. With his colleague Keaton, he returns to the world of gesture, movement and expression, coming back to the place where he belongs—his home—and honoring it, returning to pure clownery. There could be no more fitting climax to the film Chaplin envisioned as his last. In the event, it was the fitting climax to his career in America.

The premiere of *Limelight* was held in London, and when Chaplin embarked with his family to attend, the United States government rescinded his reentry permit—he would have to defend himself in hearings conducted by the Immigration Board of Inquiry if he tried to come back to the country. The longstanding concern about Chaplin's political beliefs had not abated, and his attempts to save his friend, musician Hanns Eisler—an admitted commu-nist—from deportation in 1947 had done nothing to calm suspicions.[4] And so the comedian who had arrived in America as a penniless music hall trouper in 1912 and had stayed to help create the premiere art form of the twentieth cen-tury, becoming a millionaire in the process, was now effectively being thrown out, along with his family, of the country which had been his home for forty years. He would settle and spend the rest of his life in Switzerland.

For Calvero, his era is ending too—after his triumph, he has a heart attack.

He is carried from the limelight and is laid down on a couch in the wings—just as Columbine had reclined on a couch in the ballet, and as Terry had lain supine in Calvero's apartment. Now it is Terry who is dancing on the stage as Calvero finally surrenders to the void which has stalked him — we see the rather horrible image of a sheet being drawn over his face. In his embrace of death he is redeemed, for as Columbine had been, he is resurrected — through Terry's dance, the "dance" which has always been so important to Chaplin's work, Calvero lives on — through the art he has enabled to come to fruition, he defeats death, gives meaning and significance to his life. In his death, resultant of his own dedication to his art, he performs the ultimate act of self-sacrifice — the sort of act so important to the Tramp — freeing Terry to find real love with Neville. In Calvero's death, and in Terry's dance, Chaplin resolves his dilemma as an aging clown, as a dispossessed artist in the aftermath of sound, as a sufferer of his audience's indifference and hostility, as a man beset by fears of being a walking anachronism, a memento of days gone by, by fears of rejection and death. For as he embraces his essential identity in his act with Keaton, his authentic art beyond the philosophizing and pamphleteering, he affirms the undying transcendence of that art. In this sense, the action of the United States government was an anticlimax, for here Chaplin writes the final words on his artistic career, he officiates at his own funeral, and prophesies in no uncertain terms on the eternal resurrection his art will facilitate over all the coming days to the end of time.

Less a film than a "great hunk of celluloid history and emotion," as one contemporary reviewer put it,[5] *Limelight* is a passionate, self-indulgent, monumental production which features Chaplin's most classical score, a Chaplin ballet, three music hall ditties composed by Chaplin, several pantomimes, and his acting in a role more like himself — in a literal sense, at least — than any he had portrayed before: in Calvero's scene with his booking agent we get a glimpse of the canny young man who negotiated his terms with Mack Sennett. He unites himself to his forbears, his parents, his whole time and era, and situates them in eternity as they disappear from temporal reality — with Buster Keaton at his side, he slides into the vast immeasurable voids of the universe. "Chaplin is dead! The Tramp is dead!" the final frames proclaim. "Long live Chaplin! Long live the Tramp!"

16

The King in Exile

After officiating at his own funeral we see him come, in typical Chaplin manner, prancing neatly down the steps from an airplane. He is now a king, recently dethroned in a revolution, seeking refuge in — of all places — America. He makes his way to the well-appointed arrivals area, quite a change from the less impressive circumstances the Tramp found himself in after his entry to the Land of the Free in *The Immigrant*. But like the restraining rope thrown brutally over the Tramp and his fellow passengers in that earlier film as they approached the Statue of Liberty, King Shadov here encounters his own difficulties: "I am deeply moved by your warm friendship and your hospitality," he notes as the authorities take his fingerprints. "This big-hearted nation has already demonstrated its noble generosity to those who come to seek refuge from tyranny."

Coming five years after *Limelight*, *A King in New York* is Chaplin's riposte to Department of Immigration and Naturalization of America and its termination of his reentry permit. If the United States felt that it could throw the Tramp from its shores without the little fellow racing back to plant a kick on its behind, it hadn't done its research. Chaplin's final starring film, and his first produced outside of America, is, for the first three-quarters of its running time, a vicious satire of American life. The king who arrives on those hallowed shores has come with a new atomic plan which will "revolutionize society and bring about a utopia." He was thrown out of his own country by forces which wanted to use that atomic energy for weapons. In America, no one cares for his plans for utopia — all they're interested in is money, violence, sex and noise. It's a place where everything and everyone's for sale, where only the crassest needs and desires are met, where human dignity is trampled beneath the overpowering tides of commerce.

A King in New York is at its best when it is at its broadest, and these early scenes, when King Shadov announces to his Ambassador Jaumais his desire to see "This wonderful, wonderful America ... Its youth, its genius, its vitality!," sparkle with a bright, merry viciousness. They go out into the streets of New York and find themselves shoved and boxed in by the aimlessly milling crowd as sirens scream through the cacophonous night and an appalling pop song plays: "When I think of a million dollars, tears come to my eyes." They retire to a theater where a rock 'n' roll band performs before a screaming, hysterical crowd of teenagers. "Do you think this sort of thing is healthy?" Shadov notes to his ambassador. The trailers before a movie begin playing, advertising such entertainments as *Killer With a Soul* ("Bring the family!"), *Man or Woman?* (Chaplin's comment on the first famous transsexual, Christine Jorgensen of Denmark), and a Western shoot-'em-up in which the shots ring out like cannons. Even when they seek refuge in a restaurant, a clamorous band begins playing so loudly that Shadov must mime his orders of caviar and turtle soup for the waiter — a nice bit of silent comedy Chaplin is able to work in.

Included here as well is a strange subplot in which King Shadov's wife visits him — theirs was an arranged marriage, and she has come to seek a divorce, allowing Chaplin to indulge in a little melancholy for unrequited love, though the theme is never really explored. She departs, and the king meets up with Anne Kay, a flamboyant advertising executive who's bathing in the hotel suite next to his: when the king spies her through his keyhole, he transforms from the stoic, wise philosopher — he has some of the sad dignity of Calvero — to a silent film comic, in a short interlude of pantomime which is shoved into the film without regard for tone, evidently because Chaplin simply felt like doing it. It is still pleasurable to see the 67 year old comedian move with charm and grace, and impressive to see him go into his final balletic flourish as he as he dances off from the woman in an overflow of erotic excitement, leaping sideways into a tub of water.

Anne Kay is the brash, lively side of America which Chaplin likes. She invites the king to a dinner party which she's rigged up with hidden cameras, for the purpose of broadcasting live television commercials. As part of her dinner conversation with the king she works in plugs for deodorant and toothpaste — to his increasing self-conscious discomfort — and she encourages him to stand and recite Hamlet's "To be or not to be" soliloquy, which he does, unknowingly, into a camera. The performance makes him famous and in demand for television commercials. Since the king's fortune has been stolen by his prime minister, he is forced to do the ads, and his entry into America's hysterical materialism is through Anne. Forgetting his plans for utopia for the moment, he does a commercial for Royal Crown whiskey in which he spews the alcohol into the lens, coughing with pained distaste. The ad becomes a hit, and Anne convinces him to have a facelift, to get rid of those "wattles." He does so, and his face becomes hideously grotesque — warned not to smile or laugh, he ends up in a night club where a slapstick comedy team are performing, suffering mightily to keep his features rigid. The music introducing the team and the routine the team performs are suspiciously similar to those of the team formed by Chaplin's old Karno roommate Stan Jefferson (later Laurel).

All of this is a wicked portrait of a society in which there is only the

exploiter and the exploited, where only the vulgar and the bombastic thrive—
the dumb, drunk Americans waiting for the king to arrive at the dinner party,
complaining of their "swollen kneecaps," are similar in their coarseness to Verdoux's victims. From the perspective of fifty years later, Chaplin's commentary
on life as a commercial seems to anticipate reality television, and his routine
on plastic surgery seems remarkably prescient—as well as showing a winning
self-deprecation about the toll time had taken on his own features.

It's all sharp and audacious fun, and there's a mischievous, puckish delight
Chaplin is taking in his satire which is reminiscent of the Keystones. We are
able to look beyond the notable shabbiness of the filmmaking—at least some
of which is attributable to new, unfamiliar British methods—and the unconvincing standing-in London does for New York, and the British actors attempting to maintain American accents, because of the energy of Chaplin's ridicule.
The film only begins to lag when Chaplin retreats from his mining of America's insanity for gags to contemplate his own trauma at being hounded and
driven from the country.

At an alternative school he's visiting, the king meets a young boy named
Rupert Maccabbee (played by Chaplin's son Michael). The boy is a political
firebrand who, when we first discover him, is reading Karl Marx, and who goes
into a tirade about "political power" and the oppression of passports at the
slightest provocation. Chaplin uses the character to express many of his own
political sentiments while at the same time maintaining an affectionate, ironic
distance from them. In Rupert's response when someone asks him if he's a communist, given the book he's reading: "Do I have to be a communist to read Karl
Marx?," Chaplin's implicit comment is similar to his own later diagnosis of his
problems in America: "I was not a communist, but I refused to fall in line by
hating them."[1] Also affirmed is the absurdity of seeking to protect free speech
and democracy by clamping down on the exchange of ideas. "Committees are
searching men's minds, are controlling men's thoughts!" Rupert fulminates
later: "Those who stand up for their rights are boycotted—condemned without trial!" The boy expresses the political oppression underneath the glitter and
the wild promise of America, the other side of its manic materialism.

Later, Rupert seeks Shadov out, trying to escape from the hounding he
suffers because of his beliefs; it transpires that his parents are bring investigated
by the House Un-American Activities Committee, the body which interrogated
suspected Communists during the McCarthy era. Rupert's father refuses to
name names and so is sentenced to a year in prison for contempt of court. The
persecution of the boy's parents is almost certainly intended to be reminiscent
of the trial of Julius and Ethel Rosenberg, a couple who were executed in 1951
for being suspected spies (the suspicions were later proven to be, in part, correct). In uniting their plight with his own, Chaplin is commenting on the very
human toll the political paranoia of the time exacted. When the king is accused
too of being a communist because of his relationship with Rupert, the ominous

fear which descends when the entire force of a government is brought to bear on one's fate is portrayed.

Chaplin himself never testified before the Committee, but the king's testimony is a proxy version of what the aged comedian once claimed he'd have done if called: attend in the costume of the Tramp and perform lots of "business," reducing the entire occasion to a shambles.[2] Here, the king arrives with his finger stuck in a fire hose — the situation is set up in a rather long and protracted sequence — but before the Committee can question him, someone attaches the end of the hose to a pipe and a cascade of water bursts forth, blasting the senators out of their chairs.

It would take more than the old water hose buffoonery to deal with the lasting effects of Cold War persecution, as Chaplin well knew — and the boy Rupert is traumatized and spiritually destroyed as he is forced to testify against his parents in order to save himself. In his final meeting with the king the boy's political fire is gone, and he is a whimpering wreck of his former self. He has been broken by the system: he's a reflection of the trauma suffered by Chaplin, and of the very real pain which was resultant of the political manias of the day.

The king, however, is cleared of communism, and makes plans to leave the country: "Don't judge by what's going on today," the attractive young advertising executive says — with whom, Chaplin implies, the old king is having a casual sexual affair — "It's just a passing phase." "In the meantime, I'll sit it out in Europe," the king observes suavely, pulling his dapper gloves over his fingers. Thus, Chaplin rewrites his own story: here he is not thrown out of America — he chooses to leave the place with a sense of relief, and as the film displays abundantly, he is damned wise to do so.

A King in New York is the most one-dimensional of Chaplin's features — here the message really does take center stage, and subtlety and polish are jettisoned. The film suffers from a lopsided construction: the almost cartoonlike succession of satirical gags in the first half doesn't jibe with the very serious plight of Rupert in the second. In any case, the tragic nature of the boy's story is dealt with only peripherally, inadequately, as if the pain was still too fresh for Chaplin to go any deeper. The film has the feeling of one that "had" to be made for Chaplin's psychological well-being. He made it in full knowledge that it would never play in America, and not necessarily because of the sentiments expressed in the film: the feature before, the entirely apolitical *Limelight*, had been largely banned there after he left the country. Later, Chaplin seemed to become uncomfortable about the picture, never mentioning it in his autobiography, and confessing to being "disappointed" by it in a later book.[3] But there is much that is vigorous and inventive in its gags, the crudity of its construction joining with the hostility expressed to unite it, in a strange way, with the Keystone shorts which had brought Chaplin to fame. Chaplin acquits himself admirably in his last starring role, remaining a magnetic, enigmatic presence to the end.

After this, Chaplin released a compilation film, *The Chaplin Revue* (1959), composed of three of his First Nationals: *A Dog's Life*, *The Pilgrim*, and *Shoulder Arms*: he composed new scores for the films, and narrated intros between them. He then set to work on his autobiography, writing over several years a 500-page book which is one of the more remarkable documents over created by an entertainer. It is titled *My Autobiography* (1964), and the strange redundancy of the title is mirrored by the duality which exists within the book's pages. Critics have rightly hailed the book's first third as one of the most evocative depictions of a Victorian childhood by anyone ever — the stories of Chaplin's impoverished boyhood unfold like tales of Dickens, with unforgettable portraits of mercy and terror. The narrative current runs strong up until the point where Chaplin attains success: after this, the focus is often on the famous and celebrated with whom Chaplin socialized. The interest displayed by Chaplin in people considerably less interesting than himself makes one wonder if he always felt himself an outsider looking in, an impostor like the Tramp in *The Count* or *The Idle Class*. Some have lamented how little there is in the book on the creation of his films — but then, in the case of his best work, these were primarily physical, non-verbal activities. The viewpoint expressed in the book is alternately pompously arrogant or disarmingly self-deprecating, it is at times surprisingly frank and at others frustratingly reticent, and if his choice of words sometimes seems pedantic, there is also the unashamed and sincere joy in vocabulary which is the domain of the self-educated.

Not long after the publication of Chaplin's life story, the longest relationship of that life ended when his half-brother Sydney died in 1965. The elder sibling had long ago stated his desire to save a quarter of a million dollars and then to retire; at the time of his death he had been living a life of leisure in the south of France for thirty years, having saved, as Chaplin noted, "considerably more than" a quarter of a million dollars.[4]

Buoyed by the international acclaim afforded him by the publication of his memoirs, Chaplin felt energized to begin production of another film. He refurbished a script called *Stowaway*, a romantic comedy he'd written for his wife Paulette Goddard back in the thirties, with Gary Cooper envisioned as the male lead at that time. He updated and modified the story, retitling it *A Countess from Hong Kong*, and after engaging two of the most glamorous stars of the time for the lead roles — Marlon Brando and Sophia Loren — the 77 year old Chaplin began production on what would be his final cinematic contribution.

It is quite remarkable that Chaplin took on the intensive work of creating another motion picture when he was at an age when virtually all of his peers were dead — the great defining artistic phenomenon of 1967, the Beatles' *Sgt. Pepper's Lonely Heart's Club Band* album, featured as its packaging a pastiche of the World War I–era graphics which had been current when Chaplin began his film career. Perhaps he felt that the light farce of the script wouldn't be too taxing to realize: the tale is of an American diplomat meeting a displaced

Russian refugee — a countess who survives by dancing in a dance hall — while on a trip to Hong Kong. She stows away in his stateroom in hopes of finding a new life for herself; he discovers her out at sea, and the rest of the film consists of their hiding her from the authorities onboard the ship. With time, they fall in love — she is without a passport, so they wed her to the diplomat's valet in order to get her into America. When the diplomat's estranged wife comes aboard at Hawaii, they pretend the countess is the wife of the diplomat's assistant. In the end, the diplomat leaves his wife for the countess.

The film is a mistake. Perhaps a younger Chaplin might have been able to liven up the proceedings with a few choice pieces of business; in any case, he likely would have been able to invest the film as a whole with an internal energy and rhythm — so crucial to farce — which seems quite beyond the ability of the older artist. There is a real lack of momentum and urgency: for the greater part of the time we are offered nothing more involving than the repeated gag of someone opening a stateroom door, causing everyone to scurry and hide. The diplomat's stateroom is the setting for virtually the entire production, causing it to be Chaplin's most claustrophobic film. Marlon Brando, for all his greatness as an actor, is no comedian, and Sophia Loren, though pleasing and likable, fares little better — the actors seem uncertain and ill-at-ease, hamstrung by a script which is perfunctory and slight. The one credible comic performance is a cameo by Margaret Rutherford playing an eccentric old woman on board the ship who spends the entire journey seasick in her room.

Certainly one can discern themes in the film which have surfaced before — Natascha, the countess, is one of Chaplin's "fallen women," a dance hall girl like Edna in A Dog's Life, or Georgia in The Gold Rush, and like the earlier characters she is engaged in a spirited quest for survival; in stowing away in the diplomat's stateroom she is, as she says, seeking "escape from dance halls and prostitution." The dilemma of Ogden Mears, the diplomat, and his loveless marriage are typical of Chaplin's realistic perspective on adult situations. The shipboard setting also allows Chaplin to return to his continuing obsession with seasickness as a source of humor — an entire segment is devoted to the ship rocking from side to side as had happened in Shanghaied, The Immigrant, and A Day's Pleasure, with the resultant mouth-covering and frenzied dashes to find somewhere to vomit. Chaplin himself was evidently unable to resist the temptation to join in, and so donned a costume and appears in a quick cameo, making his last screen appearance as a chubby white-haired geriatric ship steward, gulping as he tries to ward off nausea.

The long, low-energy, plodding, ill-conceived film — Chaplin's first in color and in widescreen format — was released and savaged by the critics. Though Chaplin feistily dismissed the reviewers as "bloody idiots"[5] there is little doubt he took the film's failure hard; it is likely that in the aftermath he suffered a series of mini-strokes. The most positive aspect of A Countess from Hong Kong is its music — one of the themes, "This Is My Song," was recorded by Petula

Clark and became an international hit. The song, whose lyrics, unlike those of Chaplin's earlier hit "Smile" (taken from *Modern Times*), were Chaplin's own.

Chaplin's musical compositions are the most notable works of his later creative life. In 1970 he rereleased *The Circus* with a new score, which included a song, "Swing, Little Girl," sung by Chaplin himself; in 1971 he composed scores for *The Idle Class*, and most evocatively, *The Kid*. In 1972 an appearance of rapprochement with the United States occurred when the Academy of Motion Picture Arts and Sciences offered Chaplin an honorary Oscar; the government offered him a reentry visa (for just ten days), and Chaplin returned to America for an emotional ceremony — his son Sydney noted that he returned simply as publicity for the profitable rerelease of his old films.[6] In 1975, as if in a dream sequence from one of his productions, he was knighted at Buckingham Palace, scant miles away from where he had watched his mother go mad in their poverty-ridden apartment. That same year he rereleased his dramatic film *A Woman of Paris* of fifty years before, composing a new score for it. Throughout these last nine years he worked on a script for a film called *The Freak*; the tale of a girl born with wings, it was, as he described it, "a story about an angel." Perhaps, as in *The Kid*, it was to be one last flight to Paradise before the inevitable awakening to bitter reality. As Chaplin's health failed, the proposed film ceased to be a possibility, and in his final years, as his son Eugene related, the aged comedian compulsively read and reread Dickens' *Oliver Twist*[7]— all the while, as his other son Michael noted, the elderly clown "drifted away."[8] Though the tribulations of Dickens' young man alone on the streets of London predated Chaplin's own boyhood by fifty years, the aged clown evidently experienced kinship with the orphan's plight on those hard streets, so that amongst all the various roles he played throughout his life — clown, songwriter, political provocateur, scenarist, poet, auteur, composer, international playboy, dancer, athlete, director, satirist, actor, cinematic pioneer, knight, exile — it was the transient unknown one with nothing, the solitary unaccepted one battling fate out in the rough streets, facing the undiluted injustice of existence full force — the Tramp — which remained foremost in his consciousness at the time of his death at the age of 88, December 25, 1977.

Filmography

The Keystone Film Company (1914). All films produced by Mack Sennett.

Making a Living— One reel — Released February 2, 1914. Directed by Henry Lehrman. Costarring Virginia Kirtley, Alice Davenport, Henry Lehrman, Minta Durfee, Chester Conklin.

Kid Auto Races at Venice— Half-reel — Released February 7, 1914. Directed by Henry Lehrman. Costarring Henry Lehrman, Frank D. Williams, Billy Jacobs.

Mabel's Strange Predicament— One reel — Released February 9, 1914. Directed by Henry Lehrman and Mack Sennett. Costarring Mabel Normand, Chester Conklin, Alice Davenport, Harry McCoy, Chester Conklin.

Between Showers— One reel — Released February 28, 1914. Directed by Henry Lehrman. Costarring Ford Sterling, Chester Conklin, Emma Clifton.

A Film Johnnie— One reel — Released March 2, 1914. Directed by George Nichols. Costarring Roscoe Arbuckle, Virginia Kirtley, Minta Durfee, Mabel Normand, Ford Sterling, Mack Sennett.

Tango Tangles— One reel — Released March 9, 1914. Directed by Mack Sennett. Costarring Ford Sterling, Roscoe Arbuckle, Chester Conklin, Minta Durfee.

His Favorite Pastime— One reel — Released March 16, 1914. Directed by George Nichols. Costarring Roscoe Arbuckle, Peggy Pearce.

Cruel, Cruel Love— One reel — Released March 26, 1914. Directed by George Nichols. Costarring Chester Conklin, Minta Durfee, Alice Davenport.

The Star Boarder— One reel — Released April 4, 1914. Directed by George Nichols. Costarring Minta Durfee, Edgar Kennedy, Gordon Griffith, Alice Davenport.

Mabel at the Wheel— Two reels— Released April 18, 1914. Directed by Mabel Normand and Mack Sennett. Costarring Mabel Normand, Harry McCoy, Chester Conklin, Mack Sennett, Al St. John, Fred Mace.

Twenty Minutes of Love— One reel — Released April 20, 1914. Directed by Charles Chaplin. Costarring Minta Durfee, Edgar Kennedy, Gordon Griffith, Chester Conklin, John Swickard, Hank Mann. Chaplin's directorial debut.

Caught in a Cabaret— Two reels— Released April 27, 1914. Directed by Mabel Normand. Costarring Mabel Normand, Harry McCoy, Chester Conklin, Edgar Kennedy, Minta Durfee.

Caught in the Rain— One reel — Released May 4, 1914. Directed by Charles

Chaplin. Costarring Mack Swain, Alice Davenport, Alice Howell.

A Busy Day— Half-reel — Released May 7, 1914. Directed by Charles Chaplin. Costarring Mack Swain, Phyllis Allen.

The Fatal Mallet— One reel — Released June 1, 1914. Directed by Mack Sennett. Costarring Mack Sennett, Mabel Normand, Mack Swain.

Her Friend the Bandit— One reel — Released June 4, 1914. Director unknown. Costarring Mabel Normand, Charles Murray. No print of the film is known to exist.

The Knockout— Two reels— Released June 11, 1914. Directed by Charles Avery. Chaplin plays a supporting role in this film featuring Roscoe Arbuckle. Costarring Minta Durfee, Edgar Kennedy, Al St. John, Hank Mann, Mack Swain, Mack Sennett.

Mabel's Busy Day— One reel — Released June 13, 1914. Directed by Mabel Normand. Costarring Mabel Normand, Chester Conklin, Slim Summerville, Billie, Bennett.

Mabel's Married Life— One reel — Released June 20, 1914. Directed by Charles Chaplin. Costarring Mabel Normand, Mack Swain, Alice Howell, Hank Mann.

Laughing Gas— One reel — Released July 9, 1914. Directed by Charles Chaplin. Costarring Fritz Schade, Alice Howell, Joseph Sutherland, Slim Summerville.

The Property Man— Two reels— Released August 1, 1914. Directed by Charles Chaplin. Costarring Fritz Schade, Phyllis Allen, Alice Davenport, Charles Bennett, Mack Sennett.

The Face on the Bar Room Floor— One reel — Released August 10, 1914. Directed by Charles Chaplin. Based on the poem by Hugh Antoine d'Arcy. Costarring Cecile Arnold, Fritz Schade, Vivian Edwards, Chester Conklin, Harry McCoy, Hank Mann.

Recreation— Half-reel — Released August 18, 1914. Directed by Charles Chaplin. Costarring Charles Murray, Norma Nichols.

The Masquerader— One reel — Released August 27, 1914. Directed by Charles Chaplin. Costarring Roscoe Arbuckle, Chester Conklin, Charles Murray, Fritz Schade.

His New Profession— One reel — Released August 31, 1914. Directed by Charles Chaplin. Costarring Minta Durfee, Fritz Schade, Charles Parrott (later Charley Chase).

The Rounders— One reel — Released September 7, 1914. Directed by Charles Chaplin. Costarring Roscoe Arbuckle, Phyllis Allen, Minta Durfee, Al St. John, Fritz Schade.

The New Janitor— One reel — Released September 24, 1914. Directed by Charles Chaplin. Costarring Fritz Schade, Jack Dillon, Minta Durfee, Al St. John.

Those Love Pangs— One reel — Released October 10, 1914. Directed by Charles Chaplin. Costarring Chester Conklin, Cecile Arnold, Vivian Edwards, Edgar Kennedy.

Dough and Dynamite— Two reels— Released October 26, 1914. Directed by Charles Chaplin. Costarring Chester Conklin, Fritz Schade, Norma Nichols, Cecile Arnold, Vivian Edwards, Phyllis Allen, Jack Dillon, Edgar Kennedy.

Gentlemen of Nerve— One reel — Released October 29, 1914. Directed by Charles Chaplin. Costarring Mack Swain, Mabel Normand, Chester Conklin, Phyllis Allen, Edgar Kennedy, Charles Parrott (later Charley Chase).

His Musical Career— One reel — Released November 7, 1914. Directed by Charles Chaplin. Costarring Mack Swain,

Charles Parrott (later Charley Chase), Fritz Schade, Joe Bordeaux, Alice Howell, Norma Nichols.

His Trysting Place— Two reels— Released November 9, 1914. Directed by Charles Chaplin. Costarring Mabel Normand, Mack Swain, Phyllis Allen.

Tillie's Punctured Romance— Six reels. Released November 14, 1914. Directed by Mack Sennett. Based on the play

Tillie's Nightmare— Costarring Marie Dressler, Mabel Normand, Mack Swain, Charles Bennett, Charles Murray, Charles Parrott (later Charley Chase), Edgar Kennedy, Harry McCoy, Minta Durfee, Phyllis Allen, Alice Davenport, Slim Summerville, Al St. John.

Getting Acquainted— One reel — Released December 5, 1914. Directed by Charles Chaplin. Costarring Phyllis Allen, Mack Swain, Mabel Normand, Harry McCoy. Edgar Kennedy, Cecile Arnold.

His Prehistoric Past— Two reels— Released December 7, 1914. Directed by Charles Chaplin. Costarring Mack Swain, Gene Marsh, Fritz Schade, Cecile Arnold, Al St. John.

The Essanay Film Manufacturing Company (1915–16). All films are produced by Jesse T. Robbins. All films are directed and written by Charles Chaplin unless otherwise noted.

His New Job— Two reels— Released February 1, 1915. Costarring Ben Turpin, Charlotte Mineau, Charles Insley, Leo White, Frank J. Coleman, Bud Jamison, Gloria Swanson, Agnes Ayres, Billy Armstrong.

A Night Out— Two reels— Released February 15, 1915. Costarring Ben Turpin, Bud Jamison, Edna Purviance, Leo White, Fred Goodwins.

The Champion— Two reels— Released March 11, 1915. Costarring Lloyd Bacon, Edna Purviance, Leo White, Bud Jamison, Billy Armstrong, Ben Turpin.

In the Park— One reel — Released March 18, 1915. Costarring Edna Purviance, Leo White, Margie Reiger, Lloyd Bacon, Bud Jamison, Billy Armstrong, Ernest Van Pelt.

A Jitney Elopement— Two reels— Released April 1, 1915. Costarring Edna Purviance, Fred Goodwins, Leo White, Lloyd Bacon, Paddy McGuire, Carl Stockdale, Bud Jamison.

The Tramp— Two reels— Released April 11, 1915. Costarring Edna Purviance, Fred Goodwins, Lloyd Bacon, Paddy McGuire, Billy Armstrong, Leo White, Ernest Van Pelt.

By the Sea— One reel — Released April 29, 1915. Costarring Billy Armstrong, Margie Reiger, Bud Jamison, Edna Purviance, Paddy McGuire, Carl Stockdale.

Work— Two reels— Released June 21, 1915. Costarring Charles Insley, Edna Purviance, Billy Armstrong, Marta Golden, Leo White, Paddy McGuire.

A Woman— Two reels— Released July 12, 1915. Costarring Edna Purviance, Marta Golden, Charles Insley, Margie Reiger, Billy Armstrong, Leo White.

The Bank— Two reels— Released August 9, 1915. Costarring Edna Purviance, Carl Stockdale, Billy Armstrong, Charles Insley, Lawrence A. Bowes, John Rand, Leo White, Bud Jamison, Fred Goodwins, Frank J. Coleman, John Rand, Lloyd Bacon.

Shanghaied— Two reels— Released October 4, 1915. Costarring Edna Purviance, Wesley Ruggles, John Rand, Bud Jamison, Billy Armstrong, Lawrence A. Bowes, Paddy McGuire, Leo White, Fred Goodwins.

A Night in the Show— Two reels— Released November 20, 1915. Costarring Edna Purviance, Charlotte Mineau, Dee Lampton, Leo White, Wesley Ruggles, John Rand, James T. Kelley, Paddy McGuire, May White, Bud Jamison, Phyllis Allen.

Charlie Chaplin's Burlesque on Carmen— Four reels— Released April 22, 1916. Compiled by Leo White. Costarring Edna Purviance, Ben Turpin, Leo White, John Rand, Jack Henderson, May White, Bud Jamison, Wesley Ruggles, Frank J. Coleman, Lawrence A. Bowes. The film was expanded to double its intended length by Leo White after Chaplin left Essanay.

Police— Two reels— Released May 27, 1916. Costarring Edna Purviance, Wesley Ruggles, James T. Kelley, Leo White, John Rand, Fred Goodwins, Billy Armstrong, Bud Jamison.

The Mutual Company (1916–1917). All films directed and written by Charles Chaplin.

The Floorwalker— Two reels— Released May 15, 1916. Photographed by Frank D. Williams. Costarring Eric Campbell, Edna Purviance, Lloyd Bacon, Albert Austin, Lloyd Bacon, Leo White, Charlotte Mineau, James T. Kelley.

The Fireman— Two reels— Released June 12, 1916. Photographed by Frank D. Williams. Costarring Edna Purviance, Lloyd Bacon, Eric Campbell, Leo White, Albert Austin, John Rand, James T. Kelley, Frank J. Coleman.

The Vagabond— Two reels— Released July 10, 1916. Photographed by Frank D. Williams. Costarring Edna Purviance, Eric Campbell, Leo White, Lloyd Bacon, Charlotte Mineau, Albert Austin, John Rand, James T. Kelley, Frank J. Coleman.

One A.M.— Two reels— Released August 7, 1916. Photographed by Rollie Totheroh. Costarring Albert Austin.

The Count— Two reels— Released September 4, 1916. Photographed by Rollie Totheroh. Costarring Edna Purviance, Eric Campbell, Leo White, May White, Charlotte Mineau, Albert Austin, Stanley Sanford, John Rand, James T. Kelley, Leota Bryan.

The Pawnshop— Two reels— Released October 2, 1916. Photographed by Rollie Totheroh. Costarring Henry Bergman, Edna Purviance, John Rand, Albert Austin, Wesley Ruggles, Eric Campbell, James T. Kelley, Frank J. Coleman.

Behind the Screen— Two reels— Released November 13, 1916. Photographed by Rollie Totheroh. Costarring Eric Campbell, Edna Purviance, Henry Bergman, Lloyd Bacon, Albert Austin, John Rand, Leo White, Frank J. Coleman, Charlotte Mineau, Leota Bryant.

The Rink— Two reels— Released December 4, 1916. Photographed by Rollie Totheroh. Costarring Edna Purviance, James T. Kelley, Eric Campbell, Henry Bergman, Lloyd Bacon, Albert Austin, Frank J. Coleman, John Rand, Charlotte Mineau, Leota Bryan.

Easy Street— Two reels— Released January 22, 1917. Photographed by Rollie Totheroh. Costarring Edna Purviance, Eric Campbell, Albert Austin, Henry Bergman, Loyal Underwood, Janet Miller Sully, Charlotte Mineau, Tom Wood, Lloyd Bacon, Frank J. Coleman, John Rand.

The Cure— Two reels— Released April 16, 1917. Photographed by Rollie Totheroh. Costarring Edna Purviance, Eric Campbell, Henry Bergman, Albert Austin, John Rand, James T. Kelley, Frank J. Coleman, Leota Bryan, Tom Wood, Janet Miller Sully, Loyal Underwood.

The Immigrant— Two reels— Released June 17, 1917. Photographed by Rollie Totheroh. Costarring Edna Purviance, Kitty Bradbury, Albert Austin, Henry Bergman, Loyal Underwood, Eric Campbell, Stanley Sanford, James T. Kelley, John Rand, Frank J. Coleman, Tom Harrington.

The Adventurer— Two reels— Released October 22, 1917. Photographed by Rollie Totheroh. Costarring Edna Purviance, Henry Bergman, Marta Golden, Eric Campbell, Albert Austin, Toraichi Kono, John Rand, Frank J. Coleman, Loyal Underwood, May White, Janet Miller Sully, Monta Bell.

First National (1918–1923).

A Dog's Life— Three reels— Released April 14, 1918. Photographed by Rollie Totheroh. Costarring Edna Purviance, Mut, Sydney Chaplin, Henry Bergman, Charles Reisner, Albert Austin, Tom Wilson, M.J. McCarty, Mel Brown, Charles Force.

Shoulder Arms— Three reels— Released October 20, 1918. Photographed by Rollie Totheroh. Costarring Edna Purviance, Sydney Chaplin, Jack Wilson, Henry Bergman, Albert Austin, Tom Wilson, John Rand, Park Jones, Loyal Underwood.

The Bond— Half-reel— Released December 16, 1918. Photographed by Rollie Totheroh. Costarring Edna Purviance, Sydney Chaplin, Henry Bergman, Dorothy Rosher. A propaganda film in support of war bonds.

Sunnyside— Three reels— Released June 15, 1919. Photographed by Rollie Totheroh. Costarring Edna Purviance, Tom Wilson, Tom Terriss, Henry Bergman, Loyal Underwood, Tom Wood, Helen Kohn, Olive Burton, Willie Mae Carson, Olive Alcorn.

A Day's Pleasure— Two reels— Released December 15, 1919. Photographed by Rollie Totheroh. Costarring Edna Purviance, Marion Feducha, Bob Kelly, Jackie Coogan, Tom Wilson, Babe London, Henry Bergman, Loyal Underwood, Albert Austin, Jessie Van Trump.

The Kid— Six reels. Released February 6, 1921. Photographed by Rollie Totheroh. Costarring Edna Purviance, Jackie Coogan, Baby Hathaway, Carl Miller, Granville Redmond, May White, Tom Wilson, Henry Bergman, Charles Reisner, Raymond Lee, Lillita McMurray, Edith Wilson, Baby Wilson, Nelly Bly Baker, Albert Austin, Jack Coogan Sr.

The Idle Class— Two reels— Released September 25, 1921. Photographed by Rollie Totheroh. Costarring Edna Purviance, Mack Swain, Henry Bergman, Allan Garcia, John Rand, Rex Storey, Lillian McMurray, Lillita McMurray, Loyal Underwood.

Pay Day— Two reels— Released April 2, 1922. Photographed by Rollie Totheroh. Costarring Phyllis Allen, Mack Swain, Edna Purviance, Sydney Chaplin, Albert Austin, John Rand, Loyal Underwood, Henry Bergman, Allan Garcia.

The Pilgrim— Four reels— Released February 26, 1923. Photographed by Rollie Totheroh. Costarring Edna Purviance, Kitty Bradbury, Mack Swain, Loyal Underwood, Charles Reisner, Dinky Dean, Sydney Chaplin, May Wells, Henry Bergman, Tom Murray.

United Artists. All films produced by Charles Chaplin.

A Woman of Paris— Eight reels. Released October 1, 1923. Assistant director: Edward Sutherland. Photographed by Rollie Totheroh with Jack Wilson. Art director: Arthur Stibolt. Starring Edna Purviance, Adolphe Menjou, Carl Miller, Lydia Knott, Charles French, Clarence Geldert, Betty Morrissey, Malvina Polo,

Henry Bergman, Harry Northrup, Nelly Bly Baker. Chaplin contributes a cameo as a porter.

The Gold Rush— Nine reels. Released June 26, 1925. Assistant directors: Charles Reisner, Edward Sutherland, Henrie d'Abbadie d'Arrast. Photographed by Rollie Totheroh, with Jack Wilson, Mark Marlatt. Art director: Charles D. Hall. Costarring Georgia Hale, Mack Swain, Tom Murray, Betty Morrissey, Kay Delseys, Joan Lowell, Malcolm Waite, Henry Bergman, John Rand, Heinie Conklin, Albert Austin, Allan Garcia, Tom Wood, Stanley Sanford.

The Circus— Seven reels. Released January 6, 1928. Assistant director: Harry Crocker. Photographed by Rollie Totheroh, with Jack Wilson, Mark Marlatt. Art director: Charles D. Hall. Costarring Merna Kennedy, Allan Garcia, Harry Crocker, Henry Bergman, Stanley Sanford, George Davis, Betty Morrissey, John Rand, Armand Triller, Steve Murphy.

City Lights— Eight reels. Released February 27, 1931. Assistant directors: Harry Crocker, Henry Bergman, Albert Austin. Photographed by Rollie Totheroh, with Mark Marlatt, Gordon Pollock. Music by Charles Chaplin. Music director: Alfred Newman. Art director: Charles D. Hall. Costarring Virginia Cherrill, Florence Lee, Harry Myers, Hank Mann, Eddie Baker, Tom Dempsey, Eddie McAuliffe, Willie Keeler, Allan Garcia, Henry Bergman, Albert Austin, John Rand, Tiny Ward, Robert Parrish.

Modern Times— Eight reels. Released February 11, 1936. Assistant directors: Carter De Haven, Henry Bergman. Photographed by Rollie Totheroh with Ira Morgan. Music by Charles Chaplin. Music director: Alfred Newman. Art director: Charles D. Hall. Costarring Paulette Goddard, Henry Bergman, Stanley J.

Sanford, Chester Conklin, Hank Mann, Louis Natheaux, Stanley Blystone, Allan Garcia, Sam Stein, Juana Sutton, Dr. Cecil Reynolds, Myra McKinney.

The Great Dictator— 126 minutes. Released December 16, 1940. Assistant directors: Dan James, Robert Meltzer, Wheeler Dryden. Photographed by Karl Struss, Rollie Totheroh. Music by Charles Chaplin. Musical director: Meredith Willson. Art director: J. Russell Spencer. Costarring Paulette Goddard, Jack Oakie, Henry Daniell, Reginald Gardiner, Billy Gilbert, Maurice Moskovitch, Emma Dunn, Bernard Gorcey, Paul Weigel, Grace Hayle, Carter de Haven, Chester Conklin, Hank Mann, Eddie Gribbon, Richard Alexander, Leo White.

Monsieur Verdoux— 122 minutes. Released April 11, 1947. Assistant directors: Robert Florey, Wheeler Dryden. Photographed by Curt Courant, Rollie Totheroh. Music by Charles Chaplin. Music director: Rudolph Schrager. Art director: John Beckman. Costarring Martha Raye, Isobel Elsom, Marilyn Nash, Robert Lewis, Mady Correl, Allison Roddan, Audrey Betz, Ada-May, Marjorie Bennett, Helen High, Margaret Hoffman, Irving Bacon, William Frawley, Fritz Leiber.

Limelight— 143 minutes. Released October 23, 1952. Assistant director: Robert Aldrich. Assistant producers: Wheeler Dryden, Jerome Epstein. Photography: Karl Struss. Photographic consultant: Rollie Totheroh. Music by Charles Chaplin. Music director: Ray Rasch. Songs by Charles Chaplin, Ray Rasch. Art director: Eugene Lourie. Choreography: Charles Chaplin, Andre Eglevsky, Melissa Hayden. Costarring Claire Bloom, Buster Keaton, Sydney Chaplin, Norman Lloyd, Marjorie Bennett, Wheeler Dryden, Nigel Bruce, Barry Bernard, Leonard Mudie, Snub Pollard, Loyal Underwood, Charles Chaplin Jr.,

Geraldine Chaplin, Michael Chaplin, Josephine Chaplin.

Attica–Archway

A King in New York—105 minutes. Released September 12, 1957. Assistant Director: Rene Dupont. Associate producer: Jerome Epstein. Photography: George Perinal. Music by Charles Chaplin. Arranged by Boris Sarbeck. Conducted by Leighton Lucas. Art director: Allan Harris. Costarring Oliver Johnston, Dawn Addams, Maxine Audley, Jerry Desmonde, Sidney James, Joan Ingrams, Michael Chaplin, John McLaren, Harry Green, Robert Arden.

Universal

A Countess from Hong Kong—120 minutes. Released January 2, 1967. Assistant Director: Jack Causey. Produced by Jerome Epstein. Photography by Arthur Ibbetson. Art director: Robert Cartwright. Music: Charles Chaplin. Musical director: Lambert Williamson. Musical associate: Eric James. Starring Marlon Brando, Sophia Loren, Sydney Chaplin, Tippi Hedren, Patrick Cargill, Margaret Rutherford, Michael Medwin, Oliver Johnston, John Paul, Angela Scoular, Geraldine Chaplin. Chaplin makes a cameo appearance as an aged ship steward.

As of this writing, all of the Chaplin Keystones are being restored in an international project by the British Film Institute, Progetto Chaplin and Lobster Films. Until the completion of this project, these seminal films circulate in much the same way as they have over the past ninety years — in versions whose tattered decrepitude testify to the great popularity of the original prints, as well as to their status as public domain works. The

Keystone films can be found repackaged on a vast array of cheap DVD and VHS products, sometimes confusingly retitled; an exception to this is David Shepard's restoration of *Tillie's Punctured Romance*, available from Image Entertainment. A definitive collection of the Keystones does not exist at present: one of the better bets for now is Brentwood's *Charlie Chaplin: 57 Classics* DVD set, which features 26 of the 35 films Chaplin made at Keystone, along with substandard versions of his later Essanay and Mutual work.

Chaplin's Essanay work is better represented by David Shepard's restorations, available on DVD through Image Entertainment. The series includes Shepard's recreation of *Charlie Chaplin's Burlesque of Carmen* as Chaplin himself intended it, as referred to in this text.

The twelve short films Chaplin made at Mutual are best represented by *The Chaplin Mutual Comedies: 90th Anniversary Edition*. The restorations — again by David Shepard — allow these important works to look as good as they have at any time since their release. The package includes the thorough if somewhat hagiographic 1975 documentary, *The Gentleman Tramp*, as well as *Chaplin's Goliath*, a 1996 documentary on Eric Campbell originally made for Scottish television.

All of Chaplin's films from his First National era through to *A King in New York* are available in two box sets sanctioned by the Chaplin estate, put out by MK2. The packages include deleted scenes among a variety of extras, as well as Richard Schickel's begrudging documentary *Charlie: His Life and Art*. It might be noted that the versions of *A Dog's Life*, *The Pilgrim*, and *Shoulder Arms* here are from the 1959 compilation *The Chaplin Revue*, and suffer from the "stretch printing" used in that film. Stretch printing, by which frames were reprinted to match the film with a soundtrack, lessens the effectiveness of the movement in the films: since Chaplin's art is movement, it might be best to seek out the restorations of these works produced by David Shepard for Image Entertainment.

The "stretch printing" dilemma was later solved, as the other First National titles on the MK2 set are fine. The set also includes, thankfully, Kevin Brownlow's restoration of the original 1925 version of *The Gold Rush*, as well as the later 1942 Chaplin-narrated version, which is—unfortunately, in this writer's opinion—more prevalent today.

A Countess from Hong Kong is available from Universal on DVD.

Other documentaries of interest are *The Unknown Chaplin*, the DVD of the original BBC series in which Kevin Brownlow and David Gill unearthed a vast trove of Chaplin outtakes dating from his Mutual days to *Modern Times*. This excellent series shows how Chaplin created his art extemporaneously on camera, and features lengthy routines excised from *The Circus* and *City Lights* which would have been the highlights of the works of any other comedian.

As well, there is *Charlie Chaplin: The Forgotten Years*, an odd and moving film made for Swiss television on Chaplin's declining years in Switzerland.

Chapter Notes

Chapter 1

1. Quoted in Leonard Maltin, *The Laurel and Hardy Book* (New York: Curtis Books), p. 9.
2. Paulette Goddard, as quoted in "It Happened One Night" by Earl Wilson, *New York Post*, April 14, 1972.
3. Quoted in David Robinson, *Chaplin: His Life and Art* (Winnipeg: Paladin Books, 1986), p. 631.

Chapter 2

1. Gerald Mast and Bruce F. Kawin, *A Short History of the Movies* (London: Longman, 2003), p. 11.
2. David Shipman, *The Story of Cinema*, vol. 1: *From the Beginnings to Gone with the Wind* (London: Hodder and Stoughton, 1982), p. 17.
3. Shipman, *The Story of Cinema*, pp. 18–9.
4. Charles Chaplin, *My Autobiography* (London: The Bodley Head, 1964), p. 146.
5. Ibid., p. 15.
6. Robinson, *Chaplin: His Life and Art*, p. 18.
7. Chaplin, *My Autobiography*, p. 16.
8. Ibid., p. 18.
9. Robinson, *Chaplin: His Life and Art*, p. 47.
10. Ibid., p. 95.
11. Ibid., p. 110.
12. Ibid., p. 93.
13. Richard Anobile, *The Marx Brothers Scrapbook* (New York: Darien House, 1973), p. 14.
14. Charlotte Chandler, *Hello, I Must Be Going: Groucho and his Friends* (New York: Doubleday, 1978), p. 461.
15. Robinson, *Chaplin: His Life and Art*, p. 98.
16. Chaplin, *My Autobiography*, p. 143.
17. Maltin, *The Laurel and Hardy Book*, p. 10.
18. Chaplin, *My Autobiography*, pp. 149–50.
19. Op. cit.
20. Ibid., p. 152.
21. Ibid., p. 188.
22. Charles Chaplin, *My Life in Pictures* (New York: Grosset and Dunlap, 1975), p. 279.
23. Chaplin, *My Autobiography*, p. 157.
24. Robinson, *Chaplin: His Life and Art*, p. 133.
25. Chaplin, *My Autobiography*, p. 160.
26. Robinson, *Chaplin: His Life and Art*, p. 132.
27. Ibid., p. 131.

Chapter 3

1. Chaplin, *My Autobiography*, p. 164.
2. Ibid., p. 169.
3. Robinson, *Chaplin: His Life and Art*, p. 189.
4. Ibid., p. 141.
5. Ibid., p. 159.
6. Ibid., p. 144.
7. Ibid., p. 437.
8. Quoted in *The National Enquirer*, 1971.
9. Chaplin, *My Autobiography*, p. 253.
10. Ibid., p. 330.

11. Ibid., p. 304.
12. Ibid., p. 291.
13. Chaplin, *My Life in Pictures*, p. 31.
14. Robinson, *Chaplin: His Life and Art*, p. 145.
15. Chaplin, *My Autobiography*, p. 173.

Chapter 4

1. Chaplin, *My Autobiography*, p. 188.
2. Ibid., p. 205.
3. Robinson, *Chaplin: His Life and Art*, p. 167.
4. Ibid., p. 171.
5. Ibid., p. 178.
6. Ibid., p. 192.

Chapter 5

1. Chaplin, *My Autobiography*, p. 208.
2. Ibid., p. 230.

Chapter 6

1. Chaplin, *My Autobiography*, p. 230.
2. Robinson, *Chaplin: His Life and Art*, p. 746.

Chapter 7

1. Chaplin, *My Autobiography*, pp. 220–1.
2. Ibid., p. 291.
3. Robinson, *Chaplin: His Life and Art*, p. 298.

Chapter 8

1. Robinson, *Chaplin: His Life and Art*, p. 302.
2. Ibid., p. 321.
3. Chaplin, *My Autobiography*, p. 216.
4. Robinson, *Chaplin: His Life and Art*, p. 319.

Chapter 9

1. Pierre Berton, *Klondike* (Toronto: McClelland and Stewart, 1958), p. 244.
2. Ibid., pp. 43–48.
3. Chaplin, *My Autobiography*, pp. 299–300.
4. Robinson, *Chaplin: His Life and Art*, p. 337.

5. Chaplin, *My Autobiography*, p. 208.
6. Op. cit.

Chapter 10

1. Robinson, *Chaplin: His Life and Art*, p. 360.

Chapter 11

1. Shipman, *The Story of Cinema*, p. 200.
2. Ibid., p. 201.
3. Robinson, *Chaplin: His Life and Art*, p. 411.
4. Ibid., p. 577.
5. Chaplin, *My Autobiography*, p. 323.
6. Op. cit.

Chapter 12

1. Buster Keaton with Charles Samuels, *My Wonderful World of Slapstick* (New York: Doubleday, 1960), p. 126.
2. Robinson, *Chaplin: His Life and Art*, p. 389.
3. Chaplin, *My Autobiography*, p. 411.
4. Ibid., p. 377.
5. Ibid., p. 33.
6. Robinson, *Chaplin: His Life and Art*, p. 458.

Chapter 13

1. Ian Kershaw, *Hitler* (London: Longman, 1991), p. 27.
2. Op. cit.
3. Ibid., p. 28.
4. David Welch, *Hitler: Profile of a Dictator* (London: Routledge Press, 1998), p. 16.
5. Ibid., p. 15.
6. Ibid., p. 18.
7. Kershaw, *Hitler*, p. 142.
8. Welch, *Hitler: Profile of a Dictator*, p. 20.
9. Ibid., pp. 14–15.
10. Robinson, *Chaplin: His Life and Art*, p. 493.
11. Chaplin, *My Autobiography*, p. 316.
12. Op. cit.
13. Ibid., p. 386.

14. Garson Kanin, *Hollywood* (New York: Viking Press, 1974), pp. 157–58.

15. Robinson, *Chaplin: His Life and Art*, p. 155.

16. Chaplin, *My Autobiography*, p. 399.

17. Ibid., p. 388.

18. Robinson, *Chaplin: His Life and Art*, p. 484.

19. Chaplin, *My Autobiography*, p. 382.

20. Ibid., pp. 387–88.

21. Robinson, *Chaplin: His Life and Art*, p. 508.

22. Chaplin, *My Autobiography*, p. 322.

23. Quoted in James Bacon, *Hollywood Is a Four Letter Town* (Chicago: Henry Regnery, 1976), p. 29.

24. Keaton, *My Wonderful World of Slapstick*, p. 269.

Chapter 14

1. Chaplin, *My Autobiography*, p. 412.

2. Ibid., p. 411.

3. Robinson, *Chaplin: His Life and Art*, p. 437.

4. Ibid., p. 632.

5. Chaplin, *My Autobiography*, p. 444.

Chapter 15

1. Chaplin, *My Autobiography*, p. 216.

2. Ibid., p. 448.

3. Ibid., p. 447.

4. Robinson, *Chaplin: His Life and Art*, p. 547.

5. Ibid., p. 570.

Chapter 16

1. Chaplin, *My Autobiography*, p. 458.

2. Robinson, *Chaplin: His Life and Art*, p. 547.

3. Chaplin, *My Life in Pictures*, p. 306.

4. Chaplin, *My Autobiography*, p. 348.

5. Robinson, *Chaplin: His Life and Art*, p. 615.

6. Quoted in Pam Grady, "Inheriting the Limelight," July 14, 2004, filmstew.com.

7. Robinson, *Chaplin: His Life and Art*, p. 628.

8. Quoted on DVD, *Charlie Chaplin: The Forgotten Years.*

Bibliography

Anobile, Richard. *The Marx Brothers Scrapbook*. New York: Darien House, 1973.

Bacon, James. *Hollywood Is a Four Letter Town*. Chicago: Henry Regnery, 1976.

Berton, Pierre. *Klondike*. Toronto: McClelland and Stewart, 1958.

Chandler, Charlotte. *Hello, I Must Be Going: Groucho and His Friends*. New York: Doubleday, 1978.

Chaplin, Charles. *My Autobiography*. London: Bodley Head, 1964.

_____. *My Life in Pictures*. New York: Grosset and Dunlap, 1975.

Kanin, Garson. *Hollywood*. New York: Viking Press, 1974.

Keaton, Buster, with Charles Samuels. *My Wonderful World of Slapstick*. New York: Doubleday, 1960.

Kershaw, Ian. *Hitler*. London: Longman, 1991.

Maltin, Leonard, ed. *The Laurel and Hardy Book*. New York: Curtis Books, 1973.

Mast, Gerald, and Bruce F. Kawin. *A Short History of the Movies*. London: Longman, 2003.

Robinson, David. *Chaplin: His Life and Art*. Winnipeg: Paladin Books, 1986.

Shipman, David. *The Story of Cinema*, Vol.1: *From the Beginnings to Gone with the Wind*. London: Hodder and Stoughton, 1982.

Welch, David. *Hitler: Profile of a Dictator*. London: Routledge Press, 1998.

Index